Front Range Descents

HEATHER UNGER

Spring & Summer
Skiing & Snowboarding
In Colorado's Front Range

Ron Haddad & Eileen Faughey

Foreword by Louis Dawson

Photo by Al Desetta

Purpose

To enable skiers and snowboarders who possess at least intermediate skills to locate descent routes, to plan approaches sensibly, and to develop a heightened appreciation for these mountains. Advanced and expert skiers and snowboarders will find many challenging routes described in this guide.

This book is not a "how to" guide. There are resources listed in the Appendix that can help you with technique, outdoor skills, and equipment. If you are new to the sport or you are unfamiliar with the Front Range, consider hiring a guide.

Disclaimer

Backcountry skiing and snowboarding are hazardous. People have been injured or killed while engaging in these activities.

This book is not intended to teach you the skills that are needed to reduce the risk of accidental injury or death. It is solely intended to point the way to a variety of backcountry routes and peaks. Only regular visits to the mountains can help you acquire the various skills that are needed to succeed in meeting your objectives.

We have made every effort to verify the data and the route descriptions. Despite our best efforts, errors may exist. If you discover any errors, we would appreciate learning about them. The authors assume no responsibility for problems that may arise from using this book.

Published by *Sigma Books*
P.O. Box 21175
Boulder, Colorado 80308

Printed in the United States
ISBN: 0-9650412-3-9

Front Cover: Clark Bowl (May). Inset – Sawtooth Mtn. (June)
Title Page: Unnamed peak in the Elk Mountains (June)
Back Cover: Top – Bard Peak (May). Bottom – Stanley Slide Path (May)

Design, photography, and illustrations by the authors except where credited.

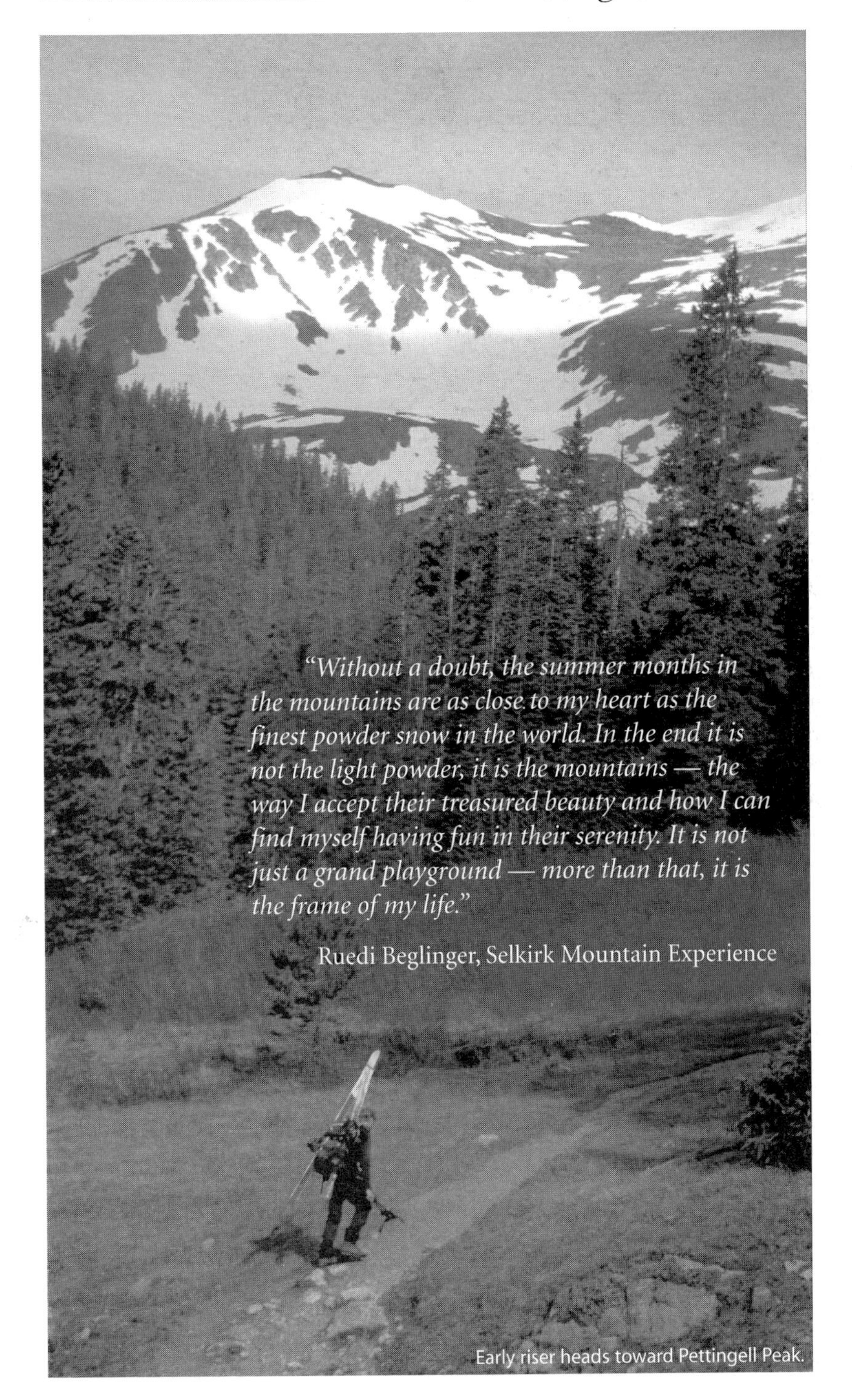

"Without a doubt, the summer months in the mountains are as close to my heart as the finest powder snow in the world. In the end it is not the light powder, it is the mountains — the way I accept their treasured beauty and how I can find myself having fun in their serenity. It is not just a grand playground — more than that, it is the frame of my life."

Ruedi Beglinger, Selkirk Mountain Experience

Early riser heads toward Pettingell Peak.

Contents

Foreword

After more than three decades of ski mountaineering, I'm still fascinated by the phenomenal number of skiable peaks and routes we have in Colorado. Our fifty four 14,000 foot peaks are all skiable, most by quality routes. Beyond the fourteeners we have about six hundred stupendous peaks topping 13,000 feet, and thousands more below that.

I'll admit to a weakness for the fourteeners. I've loved writing about them, skiing from their summits, photographing them, and simply gazing at them. Nevertheless, I've spent many a fine day skiing Colorado's other mountains. Thus I'm excited about this guidebook, as it includes several fourteeners, but gives equal billing to many other worthy peaks. One of those sticks in my mind like I'm still there.

My friend Russ and I are on Buffalo Mountain in Summit County. As the warm springtime sun lofts through a stunning indigo sky, we switchback up a series of huge, open, south-facing slopes blanketed by perfect velvet snow. We're tempted — but want something special. So we go on faith and head over the summit, where a stunning snow-filled slot drops down the north face like the swipe of a huge white paintbrush.

Standing at the top, I'm as ready as a ski mountaineer can be. Sun hit the couloir only minutes ago. Perfect. The warming snow will easily edge a ski, but it's still firm, without the sticky slush that'll soon form on the surface. My skis are engineered for high mountain skiing, waxed and sharp. My sun-warmed leg muscles are fluid and flexible.

I launch. My skis rebound gently from each edgeset, sending warm quakes up my spine. Every turn pauses with a gliding float. Coming down from each soaring moment, I carve a perfect arc, a curve so fair you could use it as the template for a yacht hull.

Twenty turns, thirty turns....Then it happens. My mind stops. I'm not thinking, only feeling. In each turn I reach a point where the next simply occurs, dictated by the snow, the length of the arc, and the tension in my skis. I relax into a centered stance that feels almost as if I'm sinking into an easy chair — a tranquil observer with the snow and the planet turning under me.

Overcome by peace and joy, I stop about halfway down. I've visited the zone, the place athletes train lifetimes for, give up their careers for, sacrifice almost everything for.

Russ pulls in next to me and smiles. Our words are few. A lifelong seeker of the carve, he knows where I've just been. We gaze up at our tracks. Melt water trickles like music down rocks on the sides of the couloir. Russ quietly pushes off; I follow. In the silence, under the sun, we make a set of figure eights to the bottom of the run — brothers in the zone.

Ever since that day on Buffalo I've had my deepest appreciation of the places ski mountaineering can take us — in body and in spirit. We backcountry skiers are privileged. For a season in our lives, our skills and health bless us with recreation beyond the capabilities of most people. What's more, we own vast areas of public land in Colorado where we can practice our craft in virtual solitude, thus insuring most of our trips will be brilliant adventures — with a few perhaps taking us to the zenith.

So why a guidebook? Why chance adding more people to the mix? Why risk taking away the solitude that contributes to our peak experiences?

This guidebook wraps a fine gift. The gift is our Colorado mountain terrain, a land so vast we can easily enjoy it without crowding, provided we don't follow each other to the same places. By ranging farther with the help of Ron and Eileen's information, you'll easily find places where it's only you, a few friends, perfect snow — and perhaps the peak turns of your life.

Louis Dawson, 2003

Preface

I first traveled to Colorado to ski in March,1979. After landing at the old Stapleton Airport in Denver, I rented a car at about eight o'clock in the evening. With indescribable anticipation I drove west on I-70 and then to the top of Loveland Pass. The night was crystal clear and the moon was full. Around ten o'clock I got out of the car and inhaled deeply the calm and noticeably thin, cold air. Within minutes a van loaded with skiers arrived at the Pass. Six guys in downhill boots hobbled out, snapped into their skis, and dropped off the slope to the west. In a flash I had uncovered backcountry skiing in high mountains.

I never thought about skiing in the same way since that moment. Even though I still enjoyed skiing at ski resorts, I thought of the resorts as a training ground for backcountry skiing. Although I was living in the East where skiing is strictly a winter activity, I knew that in the Rockies snowfields lingered into the summer months, meaning there was a way to extend the ski season by many weeks.

My first summer ski trip to Colorado occurred in early June 1983. My first summer ski run was down the west side of Loveland Pass. It had been an exceptionally high snow year. The mountains were blanketed with perfect corn snow down to an elevation of 10,000 feet. My partners and I skied every line around Loveland Pass and later drove southwest to ski some more in the mountains outside of Aspen. We were hooked. From each summit we could see countless others mantled in white. The possibilities for ski descents seemed, literally, endless.

During every summer that followed, I traveled west to ski — Montana's Beartooths, California's Sierras, and, of course, Colorado. I was drawn to the mountains by the same things no matter where I chose to ski: warm weather and long sunny days, pine-scented breezes, rushing streams, fresh wildflowers, and long runs on reliable corn snow. These were, and still are, the constants.

But significantly some things have changed since my earliest forays into the backcountry. Ultralight alpine touring equipment; sturdier, more user-friendly free-heel equipment; packs designed for carrying skis or snowboards conveniently. These, plus an expanding culture of backcountry skiing have helped to make Colorado's mountains, winter or summer, accessible to growing numbers of skiers and snowboarders.

My love affair with spring and summer skiing culminated, in 1996, with the publication of *Indian Peak Descents*. With that slim volume, my wife Eileen and I dipped our toes into the guidebook-writing waters. The success of that effort and the encouragement of friends and strangers who share our enthusiasm for spring snow have lead us to expand our coverage and to write this guide.

Ron Haddad, 2003

June, 1983 — Relaxing at the foot of North Maroon Peak, Elk Mountains of central Colorado.

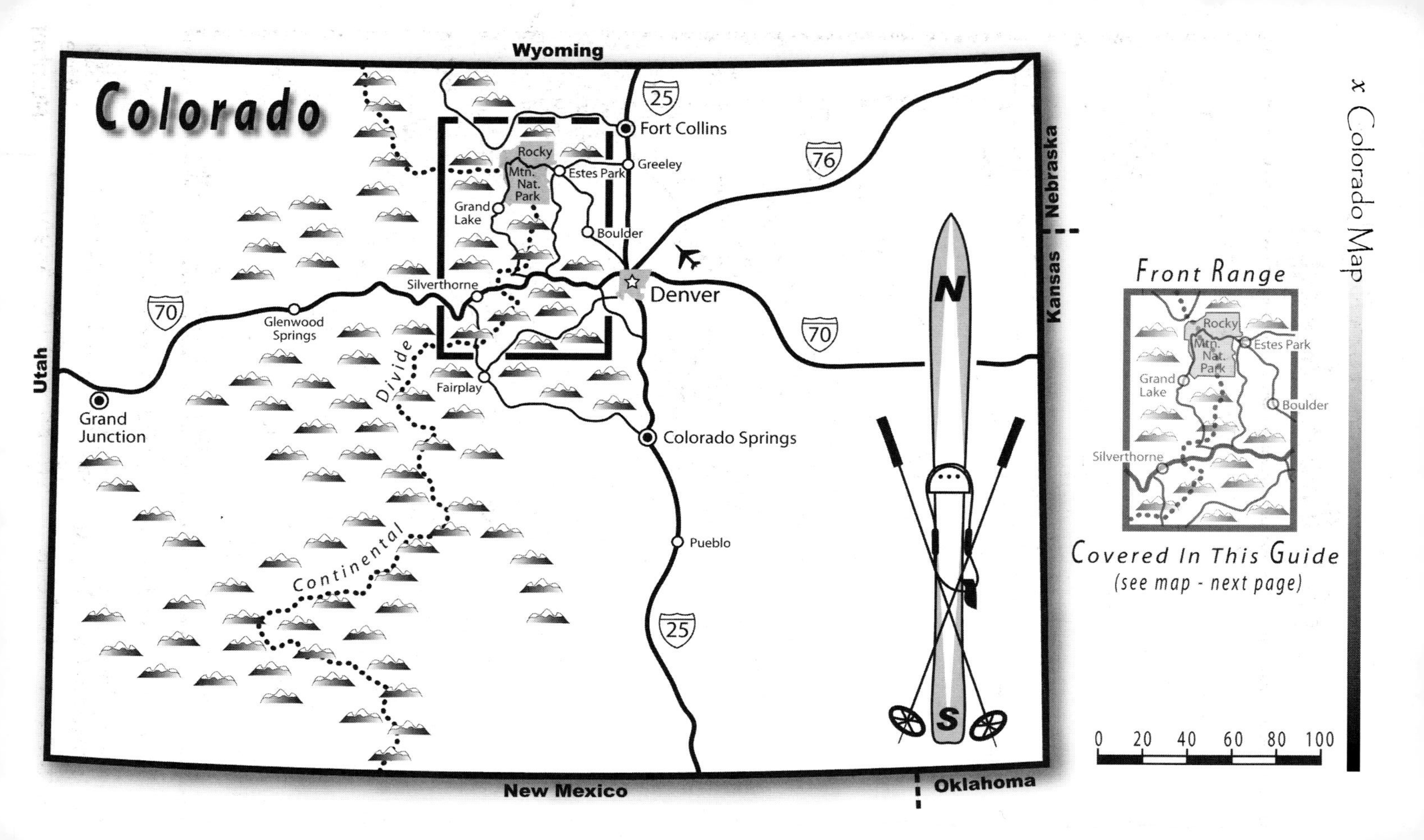
Colorado
Wyoming
Nebraska
Kansas
Utah
New Mexico
Oklahoma
25
76
70
Fort Collins
Greeley
Rocky Mtn. Nat. Park
Estes Park
Grand Lake
Boulder
Silverthorne
Denver
Glenwood Springs
Fairplay
Grand Junction
Divide
Continental
Colorado Springs
Pueblo
N
S
Front Range
Covered In This Guide
(see map - next page)
0 20 40 60 80 100

The Front Range

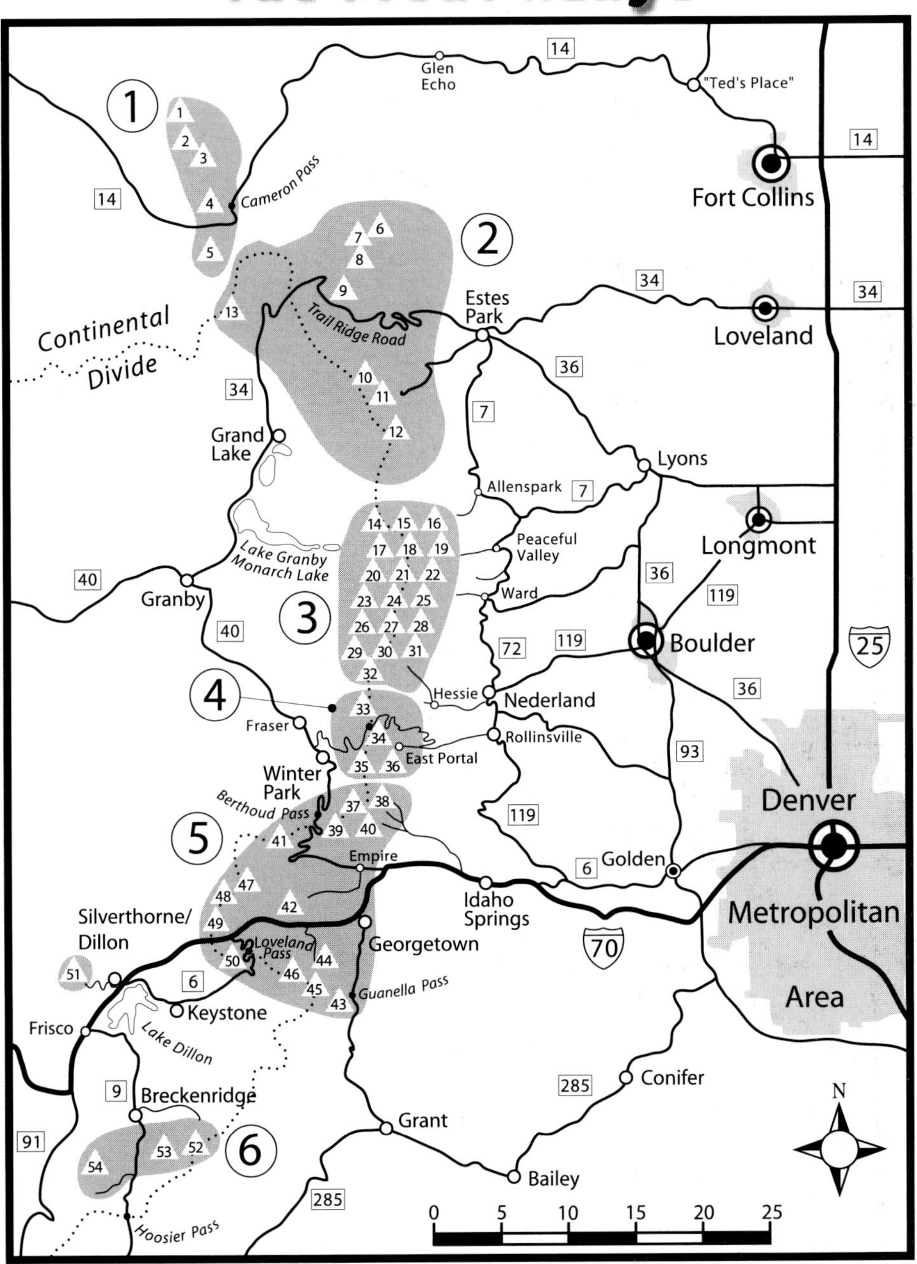

1 Cameron Pass Region

2 Rocky Mountain National Park Region

3 Indian Peaks Region

4 Rollins Pass Region

5 Interstate 70 Region

6 Summit Cty. Region

Route Number

Introduction

The Front Range

The Great Plains of the Midwest rise gently westward from the Mississippi River for eight hundred miles. Then with astonishing abruptness, the Rockies thrust upward. Nowhere is this transition more dramatic than where the high plains meet Colorado's Front Range. Over the course of a mere twenty-five miles, the elevation changes from 6000 feet above sea level to twice that number. Every physiographic, climatic, and ecological parameter is altered as a result of this elevation change. Steep-sided mountains alternate with deep canyons and glacial valleys, temperatures fall, precipitation increases, and wind speeds accelerate. All of these changes encourage snowfall and wind deposition of snow on lee aspects.

Colorado's Front Range extends 150 miles from the Wyoming border southward to Pikes Peak, west of Colorado Springs. The section of greatest interest to skiers and snowboarders is a 100-mile stretch from Clark Peak (12,951') in the Medicine Bow Mountains north of Cameron Pass, through Rocky Mountain National Park and the Indian Peaks, to Hoosier Pass at the south end of the Tenmile Range. Summit elevations range from 11,000 feet to 14,000 feet. From October through July, snow-lovers living on the plains or in the mountain towns can gaze up toward the snow-covered peaks and dream of ski descents.

All of the mountains described in this book are accessible from the metropolitan areas of Fort Collins, Denver, and Colorado Springs by driving from one to three hours. Residents of counties west of the Continental Divide and the mountain towns scattered among the foothills have even easier access.

The Snowpack

The Front Range contains pockets of snow during most of the year. In absolute terms, the amount of snow that falls directly onto the Front Range is unimpressive when compared with some other western ranges such as the San Juans, Wasatch, Sierras or Cascades. However, winter snow is transported eastward by prevailing winds that are accelerated by the gradually upsloping terrain west of the Continental Divide. These ferocious winter winds scour snow from windward slopes and deposit and compact the snow on leeward slopes east of the Divide. These are the snows that one sees plastered onto the steep mountain faces and glacial cirques that are the hallmark of east slope topography above timberline.

Until about the middle of April, the snow above timberline consists of crusty sheets of impregnable *sastrugi*, the result of ruthless battering by the wind. As spring progresses, the days lengthen, the sun rises higher in the sky, and temperatures increase. Surface snow begins to melt and water percolates deeper into the snowpack, changing the structure of snow crystals from more crystalline, cohesive forms to more rounded, less cohesive forms. At night, temperatures drop below freezing and the top few inches of the snowpack freezes solid again as ice grains become welded to their neighbors only to be re-melted the following day. Freeze, melt...freeze, melt. Throughout May and into June and July, this cycle gradually transforms the snowpack into a consolidated and uniform mass with very little free air between the ice grains. It is the upper few inches of this consolidated snowpack that softens by day and forms corn snow. To skiers and snowboarders, "velvet corn" is the spring and summer equivalent of winter's "champagne powder." Slopes that had been either too avalanche prone or too wind-packed to ski in winter are safer now and skiable.

Our Public Lands and Wilderness Areas

All of the mountains described in this book are part of our National Forest, State Forest, or National Park systems. Much of this land has been federally protected as Wilderness. In addition to the peaks themselves, these Wilderness areas feature an abundance of older forests, rushing streams, hundreds of lakes, stretches of alpine tundra, and wildlife. These Wilderness areas are a cherished resource of inestimable value.

Devil's Thumb Trail, west of Hessie—Indian Peaks Wilderness

In designating an area as a Wilderness, the intent of Congress is to protect its pristine condition and ecological values. To this end, human intrusion and amenities are minimized or eliminated. Rocky Mountain National Park, on the other hand, is sustained by a different value structure. While the Park places a high value on resource preservation, it is also committed to the concept of accessibility to the public. Roads, interpretive displays, visitor centers, campgrounds and other amenities exist to enable the public to get close to the wilderness and wildlife. The distinction between a Wilderness Area and a National Park is an important one. Wilderness Areas are set aside to serve the wilderness. National Parks are designed to serve people.

As we hike, camp, climb, ski or snowboard on our public lands, we need to accept the fact that we are visitors. It is essential that we minimize our impacts. The proximity of the Front Range to our urban centers has made it among the most heavily traveled of all the public lands in our nation. Current and future levels of use will only be acceptable if each visitor is knowledgeable about minimum-impact travel and camping techniques and about the regulations that permit or prohibit camping and campfires. There are portions of the Front Range, such as the Four Lakes Travel Zone west of Brainard Lake in the Indian Peaks, where camping has been prohibited or is severely restricted. These restrictions are necessary in order to preserve the qualities that draw us to these mountains in the first place.

Equipment

The purpose of this section is to discuss only the equipment that is relevant to ski and snowboard mountaineering. It is not intended to contain an exhaustive list of items that one needs to pack for a trip.

Free-Heel Skis, Boots, Bindings — For skiers who are looking for a combination of comfort, lightness, efficiency, and performance, one choice is "free-heel" or "telemark" gear. Don't be discouraged from fulfilling your ski mountaineering dreams just because you are not an "expert" free-heel skier. Budding free-heel skiers can enjoy many of the routes in this book.

Today's free-heel skis are practically identical to fixed-heel alpine touring skis. Similarly, free-heel boot design has also converged with alpine touring boots. The differences among the various free-heel boots have to do with weight, flexibility, fit, and the number of buckles. As boots have become heavier and stiffer, free-heel bindings have been strengthened to withstand the increase in boot-to-ski forces. Two advantages of these changes is that, first, free-heel skiers can now make less-fatiguing parallel turns as easily as they can make telemark turns, and second, skiing steep slopes is less of a gamble.

Alpine Skis, Boots, Bindings — If you prefer to use downhill skis and boots designed for ski resorts, you will need to free your heels during the approach and uphill climb. This problem can be solved by using lightweight

(2.7 pounds/pair) adapters that snap into your fixed-heel bindings. The adapter, called the *Alpine Trekker*, has an attachment for your downhill ski boot and a toe pivot so you can raise and lower your heel just as you would with an alpine touring binding (see next paragraph). When you reach the top of a ski run, you simply remove and stash the adapter, snap into your bindings, and ski down.

Courtesy Backcountry Access

The Alpine Trekker is an ingenious pair of lightweight adapters that enable a skier to use standard downhill skis and boots for skiing uphill in the backcountry.

Another choice for fixed-heel skiers is to use alpine-touring (AT) skis, boots, and bindings. AT skis are lighter and may be wider and shorter than typical downhill skis. They perform well under a variety of backcountry conditions.

Traditional AT bindings consist of a plate or steel rails that the ski boot snaps into, much like a traditional downhill binding. However, the plate is hinged at the front where it connects with the ski. The rear of the plate can be locked into the ski for skiing downhill. To ski the flats or uphill, one simply releases the back end of the plate thereby freeing the heel to move up and down. AT bindings are capable of releasing during a fall. All AT bindings come with built-in adjustable heel lifts.

Another type of AT binding manufactured by Dynafit dispenses altogether with the heavier rail/plate design. Instead, a separate binding toe piece clamps directly into the sides of the boot toe. The boot, which needs to be compatible with this toe piece, is now free to pivot up and down without being attached to a plate or rails. A separate heelpiece clamps the back of the boot for skiing downhill and can be released like any AT binding. The result is a much lighter binding (1.5 pounds/pair) and a more ergonomic pivot point closer to one's toes.

To go the complete AT route, you should purchase AT boots that are designed to snap into AT bindings. The sole is lugged and has a built in rocker for much easier climbing and walking without skis. These boots are much lighter compared with regular downhill boots (6 to 8 pounds as compared with 8 to 10 pounds), and since they are softer, are more comfortable. The forward-leaning cuff of an AT boot is releasable and generously hinged at the ankle allowing freedom of lower leg movement when one is shuffling along an approach. Don't expect the above boot-binding-ski combination to provide the level of control you may be used to with regular downhill equipment. On the other hand, the convenience, comfort, and weight savings overshadow their performance liabilities.

Courtesy Life-Link

Dynafit's Tourlite Tech 4 boots (7.2 lbs.) and Tourlite Tech bindings (1.4 lbs.) have set the standard for light weight among ski mountaineering equipment.

Snowboards — The evolution in snowboards and technique has enabled riders to employ a carving style of descent that is both powerful and graceful. The obvious limitation for snowboarders is their inability to shift their boards into uphill mode. One way to solve this problem is by using snowshoes. Using a pack that is designed to carry a snowboard and approaching on small, lightweight snowshoes, snowboarders can access any of the routes in this book. Another solution is to purchase a "split-board," a snowboard that can be separated into two halves and, along with skins, be used as a pair of skis for the approach.

Snowboarders who plan on skiing steeper routes should carry an ice axe to use when ascending or descending. Collapsible ski poles that can be attached to a pack are useful aids when approaching a descent on snowshoes or with a split board.

Skins — Ski skins enable you to travel uphill — steeply uphill. They are like having four wheel drive plus chains on your feet. (A well-kept secret is that some of us even engage our skins when descending scary wooded trails with unmentionable snow conditions.) Ski skins attach using a layer of glue on the undersurface of the skins. Skins are available for different widths of skis and some can be custom-trimmed to match the base of your skis exactly. Consider buying skins with a tail attachment.

Crampons and Ice Axe — The decision whether or not to use crampons and an ice axe when climbing a steep snow slope depends on three things: the hardness of the snow, the steepness of the slope, and your level of confidence in your ability to climb steep snow.

Heel Lifts — These have been standard equipment on AT bindings for years. Heel lifts are available also for free-heel setups. By raising your heels above your skis when skinning uphill, they reduce the degree of flexion between your feet and lower legs making uphill travel less of a chore and more efficient.

Poles — Adjustable ski poles are among skiing's great inventions. They can be extended to increase arm thrust when kicking and gliding, shortened to normal length for skiing downhill, and greatly shortened when kicking steps up a steep slope. You can purchase poles with self-arrest grips. You can also purchase these grips separately to attach to your poles. Self-arrest grips are like mini-ice axes for each hand. They are helpful climbing aids when the going gets very steep, but they are not a substitute for an ice axe should a fall occur on a very steep slope. It is a good idea to practice using them in a variety of controlled situations to get a feel for what their capabilities are.

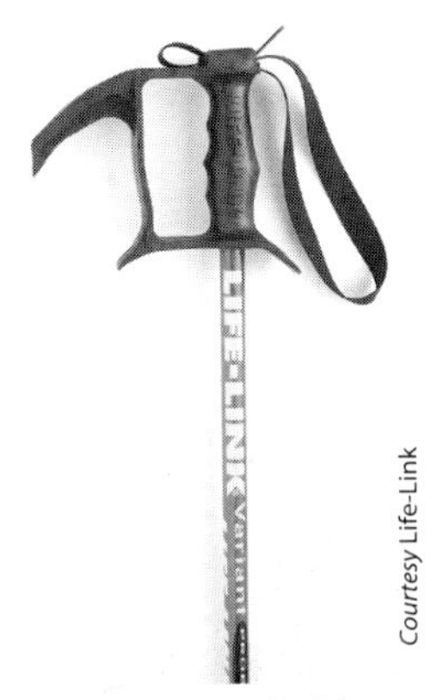

Courtesy Life-Link

Self-arrest ski poles double as handy back-scratchers.

Kneepads — Free-heel skiers who make telemark turns should wear kneepads during descents. In the spring, a slope that appears uniformly covered by deep snow can hide obstacles. Many routes are in scree and talus filled gullies where it is possible for a ski to slice down onto a hidden block of talus and cause a shattering blow to the knee.

Altimeter — For orienteering in unfamiliar terrain and for monitoring progress during an ascent, an altimeter is useful in conjunction with a topographic map and a compass. In addition to the traditional big-dial-slung-from-the-neck-type altimeter, there are also digital wristwatch/altimeters that read at one-foot intervals (who are they kidding?) and have other useful "bells and whistles."

Inclinometer — Judging the angle of steepness of a snow slope is difficult, even for experienced backcountry skiers and snowboarders. One's location in relation to the slope in question, plus subjectivity and wishful thinking, can contribute as much as plus or minus ten degrees to a person's estimation of slope angle. An inclinometer can help to answer the question, "How steep is it — really?"

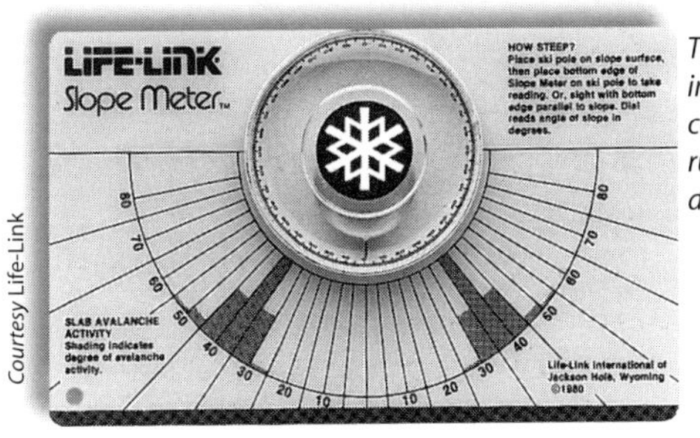

Courtesy Life-Link

This lightweight inclinometer slips easily into a pocket or zippered pack compartment. The reverse side has a ruled scale for estimating slope angles directly from U.S.G.S. topographic maps.

Global Positioning System (GPS) — Many backcountry travelers choose to carry a GPS to assist with navigation or to have something to fiddle around with during breaks. The accuracy of newer systems is astonishing. In conjunction with computer map software that can output waypoints, a great deal of uncertainty can be removed from route-finding. We need to emphasize that a GPS should not substitute for the ability to navigate by map, compass, altimeter, and a pair of eyes.

Packs — A well-designed pack is like a reliable companion. There are several excellent packs available for backcountry skiing. Look for a pack with a shovel compartment, straps along the sides for attaching skis, a generously padded hip belt for comfort and for stability when skiing downhill, and sufficient capacity for emergency supplies and extra clothing, food, and water.

For overnight outings a large backpack is needed to pack in camping gear plus ski equipment. This is how the entire arrangement looks…, …and this is how it feels.

A Few Words On Weight

Why does the issue of weight figure heavily in this discussion of equipment? First, backcountry skiing and snowboarding are physically demanding activities that often occur at elevations above 10,000 feet. Second, as the snow recedes into the alpine basins and couloirs in late spring and summer, you are forced to pack in your ski gear. Except for the demigods whose extraordinary skiing feats are heralded in ski publications, the rest of us mortals have limited muscle glycogen and lung capacities. Ascending a steep snowfield with overweight equipment strapped to a bulky pack may look good in pictures, but it is exhausting. Opt for the lightest setup that allows you to ski a slope safely and enjoyably. As with all backcountry modes of travel, it makes sense to travel as efficiently as possible in order to maximize your success rate and enjoyment without compromising on safety and dependability of equipment.

Camping on the south side of Loveland Pass in June.

Mountain Hazards

Snowslides — Earlier in the Introduction we described the freeze-melt cycle that transforms steep avalanche-prone slopes into more stable, consolidated snow that is safer to climb and to ski. In spite of the greater stability of the spring snowpack, the mountaineer needs to be aware that dangers still exist especially during April and May. During these transitional months, large amounts of water, acting as a lubricant, may accumulate between the ground and the snow. Given a suitable bed surface and slope angle on which to slide, dangerous wet slabs with the consistency of cement can result. On several occasions in the spring we've observed the aftermath of slab avalanches that ran along the ground just above treeline on inclines as low as 25 degrees. Along similar lines, smooth rock slabs that lie tilted above one's route can readily unload their snowcover as the rock warms and becomes lubricated with meltwater. Careful route selection and timing are essential to avoid this hazard, which increases as the day progresses.

An enormous June wet slide probably triggered by a collapsed cornice. Notice that the bed surface is composed of smooth rock.

Colorado's winters are notorious for posing a high slab avalanche hazard. With the onset of spring, the chances of slab avalanches occurring become less. However, it is not unusual for five to ten inches of fresh snow to fall on top of frozen, consolidated snow in late May and early June, usually above 10,000 feet. For twenty-four hours after such a storm the danger of slab avalanches reappears on slopes near or above 30 degrees.

Even when complete consolidation of the snowpack finally occurs, mountaineers must still maintain their guard. We have observed both slow and fast sluffs of heavy wet corn snow in June, typically during sunny afternoons or during a pounding bout of hail. A skier may trigger sluffing especially when the snow has had a chance to soften to a depth of four to six inches. Unlike slab avalanches, sluffs lack cohesion and are usually harmless. However, their weight makes them capable of knocking a person off balance. The observant mountaineer stays abreast of the weather history in the area of interest and constantly studies the terrain for evidence of past avalanche activity and for signs of potential avalanche hazard such as slabby rock bed surfaces. When climbing a slope that appears prone to sluffing, proceed cautiously.

Cornices — The prevailing westerly winds that transport huge amounts of snow across the Front Range are responsible for the buildup of cornices on ridgetops. Cornices can transform ridgetops into beautiful abstract sculptures. Cornices that break are another matter. Even small cornices are extremely heavy. Those that overhang precariously are very likely to break sometime during the spring. It is common to see crate-sized blocks of fractured cornices on many of the slopes described in this book. The number and size of these blocks is a sobering testament to the size of the original cornice. It is easy to envision the outcome of an encounter with hurtling blocks of hardened snow. The careful mountaineer is constantly vigilant when climbing or skiing below cornices. It is best to avoid exposure altogether even if doing so involves selecting a more circuitous route. If it is necessary to climb beneath an overhanging cornice,

A cornice such as this one is a significant hazard to a skier or snowboarder who is directly below. The hazard increases after the sun has warmed the cornice and the surrounding air.

try to predict the path that the falling snow might take down the slope and stay out of this danger zone.

Rockfall — Another hazard of spring mountain travel is rockfall. Anyone who has traveled in the mountains during the spring has probably heard the clattering of rock fall. During the winter water seeps into cracks in rocks and freezes. Expansion of the ice exerts tremendous lateral pressure on the surrounding rock causing it to fracture. As the ice that holds the rocks in place thaws, the loosened rocks are free to find a more stable resting place. Later in the summer many slopes will be littered with rock fragments that broke free earlier as a result of frost action on surrounding rock faces. Crude calculations suggest that rock fall in some zones is a daily occurrence during the spring. The presence of rocks under skis can make for an unpleasant descent. The presence of rocks careening overhead can be deadly!

Moats — Like their medieval counterparts, moats that separate rock walls from the snow are meant to be avoided. Caused by the differential melting of the snow adjacent to rock walls, moats are a common sight throughout the spring and summer seasons. No one deliberately skis into a moat, but it is easy to see how one bad turn might launch a skier moatward with serious consequences. Take note of their presence as you ascend a route.

Differential melting around a large buried boulder caused this moat to form.

Sunburn — Brilliant sunshine and long days are certainly among the joys of summer in the mountains. Unfortunately alpine bowls behave as giant reflector ovens with mountaineers the unwitting foci of their reflections. Backcountry skiers accustomed to the cold temperatures and lower sun angles of winter frequently learn the hard way just how hot and sunny alpine bowls can get. Severe sunburn invariably results from a failure to apply – and reapply – sunscreen. Neither of us can forget the second degree facial burns and subsequent blistering and peeling that we received during a trip through the High Sierras in July at a time when we were inexperienced. All exposed skin surfaces should be slathered generously with sunscreen. Long-sleeved shirts and windpants provide greater protection from the sun. To reduce overhead glare a cap with a bill should be worn. A hat with a 360° brim is even better, but remember to remove it when you are being photographed to avoid looking like a geezer. Sunglasses with side guards ("glacier glasses") are essential equipment. Keep a tube of chapstick in your pocket and apply it frequently throughout the day. Don't be fooled on overcast days. Ultraviolet rays can penetrate clouds and fog.

"Snow Burn" — A surprising characteristic of corn snow is its abrasive quality. The granules of ice that comprise spring snow have the quality of coarse sandpaper. Even a slow speed slide with skin exposed can cause a painful abrasion that at first will not feel painful because of the anesthetic action of the cold snow. On one June outing in the Maroon Bells-Snowmass Wilderness, a companion of ours received an extensive abrasion along his midriff when he "involuntarily glissaded" down a slope. Adding to his discomfort, the affected skin was precisely where his hip belt was designed to rest. While it may be sporting to ski in shorts and a tee shirt, never leave skin exposed when skiing a slope where there is a chance of falling.

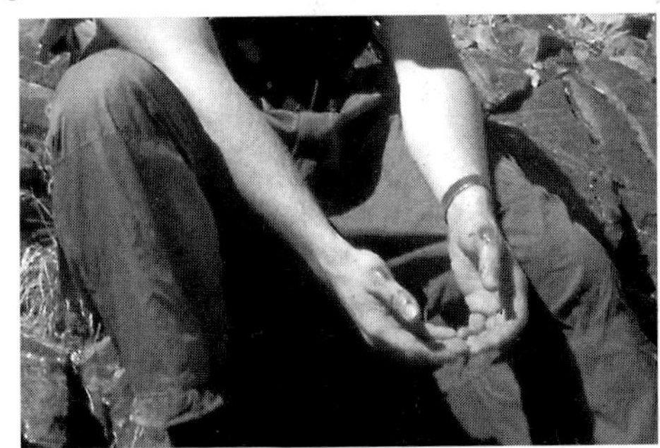

This person suffered a painful hand abrasion because he attempted an ice-axe self-arrest without wearing gloves.

Lightning — Late morning and afternoon thunderstorms are common along the Front Range during the summer. Storms develop and move in amazingly fast. Freezing rain, sleet, and hail accompanied by high winds and plummeting temperatures accompany these storms. By far the greatest hazard during a thunderstorm is lightning. Deaths from lightning strikes occur in the mountains every year. There is nothing more frightening than being trapped on or near a summit with lightning striking nearby. Every mountain traveler should know the procedures to follow during a lighting storm. Weather forecasts can be helpful in judging the likelihood of thunderstorms on a given day; but despite the rosiest forecast, storms may still develop locally. The best policy for avoiding storms is to start out early, summit and descend before noon. This way you can spend the afternoon enjoying a leisurely return to the trailhead or to camp.

Dehydration — Everyone knows that dehydration can be a serious problem when exercising at higher elevations especially in the Rockies where humidities are low. And yet many mountaineers become dehydrated to some degree in the course of a day. The main reasons for insufficient water intake are: the inconvenience of stopping to remove one's pack and drink; a reluctance to carry the extra poundage in the form of water; and the fact that the thirst sensation in humans is delayed until a person is already mildly dehydrated. Here are some strategies to avoid these problems.

- Start your water intake when you wake up and continue drinking up to a liter before you arrive at the trailhead.
- Carry two liters in your pack. Carry a half-liter water bottle on your hip belt within arms reach and take sips during the approach.
- Instead of using water bottles carry your water in a high capacity *Camelbak®* or similar system.
- Before ascending the steep final pitch of a route, take a ten-minute break to gobble some food and drink some more.
- Carry a tiny bottle of iodine tablets or solution so you can decontaminate meltwater from springs and creeks. A water filter is even better but is heavier.
- Notice the color of your urine and how frequently you pee. To put it simply, very yellow pee is bad, and pale-colored pee is good.

With so much melting snow, there's no excuse for dehydration during a spring or summer ski tour. Use your ski pole to fetch a fresh drink from hard to reach places.

Late Starts — Before concluding this section it is worth reemphasizing the importance of starting out early as a way to help avoid some of the problems that were described above. By traveling during the early morning hours the snow will be firmer, easier to walk on, and less likely to slide or sluff. Rockfall and cornice breakage are less likely especially if temperatures have dropped below freezing the night before. Since it is cooler in the morning, physical exertion is more comfortable and less taxing. By summiting before noon, there is a better chance that the top layer of snow will have thawed just enough for perfect skiing conditions. Snow that consists of deep slush is a nuisance to ski. Leaving the trailhead at seven o'clock should be early enough for routes that have relatively short approaches. Six o'clock is the recommended starting time for longer approaches. A few of the routes described can be enjoyed more fully by backpacking into a basecamp the day before and getting an early start the next day. By spending the night closer to one's destination, it is possible to ski two or three nearby routes during the morning and early afternoon.

To avoid the agony of postholing remember two simple words.— Early Start.

Explanation of Route Summaries

Each route description begins with a route number and route title followed by a table that has information needed for choosing and planning a trip. The title is usually the name of the mountain where the descent route is located. Occasionally the title refers to a feature that is not part of a major named mountain – for example, *Stanley Slide Path* or *Loveland Pass.* If the name of a mountain is in quotation marks, this means that the name is unofficial and does not appear on the U.S.G.S. map. Here is a sample table and an explanation of the subheadings that appear in the table.

Difficulty/Quality	Advanced and Expert / ☺☺☺
Season	End of May, June
Distance	8 miles
Starting Elevation	9,475'
Elevation Gain	2,725' to Ptarmigan Pass (12,200')
Access	Bear Lake Parking, Page 38
Maps	
U.S.G.S.	*McHenrys Peak*
Trails Illustrated	#200, *Rocky Mountain National Park*
Guidebook	Page 184

Difficulty/Quality – There are three difficulty ratings: Intermediate, Advanced, and Expert. The rating is determined by the slope angle that is encountered on the descent route when the snow is in ideal condition.

- Intermediate — up to 25 degrees
- Advanced — 25 to 35 degrees
- Expert — 35 to 50 degrees

However, a very short (one or two turns) steep section is not significant enough to warrant a higher rating for a route. The rating is not based on the length or difficulty of the approach and subsequent climb. An intermediate route can be skied by a person who is comfortable skiing "blue" runs at a ski area. Advanced routes require consistent and accurate telemark or parallel turns. A bombproof parallel or telemark jump turn is required on expert routes where missing the mark can result in a long slide. An inclinometer was used to measure slope angles for many of the routes in this book. We also used a trigonometric formula to derive slope angles directly from U.S.G.S. 7.5 minute topographic maps.

Advanced and expert routes should be avoided when conditions are marginal. An icy surface or snow that is severely sun-cupped is difficult and dangerous to ski. Should you decide to forfeit a ski descent because of dangerous conditions, you can spend the time taking pictures, spotting wildlife, or hanging out with friends.

There are three levels of quality:

☺ ☺☺ ☺☺☺

These three ratings are based on a slew of different factors. Very lengthy approaches reduce the rating. Outstanding scenery increases it. Narrowness of a couloir or the likelihood of an uneven snow surface reduces it. More vertical drop increases it.

Season — The routes described in this book may be skied in spring and summer after the snowpack has consolidated. March is definitely too early. The beginning of April is also too early for most of the routes. In late April some of the routes will be skiable while others are not safe to ski until June. The months given with each route are meant to give only a general idea of the best time to plan a trip. Almost all of the routes are skiable for several weeks to more than a month.

Several factors determine when and for how long a route is skiable: the depth of the winter's snowpack; the number and severity of spring snowstorms in the high country; the springtime average daily temperatures; and the amount of rainfall and cloud cover. It is not necessary to delve into these issues in detail. Instead, a couple of examples from the past few years should make it clear that predicting the onset of spring consolidation can be tricky.

1993: There was above average winter snowfall. The spring weather was normal. Consolidation came on schedule in late May and June. Good skiing was had through early August.

1994: The winter snow was almost average. April and May were hot and dry. In June the snow had the texture of July snow, that is, shallow corn on top of a hard icy base. July's snow was hard and treacherous with August almost snow free.

1995: Record amounts of snow fell during April and May. June saw a deep snowpack with an April consistency and very little consolidation. Consolidation was delayed until July with good skiing through August.

2002: Who will forget this snow season? Winter snowfall was the lowest in twenty-five years. However, four significant storms in April and May provided surprising powder conditions for those of us who hadn't auctioned off our skis. In general the spring snowpack in May resembled a June snowpack and June's resembled July's. Considering the low snowpack, the spring skiing was reasonably good, though short-lived.

The only surefire way to determine the condition of the spring snowpack is to go out and stand on it, or else talk to a reliable source who has been out skiing or climbing in the mountains.

May, 2002—The "worst" snow year in twenty-five years?
A series of spring snowstorms provided powder skiing in Kearney Bowl, Loveland Pass.

Distance — This is the round trip distance in miles from the suggested parking area to the high point on the route. Measurements were taken from the U.S.G.S. maps using a map measurer or from computer-generated maps using *TOPO!* ® software. Actual distances may vary slightly. No travel times have been suggested since it has been our experience that these vary enormously among different parties. One half to a full day should be allowed for most of the routes.

Starting Elevation — This is the elevation at the parking area or trailhead. In some cases where you will park will be determined by the amount of snow, if any, on an access road or by the condition of the road and your vehicle's ability to negotiate a rough road. These possibilities are noted where they are relevant.

Elevation Gain — This is the net gain in elevation computed by subtracting the starting elevation from the elevation given in the route title and then rounding to the nearest hundred feet. Occasionally a route may involve a loss of elevation below the parking area. These losses are only factored in when they are significant (for example, the skiing around Loveland Pass or Sundance Mountain).

Access — This is the name of the parking area or trailhead. Descriptions of these are located in the introduction to each of the six Regions.

Maps — Three map sources are cited:

- 7.5 minute U.S.G.S. maps. These are available at local outdoor stores or by mail order from the source listed in the Appendix of this book.
- Composite and annotated *Trails Illustrated Maps®* published by National Geographic. Also available at local outdoor stores.
- Our annotated maps in the back of this book. These maps were created using National Geographic's *TOPO!* ® software and annotated using graphics software.

It is advisable to carry a U.S.G.S. map on all tours. Alternatively, you can purchase the TOPO! ® software and print your own maps. Some outdoor stores have printers that use TOPO! ® software so you can print out exactly the map section that you need on waterproof plastic "paper."

Wet creek crossing enroute to Kelso Mountain.
All in a day's work for the backcountry skier.

And finally...

To view the Front Range only as a place to ski or to snowboard is to miss the point of ski mountaineering. Like mountaineering in general, ski mountaineering is a multifaceted experience. There is satisfaction to be found in the exertion of the approach, in summit views, in camaraderie, in spotting wildlife and wildflowers, as well as in the descent itself. Days are long and the sun warms the breezes. Subalpine forests are redolent with the vapor of minty resins. Streams are thunderous and swollen with meltwater. Savor the complete mountain environment and your ski descents will acquire a broader context and a more lasting meaning.

Below Ptarmigan Point. Rocky Mountain National Park

...there's more than the descent.

Mountain goats — Grays Peak summit

Elk — Rocky Mountain National Park

Ptarmigan — Diamond Peaks

Scarlet gilia

Colorado columbine

"You talkin' to me?"

Region 1

Summit Clark Peak

Cameron Pass

Skiers who are looking for an alternative to the popular venues along the I-70 corridor, Summit County, and the Indian Peaks may want to consider heading for Cameron Pass. Colorado Highway 14 follows the exceptionally scenic Poudre River from Fort Collins to the Pass. Highway 14 is the only major road to split the Front Range between the Wyoming border and the town of Granby, a stretch of seventy miles. The Medicine Bow Mountains and the Rawah Wilderness lie north of the Pass, while the Never Summer Mountains, officially part of Rocky Mountain National Park, lie to the south. Five of the routes described in this section are in the Medicine Bows north of the Pass; Lake Agnes Bowl and Mount Richthofen is the only route on the south side.

Skiing Diamond Peak. Nokhu Crags (left) and Mt. Richthofen (right) in the distance.

To reach Cameron Pass from Fort Collins, locate the merger of Colo. 14 and U.S. 287 in the heart of Fort Collins. Drive north on U.S. 287/Colo. 14 for nine miles to "Ted's Place," where there is a convenience store. Turn left (west) on the continuation of Colo. 14 and drive 73 miles to reach the Pass. There are quite a few Forest Service campgrounds along the highway. The trailheads described below are a few miles on either side of the Pass or at the Pass itself.

Parking and Trailheads

Blue Lake Trailhead Parking and Sawmill Creek Trailhead (9,550')

Located 68 miles from Ted's Place on the right (west) side of the highway. Park here for Clark Peak and the three peaks at the head of Sawmill Creek. For Sawmill Creek, walk about a quarter mile south toward Cameron Pass to a gated dirt road on the right (parking here is prohibited). This old logging road works its way into the Sawmill Creek drainage.

Cameron Pass Parking Area (10,276')

Located directly on the Pass on the right (west) side of the highway. No official trails lead from this parking area. Access to Diamond Peaks is via an avalanche runout on the west side of the parking area. There are picnic tables and a restroom.

Lake Agnes Parking Area (9,710')

Located off Hwy 14, 2.4 miles west of Cameron Pass on the left (south) side of the highway. A sign reads "Lake Agnes – American Lakes." Turn left onto the dirt road and park before the locked gate. Access Lake Agnes Cabin, Lake Agnes Bowl, and Mt. Richthofen.

Agnes Cabin is located only a mile before Lake Agnes.

April, 2002 — A fierce spring snowstorm blankets the Diamond Peaks above Cameron Pass and Highway 14.

(12,951')

Clark Peak

Difficulty/Quality .... Advanced / ☺☺
Season .... End of May, first half of June
Distance .... 12 miles
Starting Elevation ...... 9,550'
Elevation Gain .... 3,400'
Access .... Sawmill Creek Trailhead, Page 24
Maps
U.S.G.S. .... *Clark Peak, Chambers Lake*
Trails Illustrated .... #112, *Poudre River, Cameron Pass*
Guidebook .... Page 180

Clark Peak is the highest mountain in the Medicine Bows. The summit affords excellent views of the north side of Rocky Mountain National Park as well as the other mountains at the head of Sawmill Creek. The loop tour described below involves an approach via Sawmill Creek, a high traverse to the summit of Clark, and a descent into Fall Creek, which can be followed past Chambers Lake and eventually to the Blue Lake Trailhead Parking. The scenery along the entire route is outstanding. Prepare for an early start and a long day.

Park at the Blue Lake trailhead Parking and walk up highway 14 to the Sawmill Creek Trailhead (unsigned). Follow the old logging road (Sawmill Creek Trail), which is likely to be at least partially snow-covered. The road/trail is shown on the T.I. map, but not on the U.S.G.S. map. (At the first left-turning switchback, consider following a rough herd path steeply uphill for 75 yards to rejoin the road. This option saves about a quarter mile along the road.)

Soon the road opens up and becomes a straightaway with good views of Clark Peak, Peak 12,390', and Peak 12,386'. Follow the road for another mile and a half to an obvious ending blocked by forest at 10,400' and 2.3 miles from the start. Drop down a short step to the floor of the Sawmill Creek valley and walk or ski west through open forest, up a steep open slope to a flat basin at 10,800'. Continue west on snow for about a mile along the base of the steep ridge formed by Point 11,730'. A snow slope leads north to the saddle slightly west of Point 11,730'. Gaining this saddle is the key to the route.

From the saddle follow the ridge west for about half a mile to 12,200'. At this point traverse northwest to another saddle slightly north of Point 12,433'. From this saddle, the summit of Clark Peak is 0.7 mile to the north.

From the summit, ski down the southeast shoulder back to the previous saddle. Turn east and ski into the huge bowl (Clark Bowl) east of the saddle. Follow the drainage down an improbable drop into a second huge bowl. Ski down this second bowl and follow the creek drainage through intermittent meadows to 10,600'. At this point your goal is to locate the Blue Lake Trail to avoid running out of snow and ending up slogging through wet meadows or the deadfall-strewn forest. Follow Fall Creek to around 10,400', then head directly north about a quarter mile to the Blue Lake Trail. Ski and eventually hike the trail for about four miles to the Blue Lake Trailhead Parking.

Clark Peak in May. View looking northwest from the Sawmill Creek Trail. Clark Bowl is to the left of and below the summit.

Upper Sawmill Creek Peaks 12,390' and 12,386'

Difficulty/Quality .... Expert (12,390'), Advanced (12,386') / ☺☺
Season .... End of May, first half of June
Distance .... 9 miles for each peak, 11 miles for both
Starting Elevation ...... 9,550'
Elevation Gain .... 2,840'
Access .... Sawmill Creek Trailhead, Page 24
Maps
U.S.G.S. .... *Clark Peak, Chambers Lake*
Trails Illustrated .... #112, *Poudre River, Cameron Pass*
Guidebook .... Page 180

The two inviting peaks located at the head of Sawmill Creek can both be skied in the same trip. Each peak offers around 1000 vertical feet of steep skiing, not counting the return to the Sawmill Creek Trail. These peaks are clearly visible south of Clark Peak while hiking west on the trail.

Follow the route directions under Clark Peak to the point where the Sawmill Creek Trail (old logging road) ends at 2.3 miles and 10,400'. Turn left (south) and ski up a short steep step to less steep wooded, but open, terrain. After 100 feet of climb, turn west and ski toward timberline and flat open terrain at an elevation of 11,000'. This is where the routes to the peaks split.

For Peak 12,390', head slightly north of west into the basin at the foot of the peak. Gain a bench at 11,480'. The steep east face is above this bench. Climb directly toward the summit. There is a small cornice that can be passed on the left side. Ski the fall line, directly east, staying north of the ascent line.

For Peak 12,386', from the 11,000' point described above, head southwest and gain the long east ridge of the peak. Hike along this ridge west and then south to the summit. Slightly south of the summit, ski into the east-facing bowl.

Returning to the Sawmill Creek Trail from either peak is easy. Use your map and visual landmarks to locate the more southerly branch of Sawmill Creek. Follow the creek to 10,600'. From this point the creek cuts a steep-sided channel. Avoid this channel by skiing along the right bank through an old logging area. Be watchful for stumps and downed timber.

The Sawmill Creek trail starts out as an old logging road that leads to the two beautiful peaks at the head of Sawmill Creek. Peak 12,390' is on the right. Peak 12,386' is on the left. Both can be skied in a single outing.

Upper Sawmill Creek Peak (12,170')

Difficulty/Quality	Expert / ☺☺☺
Season	End of May, first half of June
Distance	9 miles
Starting Elevation	9,550'
Elevation Gain	2,600'
Access	Sawmill Creek Trailhead, Page 24
Maps	
U.S.G.S.	*Clark Peak, Chambers Lake*
Trails Illustrated	#112, *Poudre River, Cameron Pass*
Guidebook	Page 180

This beautiful peak is located just south of the two peaks described in the last section. It isn't visible, as are the others, during the hike up the Sawmill Creek Trail. It comes into view upon arriving at the flat basin above timberline (11,000'). The ski descent is a bit shorter than the previous two, but what it lacks in length it makes up for in beauty of line. It can be combined with the previous two peaks, making for a long and strenuous day of skiing.

To reach Peak 12,170', follow the previous route description for Clark Peak to the end of the Sawmill Creek Trail (road) at 2.3 miles and 10,400'. Turn left (south) and ski up a short steep step to less steep wooded, but open, terrain. After 100 feet of climb, traverse south for about a quarter mile and cross the southwest branch of Sawmill Creek. As you climb above the creek bed, the terrain opens up and the long east ridge of Peak 12,170' appears. Gain this ridge at its east end by the easiest way possible. Hike west along the ridge to the summit. The ski descent starts out with a wide northeasterly aspect, then narrows and drops to the valley floor. To return to the Sawmill Creek trail from the flat terrain below the peak, follow the description for the previous two Sawmill Creek peaks.

The irresistable descent on the north side of Peak 12,170' begins to the left of the pointed summit.

(11,781' and 11,852')

Diamond Peaks

Difficulty/Quality .... Expert (11,781'), Adv. (11,852') / ☺☺☺
Season .... Mid May, first half of June
Distance .... 2 miles
Starting Elevation ...... 10,276'
Elevation Gain .... 1,500'
Access .... Cameron Pass parking area, Page 24
Maps
U.S.G.S. .... *Clark Peak*
Trails Illustrated .... #112, *Poudre River, Cameron Pass*
Guidebook .... Page 181

Winter or spring the Diamond Peaks are the most accessible and most popular skiing destination near Cameron Pass. Springtime visitors to the Pass can ski in the morning, and then spend the afternoon bicycling, fishing, or relaxing. The view to the south of the Lake Agnes area and the Nokhu Crags is outstanding. The Diamond Peaks are clearly visible from Colorado 14 a mile and a half north of the pass near the Zimmerman Lake trailhead parking area.

Park in the Cameron Pass parking area. From the restrooms, head due west for 50 yards and locate a wide, low angled, avalanche runout that is likely to be snow-covered. Hike or ski up this path to timberline at 11,000'. The 11,781' Diamond Peak is directly in front of you. Hike or ski up the right (north) side of the peak to the ridgeline and follow it south to the summit. For Peak 11,852', follow the ridgeline north to the obvious summit. The skiing is generally better, although steeper, on Peak 11,781' due to its northeasterly, rather than easterly, exposure. The return route follows the ascent route.

The more southerly of the Diamond Peaks (11,781') is clearly visible above highway 14 about a mile before reaching the parking area at Cameron Pass.

The summit of Diamond Peak (11,781').

(12,940')

Lake Agnes Bowl and Mount Richthofen

Difficulty/Quality .... Advanced / ☺☺☺
Season .... End of May, first half of June
Distance .... 7.5 miles
Starting Elevation ...... 9,710'
Elevation Gain .... 2,300' to saddle at top of bowl, 3,200' to summit
Access .... Lake Agnes Parking Area, Page 24
Maps
U.S.G.S. .... *Clark Peak, Mount Richthofen*
Trails Illustrated .... #112, *Poudre River, Cameron Pass*
Guidebook .... Page 181

Driving south and west from Cameron Pass on Colo. 14, you get outstanding views into the huge basin above and surrounding Lake Agnes. Incredibly, reaching Lake Agnes and the snow-filled bowl above the lake is a relatively easy undertaking. The summit of Mount Richthofen is an option after reaching the saddle at the top of the bowl. Most of the route described below can be previewed from the highway.

Walk around the locked gate at the Lake Agnes parking area and walk along the road for a half a mile to a large clearing. Turn right onto another dirt road that crosses a large creek (Michigan Creek) on a bridge. Continue on this jeep road (probably snow-covered) for another mile and a half to Agnes Cabin situated in a meadow at 10,300'. (See photo on page 24.) Presently the cabin is not available to rent, but the meadow is a good place to set up a base camp.

The easiest way to Lake Agnes from this cabin is as follows. Head southeast for a few hundred feet and locate a snow-filled gully that sits at the base of the steep snow and talus-covered slopes of the Nokhu Crags. Follow this obvious line directly to Lake Agnes.

From Lake Agnes hike or ski south along the east bank of the lake. Continue south and slightly east on open snow slopes into the huge bowl above and eventually to a second higher bowl that culminates in a saddle at 12,000'. This saddle provides rare views of the Never Summer Mountains to the south.

You can drop your skis at the saddle and hike and scramble another 1000 feet to the summit of Mt. Richthofen.

From the saddle, ski directly down the bowl retracing your ascent route. It is possible to ski all the way back to the bridge that crosses the Michigan River.

From L to R — Nokhu Crags , Mt. Richthofen, Lake Agnes Bowl (center), and Mt. Mahler

Preparing to descend Lake Agnes Bowl

Region 2

Ascending Notchtop Couloir — Ptarmigan Point Cirque

Rocky Mountain National Park

Mount Fairchild

Many of us who live along the Front Range may take for granted that one of America's most famous national parks is only an hour or so drive from home. When we visit the Park it is usually to snowshoe, hike, climb or observe wildlife. So it may come as a surprise that the Park has challenging spring ski descents that complement its superb alpine climbing and spectacular and rugged scenery. There are ski descents to match every level of ability.

Access to the Park is from three directions. From the Fort Collins – Denver corridor, highways lead west to the mountain town of Estes Park. From the south, access to the Park is via Colorado Highway 7, the "Peak To Peak Highway," which also leads to Estes Park. From the west side towns of Granby and Grand Lake, U.S. Highway 34 leads north into the Park where Hwy. 34 is named "Trail Ridge Road." Trail Ridge Road traverses the Park for 48 miles connecting the resort towns of Estes Park and Grand Lake. The road's maximum elevation is 12,000 feet slightly west of Sundance Mountain. Trail Ridge Road is usually opened by Memorial Day at the end of May after snowplow crews have cleared the road.

Entrance into the Park requires a fee of $7 (five-day pass) or annual park pass ($30). Reservations are required to camp in one of the Park's four campgrounds. The camping fee is $18.

Parking and Trailheads

Lawn Lake Trailhead Parking (8,550')

Use the more northerly Fall River Entrance to the Park. The entrance station is five miles west of Estes Park. The Lawn Lake Trailhead parking is 2 miles west of the entrance station on Trail Ridge Road on the right (west) side of the road. This trailhead is used to access Mts. Ypsilon and Fairchild. There is a restroom here.

Sundance Mountain Parking (12,100')

Use the more southerly Beaver Meadows Entrance to the Park. Parking for Sundance Mountain is located 18 miles west of Estes Park along Trail Ridge road and 0.65 miles east of the "Rock Cut." This is not a developed parking lot but a widened shoulder. Park on the south side of the road. The view of immense Forest Canyon south of the road is breathtaking. Forest Canyon is the headwaters of the Big Thompson River. An easy stroll toward the saddle to the north leads to the Sundance Mountain snowfield.

Alpine Visitor Center on Trail Ridge Road (11,796')

Use the more southerly Beaver Meadows Entrance to the Park. The large parking area, visitor center, souvenir shop and snack bar are located 23 miles west of Estes Park on Trail Ridge Road. This is a cold and windy place. From the parking area, a dirt road (Fall River Road) leads east and downhill for two miles to the Chapin Pass trailhead where a marked trail leads north to Chapin Pass and access to Mount Chapin and Mount Chiquita. The road is closed to cars, so consider using a mountain bike to reach the Chapin Pass trailhead.

Bear Lake Parking (9,440')

Possibly the busiest parking lot in the Park because it enables access to so many beautiful trails and destinations. Use the more southerly Beaver Meadows Entrance to the Park. Two tenths of a mile past the entrance station, turn left (south) onto the road to Moraine Park. Stay on this road for nine miles until it dead ends at the Bear Lake parking area. Trails to Ptarmigan Point, Notchtop Mountain, and Flattop Mountain begin here. There is a restroom.

Glacier Gorge Parking (9,240')

Use the more southerly Beaver Meadows Entrance to the Park. Two tenths of a mile past the entrance station, turn left (south) onto the road to Moraine Park. Stay on this road for 8.4 miles. The Glacier Gorge Trailhead parking is located in the crook of a hairpin curve. The trail to Taylor Glacier starts just across the road. There is a restroom.

Colorado River Trailhead (9,140')

This trailhead is located on the west side of the Park just off Trail Ridge Road (U.S. 34). If you are driving from the south through Grand Lake, the trailhead is ten miles north of the Grand Lake Entrance Station on the left (west) side of the highway. If you are driving west from Estes Park, the trailhead is ten miles west of the Alpine Visitor Center (see above) on the right (west) side of the highway, at the bottom of a long series of switchbacks. From here a trail heads north along the nascent Colorado River with branches leading west into the Never Summer Mountains and Mount Cumulus. A restroom is located across the road at a different trailhead.

A blue bird morning in June. Sundance Mountain parking area.

(13,502')

Fairchild Mountain

Difficulty/Quality .... Advanced / ☺
Season .... End of May, first half of June
Distance .... 12 miles
Starting Elevation ...... 8,550'
Elevation Gain .... 5,000'
Access .... Lawn Lake Trailhead, Page 38
Maps
U.S.G.S. .... *Trail Ridge*
Trails Illustrated .... #200, *Rocky Mountain National Park*
Guidebook .... Page 182

A trip to Fairchild is one of the most committing in the Front Range. Five of the twelve miles are off trail and a portion of the trailed section also requires routefinding since the trail is covered with snow. Do not attempt to reach this mountain unless your orienteering skills are excellent. An early start is mandatory.

Fortunately, the south face of Fairchild is massive and the snow slope so prominent that it is visible from many places in the Park and even along the highways leading to the Park. The best views of Fairchild and Ypsilon, its southern neighbor, are from Trail Ridge Road just before and just after "Many Parks Curve."

Begin at the Lawn Lake Trailhead and hike for 1.2 miles to a junction. The trail straight ahead goes to Lawn Lake while the left trail is the Ypsilon Lake trail, the one you want to take. Drop to the creek and cross it on a bridge. Hike steadily uphill to where the trail flattens at about 10,300'. From this point there is usually snow and hopefully an old snowshoe/ski track. Attempt to follow the trail along the broad, forested ridge to an elevation of 10,700'. Take care to stay on the trail since clear landmarks in this area are sparse. The trail makes a short traverse slightly downhill along a steep hillside to tiny Chipmunk Lake (10,740').

From Chipmunk Lake head due north on snow (off the trail) a quarter mile to the outlet of Ypsilon Lake, one of the Park's many gems. Hike several hundred yards along the base of a steep, talus-strewn slope and locate a steep, grassy slope that leads up to a flat bench east (right) of some cliffs. Hike up this slope to the bench. From the bench drop down a snow slope to the first of the Fay Lakes (10,800').

From this lake head north along the east side of the main creek to reach the second, larger Fay Lake (11,100'). The view of the craggy Blitzen Ridge leading to the summit of Ypsilon is stunning. Curve around the west side of the lake and climb or ski north to a flat spot at 11,300' with more great views. Directly in front (north) of you is a steep, snow-filled gully. Climb to the left (west) side of the center of the gully since the snow in the gully lies on top of several short, steep ice-falls. (Remember this when you are skiing down.) After a climb of about 1000', the steepness moderates and you can "cruise" another 1000' to the summit.

The ski descent and return to the trailhead are a reversal of the approach.

Looking north toward Mount Fairchild from Trail Ridge Road.

(13,514')

Ypsilon Mountain

Difficulty/Quality .... Advanced / ☺
Season .... End of May, first half of June
Distance .... 11 miles
Starting Elevation ...... 8,550'
Elevation Gain .... 5,000'
Access .... Lawn Lake Trailhead, Page 38
Maps
U.S.G.S. .... *Trail Ridge*
Trails Illustrated .... #200, *Rocky Mountain National Park*
Guidebook .... Page 182

Like Fairchild Mountain, Ypsilon is another mountain that involves a difficult approach especially when much of the route above 10,500' is snow-covered. From Chipmunk Lake the route-finding is a bit more difficult than it is for Fairchild.

In the route description for Fairchild Mountain, follow the directions to Chipmunk Lake. At Chipmunk Lake continue northwest on the Ypsilon Lake Trail (rather than heading due north as for Fairchild). Stay on the trail for about 200 yards at which point you will see a large, unforested, talus-strewn clearing on your left. Turn off the trail and head due west into this basin. Climb west out of the basin and pick your way across snow, talus, and through forest to the steep-walled, lightly forested bowl (11,000') that sits below Chiquita Lake. From this relatively open area pick your way northwest and uphill into the drainage that originates in the bowl between Ypsilon and Chiquita. With good route-finding, you can stay on snow the entire time, eventually reaching the base (12,000') of Ypsilon's south face where a long snow slope leads north toward the summit plateau. Climb the snow slope to where the snow ends at 13,000'. You can turn around and ski the slope, or else drop your skis and head for the summit. Beyond the top of the snow slope, gentle tundra for 0.4 mile leads north to the summit. The view to the east into the Spectacle Lakes basin is incredible. Remember that the snow slope faces south and that a trip to the summit will delay your descent, which could result in the snow softening too much.

From the summit, return to your skis and ski down to 11,000'. From here try to follow your ascent route back to Chipmunk Lake. Except for a short stretch of uphill past Chipmunk Lake, you can often ski through the forest down to about 10,500' although the snow conditions are likely to be marginal. From the snowline, hike back to the Lawn Lake Trailhead.

Mount Ypsilon from the southeast

(13,069')

Mount Chiquita

Difficulty/Quality .... Expert (top of couloir), advanced to the bottom / probably ☺☺☺
Season .... End of May, June
Distance .... 10 miles from the Alpine Visitor Center; 6 miles from Fall River Road
Starting Elevation ...... Alpine Visitor Center - 11,800'; Fall River Road – 8,780'
Elevation Gain .... 1,269' from Alpine Visitor Center; 4,290' from Fall River Road
Access .... Alpine Visitor Center, Page 38
Maps
U.S.G.S. .... *Trail Ridge*
Trails Illustrated .... #200, *Rocky Mountain National Park*
Guidebook .... Page 183

Several times while driving along Trail Ridge Road past the huge Rainbow Curve parking area and rest stop, we stared in awe at the south face of Mount Chiquita. Splitting the middle of the face is a snow couloir of compelling beauty and line. We had no idea if anyone had named it, but "Banana Couloir" immediately came to mind. (Regrettably, so did "Banana Split.") Viewed head on, the Banana Couloir looks almost vertical. It isn't. In fact the average slope angle is 35 degrees, an estimation derived from the topographic map and direct observation from the bottom of the couloir. The wider top portion, we guessed, is 45 degrees based on similar couloirs elsewhere.

Two years ago in June, a couple of us hiked to the summit of Chiquita from the Alpine Visitor Center. We stood at the top of Mount Chiquita in full skiing dress. We were breathless with anticipation and oxygen deprivation, but clueless about how we would exit the valley of Chiquita Creek once we had reached the bottom of the couloir. In order to return to the Visitor Center, we considered three options. Option 1 would be to exit via the headwall at the upper end of Chiquita Creek between Mounts Chapin and Chiquita. The headwall is very steep, corniced, and bounded by cliffs. Not impossible but definitely tricky and requiring crampons and an ice axe. Option 2 would be to bushwhack over two miles down Chiquita Creek to Fall River Road, hike two more miles down the road to Trail Ridge Road, and hitchhike back to the Visitor

Center. Option 3, of course, would be to climb up the couloir and reverse the approach.

Unfortunately (or fortunately?) a huge fog bank crept in from the east, its billowy whiteness obscuring the couloir and the entire valley of Chiquita Creek. The scene reminded us of a Norwegian fjord. We lingered for a few hours in the hope that the fog bank would dissolve. It didn't. Unwilling to ski blindly into the couloir, we agreed to Option 4 – turned around and returned with our "skis between our legs."

Based on a summer excursion we made up Chiquita Creek to the bottom of the couloir, our bias in the future would be to exit via Chiquita Creek, about a two hour bushwhack. This means you would have to leave a car parked at the Endovalley picnic area, drive a second car to the Alpine Visitor Center, hike to the summit of Chiquita via Chapin Pass, ski the couloir, and return to the first car via Chiquita Creek. The suggested route down Chiquita Creek is indicated on the map on page 183. There are game trails to follow and the deadfall is moderate.

None of the above should discourage ski mountaineers with the requisite skill and stamina from attempting this route. But we have one favor to ask. If you descend the Banana Couloir (or whatever you choose to call it) or if you have already done so, please let us know what you found. If we get to it before you do, we'll share with you our impressions. Finally, if you or anyone you know about has skied this line, we'd like to know about it.

Mount Chiquita. The Banana Couloir is in the center of the photo.

(12,200')

Sundance Mountain Bowl

Difficulty/Quality	Intermediate, Advanced and Expert (lower 1/3) / ☺☺☺
Season	Memorial Day weekend, June
Distance	1.6 miles (includes uphill climb from bottom of slope)
Starting Elevation	12,050'
Elevation Gain	1,700'
Access	Sundance Mountain parking, Page 38
Maps	
U.S.G.S.	*Trail Ridge*
Trails Illustrated	#200, *Rocky Mountain National Park*
Guidebook	Page 183

When Trail Ridge Road opens for the summer (usually Memorial Day weekend), Sundance Mountain Bowl becomes a popular destination for spring skiers. This is "buy now...pay later" skiing at its best. You can get out of your car, walk several hundred yards, hop onto your skis or snowboard and drop 1,700 vertical feet into the steep valley of Fall River. Because the slope is convex, you get plenty of lower angle turns in perfect corn snow before the terrain steepens dramatically. Unfortunately there is no chairlift, team of mules, or jet pack to get you back to the top. So you have to pay. The price is roughly a mile and 1,600 uphill vertical feet of kicking steps and skinning or snowshoeing. Hopefully your descent will be so exhilarating and your turns so perfect that you will consider the price a bargain, or at least, a fair trade.

From the Sundance Mountain parking, hike north easily toward the left (west) side of a broad saddle that lies west of Sundance Mountain. The wide snow-filled bowl isn't visible until you reach the saddle. In order to squeeze out a bit of extra vertical, head for the high point of snow amid a rocky area on the west side of the top of the bowl. Ski down from this point.

As mentioned above, the top of the bowl is intermediate, the mid-section is advanced, and the bottom third is expert. Intermediate skiers can choose to ski as far as their skills and nerve allow, then return to the top, and perhaps, make repeat runs.

This bowl should be skied in the morning as soon as the top inch of snow has thawed. Later in the morning, the snow thaws out to a much greater depth. Waiting too long can mean an incredibly arduous climb especially through the steep section above the river where the snow lies atop willows and is prone to collapse.

Carving turns in perfect corn, beneath a cobalt sky, in the Sundance Mountain bowl

(12,200')

Ptarmigan Point Cirque

Difficulty/Quality .... Advanced and Expert / ☺☺☺
Season .... End of May, June
Distance .... 8 miles
Starting Elevation ...... 9,475'
Elevation Gain .... 2,725' to Ptarmigan Pass (12,200')
Access .... Bear Lake Parking, Page 38
Maps
U.S.G.S. .... *McHenrys Peak*
Trails Illustrated .... #200, *Rocky Mountain National Park*
Guidebook .... Page 184

The large snow-filled cirque bounded by Notchtop Mountain, Ptarmigan Point and Flattop Mountain is the best spring skiing destination in Rocky Mountain National Park. There are several routes of varying steepness. The snow is abundant and reliable. The approach is not unreasonably long. The scenery is superb. In May and early June you can expect the trail to be snow-covered west of the Flattop Mountain Trail cutoff. Since the Bear Lake Parking area is open year round, the bowl can be skied in May during lean snow years.

From the west end of the Bear Lake Parking area, start walking north past Bear Lake along the Fern Lake Trail. The trail climbs to the northeast and switches back to the west after 0.3 miles. Remain on this trail until you reach Lake Helene at about 2.8 miles. Much of the trail is likely to be snow-covered, and it can be easy to lose the trail.

At Lake Helene the main trail turns north, eventually dropping down to beautiful Odessa Lake. Leave the main trail here and ski or hike downhill to the north bank of Lake Helene. Follow around the edge of the lake to its west end and climb a snow slope that eventually leads to a basin at 11,000' on the south side of Notchtop Mountain. Most of the skiing options are visible from this point.

Notchtop Mountain Couloir (Expert) is visible on the northwest side of the cirque. Do not confuse this with the couloir that sits beside the southwest flank of Notchtop Mountain and that is used by climbers descending from the summit of Notchtop. The correct couloir is 200 yards further southwest. At more than 1,200 vertical feet, this is the longest continuous run in the cirque, and it is outstanding.

Due west there is a shorter slope (Advanced) below the uppermost bowl that sits below Ptarmigan Point. Meanwhile on the south side of the cirque there are two roughly parallel steep slopes (Expert) that are capped with cornices. Because of their northerly exposure, these can be skied later in the day compared to the couloir.

By climbing west up to the hanging bowl above, you can access Ptarmigan Point snowfield (Expert at the top only) and the Continental Divide. This snowfield is a good choice for skiers who are looking for a more moderate descent.

The return to the trailhead is a reverse of the approach, but noticeably quicker when most of the trail is snow covered.

View west into Ptarmigan Bowl. Ptarmigan Point is the point on the right that appears lower than the surroundings.

Notchtop Couloir as seen from the Continental Divide.
This is one of the most spectacular ski descents in the Front Range.

Skiing Notchtop Couloir

(12,324')

Flattop Mountain

Difficulty/Quality .... Intermediate + Advanced option / ☺☺☺
Season .... May, first half of June
Distance .... 6.5 miles
Starting Elevation ...... 9,475'
Elevation Gain .... 2,800'
Access .... Bear Lake Parking, Page 38
Maps
U.S.G.S. .... *McHenrys Peak*
Trails Illustrated .... #200, *Rocky Mountain National Park*
Guidebook .... Page 184

Imagine a sunny weekend in May or early June. You're thinking about a relatively easy day of skiing with friends. You envision long runs on excellent snow. An *après ski* picnic at the bottom of the hill would make a perfect addition to the experience. Where would you go? Our first choice would be Flattop Mountain.

There are two options in reaching Flattop Mountain. The first is to follow the Fern Lake Trail (see previous route description) for two miles to the bottom of the wide snow slope on Flattop's north side. Then hike or skin for 1,300 vertical feet to the top of the slope. The second, more scenic option is to follow the Flattop Mountain Trail, which branches south from the Fern Lake Trail after one mile. This trail switchbacks up the broad east ridge of Flattop, then continues along the low angled, rocky ridge top to the summit, which lies west of the main snow ski slope. This trail (two miles in length from its junction with the Fern Lake Trail) usually has snow at 10,600' and above and can be hard to follow. A bit later in the season, Colorado columbines bloom along the rocky edges of the trail. Picnickers may want to consider the first option, while skiers looking for a grand tour of Flattop should consider the second.

The easier ski run, and the one more frequently skied, is the wide slope that starts from Point 12,012'. Skiers looking for a steeper descent can hike farther west to the summit where there is an excellent convex slope that points northeast at first, then north directly toward Lake Helene. Incidentally this slope is an excellent place to view the condition of the Notchtop Couloir mentioned in the previous description. If you select the steeper alternative, it will add a mile to the return trip.

The top of the Flattop Mountain snowfield viewed from the Flattop Mountain Trail. This is one of the best intermediate descents in the Front Range.

(12,700')

Taylor Glacier

Difficulty/Quality .... Expert / ☺☺
Season .... End of May, June
Distance .... 10 miles
Starting Elevation ...... 9,240'
Elevation Gain .... 3,460'
Access .... Glacier Gorge Parking, Page 38
Maps
U.S.G.S. .... *McHenrys Peak*
Trails Illustrated .... #200, *Rocky Mountain National Park*
Guidebook .... Page 185

A visit to Taylor Glacier will take you through one of the most beautiful valleys in the National Park. The trail passes two waterfalls and three lakes, with the highest one, Sky Pond, situated below one of the Park's most popular rock climbing destinations – the Petit Grepon and the Sabre. From a high point on Taylor Glacier, you can ski 1,600 vertical feet to Sky Pond. The lower two-thirds of the glacier is advanced and eventually intermediate in difficulty.

From the Glacier Gorge parking area, cross the road to reach the trail to Glacier Gorge. After half a mile the trail passes Alberta Falls. A series of switchbacks followed by a level stretch brings you to a trail junction. The trail to the left goes to Glacier Gorge. Continue straight ahead on the trail to The Loch, a large lake. The Loch, an irresistible spot to take a quick break, is reached after about 2.5 miles. The trail continues around the north side of the lake and you are likely to encounter intermittent snow banks here. Continue further up Loch Vale and climb a snow-covered steep section that tops out at Glass Lake. The trail officially ends here, but there is a cairned climber's path that continues up the valley to Sky Pond.

From Sky Pond the route into the upper cirque and the top of the glacier is obvious. The top of the glacier is capped with a cornice. Because of the steepness many people begin skiing a hundred feet or so below the top. The snowfield is wide enough for a person to choose the best line with the best snow. A runnel or two is common.

Jordan Campbell

View of Taylor Glacier from the approach route. Sky Pond is located to the left of the skier.

(12,725')

Mount Cumulus

Difficulty/Quality .... Advanced / ☺
Season .... June
Distance .... 13 miles
Starting Elevation ...... 9,140'
Elevation Gain .... 3,600'
Access .... Colorado River Trailhead, Page 39
Maps
U.S.G.S. .... *Mt. Richthofen, Fall River Pass*
Trails Illustrated .... #200, *Rocky Mountain National Park*
Guidebook .... Page 186

The aptly-named Never Summer Mountains form the northwest boundary of Rocky Mountain National Park. There are a dozen peaks over 12,000 feet that are snow covered for much of the summer. There are excellent views of the range from the Gore Range Overlook and especially from Fairview Curve along Trail Ridge Road.

Mount Cumulus stands out among its neighbors due to its greater breadth and amount of snow cover. A trip to Mount Cumulus is a remote mountain adventure that provides a chance to visit the summit of a peak that is rarely climbed and that offers an uncommon view of the national park. The eastern flank offers a ski descent of almost 2,000 vertical feet.

From the trailhead hike north along a beautiful trail that parallels the Colorado River. After 0.6 mile a trail turns left (west) off the main trail, crosses a meadow and the Colorado River, before climbing the west side of the valley. (Note: This trail has been rerouted from the original path shown on the U.S.G. S. map. The Trails Illustrated map and the map in the back of this book show the location of the newer trail.) After about four miles, the trail reaches the Grand Ditch road, a dirt service road that parallels a large aqueduct. This aqueduct diverts western slope water across the Continental Divide for farmers, ranchers and residents of the eastern slope. (Thus the Colorado River, barely in its infancy, is deprived of precious snowmelt.)

Walk west about three quarters of a mile along the ditch road to where it crosses Opposition Creek. There is a bridge (right turn) here that crosses the aqueduct. A trail continues west along Opposition Creek. This trail is likely to be snow covered. Regardless, follow the creek for about half a mile to 10,600'. Bear away from the creek and locate a steep open slope that leads west and then northwest to timberline and the open slopes below Mt. Cumulus. From here hike or skin up 1,600 vertical feet to the summit ridge. From the summit ski directly east along a subtle ridge. The return follows the approach route.

Bob Jamieson

In this distant view of the Never Summer Mountains from the east, Mount Cumulus is the snow-covered hump in the center of the range.

Approaching Jasper Reservoir

The Indian Peaks

Driving west toward Boulder during the spring or early summer, one can't resist gazing up at the snowcovered Indian Peaks rising high above the foothills. Shadowed on the north by towering Longs Peak in Rocky Mountain National Park, the Indian Peaks stretch southward for twenty miles to Rollins Pass. The twenty-five summits range in elevation from 12,000' to 13,500' and constitute the crest of the Continental Divide in this part of the Front Range. Located about an hour, more or less, from Denver or Boulder, they are among the most accessible high mountains found near an urban population center. Because of heavy summer usage, a permit is required to camp in the Indian Peaks Wilderness Area between June 1 and September 15. However, there are sections of the Indian Peaks, such as the Four Lakes Travel Zone west of Brainard Lake, where camping has been prohibited or is extremely restricted. Permits are issued for a nominal fee at several locations that are listed on the Arapaho-Roosevelt N.F. website in the Appendix. The person that issues your permit can provide information about current restrictions.

Lake Isabelle — View west toward Navajo and Apache.

Navajo Snowfield (left) and Apache Couloir (right) are directly above the person.

The City of Boulder Watershed *— If you look at a map of the Indian Peaks Wilderness Area, you will notice that a "bite" has been taken out of the east side of the Wilderness Area. This is the 6,500-acre City of Boulder Watershed. This land is owned by the City of Boulder. The area is bounded on the north by Niwot Ridge and Navajo Peak and on the west and south by the Arapaho Peaks and the immense east shoulder of South Arapaho. The Watershed includes the relatively large Arapaho Glacier, which is a prominent landmark when viewed from points further east. Entry into the Watershed is prohibited by law. The area is patrolled regularly and trespassers, if caught, will be fined.*

Parking and Trailheads

The scenic, high elevation Peak-To-Peak Highway is the primary auto route *east* of the Continental Divide for travelers heading into the Indian Peaks. The highway winds southward from Estes Park to U.S. Highway 6, and ends two miles from Interstate 70 and seven miles east of Idaho Springs. The numbering of the Peak-To-Peak Highway can be confusing. From Estes Park southward to a fork four miles south of Allenspark, the highway is designated "Route 7." From this fork to Nederland the highway is "Route 72." From Nederland to U.S. Highway 6, which runs through Clear Creek Canyon, the highway is "Route119."

For travelers accessing the *west* side of the Indian Peaks, there are two options: Interstate 70 to Highway 40 over Berthoud Pass, then north past Winter Park to Granby and Grand Lake. Or, if it is open, one can take Trail Ridge Road (U.S. 34) from Estes Park, through Rocky Mountain National Park, to Grand Lake.

Allenspark / Rock Creek Road (8,700')

From the point on the Peak-To-Peak Highway where "Route 72" becomes "Route 7," drive north four miles and turn left (west) into the community of Allenspark After 200 yards make a right onto Ski Road (2WD dirt). Follow Ski Road for 1.3 miles to a signed fork, "Rock Creek/St. Vrain Mountain Trail." Turn left toward Rock Creek and continue downhill on a rougher road, cross a small creek, and park one-quarter mile ahead by a campsite on the left side of the road. Beyond this point, the road is 4WD dirt and becomes very steep and rough. If Rock Creek Road is in poor shape or snow covered, you can also park back at the signed fork. To reach St. Vrain Mountain, hike or ski west along Rock Creek Road. (The "St. Vrain Mountain Trail" mentioned above reaches St. Vrain Mountain via a longer and less direct route that leads past Meadow Mountain.)

Peaceful Valley / Camp Dick Campground (8,638')

Locate the hairpin turn that skirts around Peaceful Valley, a tiny settlement between Ward and Allenspark. Here the Peak-To-Peak Highway (Route 72) crosses Middle St. Vrain Creek. Turn west onto the dirt road and drive a mile to the Camp Dick campground where there is parking at the far end of the campground. Persons with high clearance 4WD or a mountain bike may attempt to continue on the rough and rocky road for four miles to the St. Vrain Glacier Trailhead. In May and early June the road is closed because of snowcover and washouts. On the north side of Middle St. Vrain Creek there is a foot trail (Buchanan Pass Trail) that leads to the same trailhead as the road. Either way the access is gentle but long. Use the road or the trail to access Ogalalla, Elk Tooth, St. Vrain Glaciers and "Red Deer Mountain."

Beaver Reservoir / Coney Flats Road (9,190')

The tiny town of Ward lies a "stone's throw" east of the Peak-To-Peak Highway (Route 72). From the more northerly of two turnoffs that lead down to Ward, drive north 2.6 miles and turn left (west) onto County Road 96, a 2WD road. (A small sign before the turnoff says "Boy Scout Camp"). Take this dirt road 2.8 miles to the signed Coney Flats Road on the right. This very rough 4WD road begins on the north side of Beaver Reservoir, and there is space for parking on the shoulder. The road, which is usually closed to vehicles due to its poor condition, climbs gently to the west and is flooded in spots. It reaches Coney Flats and the Wilderness trailhead after 3.5 miles. Be aware that the road has three major forks along its length. If you are on foot, which is likely, keep right at each of these forks. From the Wilderness trailhead you can access the Buchanan Pass Trail leading to Sawtooth Mountain or Upper Coney Lake and the bottom of the three "Coney Couloirs" on the northwest face of Mount Audubon.

Brainard Lake (10,500')

The tiny town of Ward lies a "stone's throw" east of the Peak-To-Peak Highway (Route 72). From the more northerly of two turnoffs that lead down to Ward, drive north about 100 yards and take a hard left onto the paved road to Brainard Lake. After 2.7 winding miles you'll reach the Red Rock Lake Trailhead and gate closure. The gate is closed through May and opens around the middle of June. Park here when the gate is closed.

Many people bemoan the road closure, which lasts into mid-June, but the two-mile walk or bike ride to Brainard Lake is easy and very scenic. You'll appreciate the alpenglow and the solitude. By midday the road will be much more crowded.

By mid-June, when the road is finally opened to cars, you can drive past Brainard Lake and the Pawnee Campground to one of two well-signed and spacious backcountry trailheads. The more southerly trailhead (10,500') accesses the Pawnee Pass Trail, Long Lake, Lake Isabelle, and Navajo and Apache Peaks. The more northerly one (10,480') accesses Mitchell and Blue Lakes and the trails to Mount Audubon, Paiute Peak, and Mount Toll. These trailheads have restrooms. Once the road is opened visitors to Brainard Lake are charged a reasonable day-use fee. Early birds aren't exempt and are asked to pay the fee when they leave.

View northwest from Lefthand Reservoir toward six of the Indian Peaks. From left to right — Apache, Shoshone, "Pawshoni," Pawnee, Toll, Paiute.

Fourth of July Trailhead (10,130')

The large town of Nederland is located along the Peak-To-Peak Highway (Route 72) about fifteen miles west of Boulder. From the traffic circle in the center of Nederland, drive south 0.6 mile on the Peak-To-Peak Highway and turn right (west) at a sign for Eldora. Stay on this valley road, which leads to the tiny settlement of Eldora after three miles. This "Eldora" is different than the nearby ski area with the same name. Another mile and the pavement ends. Continue on the 2WD dirt road for 0.8 mile to a "Y". Take the signed right fork and drive four miles to the rustic Buckingham Campground and Fourth of July Trailhead, and park in the trailhead parking area, which has a restroom. The Arapaho Pass Trail begins here and leads 3.5 miles west to Arapaho Pass. From the trail you can access North and South Arapaho Peak, Mount Neva and "Jasper Peak."

Hessie Trailhead (9,000')

Follow the directions above for the Fourth of July Trailhead. When you reach the "Y" intersection along the dirt road that leads west from the town of Eldora, take the left fork. This 4WD road is often flooded. You can take it 0.3 mile to the Hessie townsite and park. Less amphibious travelers can park back at the "Y" and hike along a good trail through the forest on the north side of the flooded road.

From the town site (marked by a large sign) the official "Hessie Trailhead" is a short walk further west where a solid bridge crosses the North Fork of Middle Boulder Creek. This is an important (and busy) trailhead that accesses three major drainages and four trails: the Jasper Lake/Devil's Thumb Trail, the Woodland Lake Trail, the King Lake Trail, and the Lost Lake Trail. Use this Jasper Lake/Devil's Thumb Trail if you intend to camp and ski in the huge bowls ("Devil's Thumb Bowl," "Storm Lakes Bowl," and Challenger Glacier) directly west at the head of the main valley.

Monarch Lake Trailhead (8,346')

Monarch Lake is the quiet and diminutive eastern annex to the much larger and busier Lake Granby. It sits on the western boundary of the Indian Peaks Wilderness and is the jump off point for several long and beautiful trails that lead eastward through deeply cleft valleys. These valleys culminate in higher alpine basins and cirques at the western foot of the Continental Divide. By Memorial Day, most of the snow has melted from these trails up to about 10,000' enabling climbers and ski mountaineers to access some of the most beautiful and remote backcountry to be found anywhere in Colorado.

There are two very different ways to reach Monarch Lake – via I-70 and Berthoud Pass (U.S. 40) or via Trail Ridge Road. Denverites prefer the I-70 route. Take I-70 west to Hwy. 40 west. Go 46 miles over Berthoud Pass to Granby. At Granby proceed north on Hwy. 34 for five miles to the Arapaho Bay access road (County Route 6). Turn right and drive one mile on a paved road and nine miles on 2WD dirt to the parking area at Monarch Lake. From Denver this route takes roughly two hours to drive.

The more scenic route is to drive over Trail Ridge Road, which usually is plowed and opened by Memorial Day. Trail Ridge Road begins in the town of Estes Park. In Estes Park locate Hwy. 34 west, the National Park bypass, and drive five miles to the Park entrance and the start of Trail Ridge Road. Drive across the Park, exit the Park, pass Grand Lake on the left and, 9.5 miles from Grand Lake, turn left onto the Arapaho Bay access road described in the preceding paragraph. This route takes about three and a half hours from Denver, or longer if you stop to ogle the elk.

There is a ranger cabin located 50 yards west of the parking area at Monarch Lake. You can pick up a Wilderness camping permit here. The trail starts out from the ranger cabin and heads west along the north side of Monarch Lake. After three miles the trail splits. The Buchanan Pass Trail branches left and the Cascade Creek Trail branches right. The Cascade Creek Trail leads to the magnificent Lone Eagle Cirque and Fair Glacier, eight miles from Monarch Lake.

(13,138')

Ogalalla Peak

Difficulty/Quality .... Expert / ☺
Season .... Late May, early June
Distance .... 19 miles
Starting Elevation ...... 8,638'
Elevation Gain .... 4,500'
Access .... Peaceful Valley / Camp Dick Campground, Page 60
Maps
U.S.G.S. .... *Allenspark, Isolation Peak*
Trails Illustrated .... #102, *Indian Peaks-Gold Hill*
Guidebook .... Pages 187 and 188

Ogalalla stands at the head of Middle St. Vrain Creek. Because of its distance from major trailheads, Ogalalla is among the more obscure thirteeners and is seldom visited. Skiers and snowboarders who are willing to make the long trek to the summit are rewarded with outstanding views of Rocky Mountain National Park, the northern Indian Peaks, and several remote peaks and valleys located west of the Divide. The steep southeast face of Ogalalla is interrupted in only one place by a wide and steep slope ("Ogalalla Express") that leads to the ridgetop only minutes from the summit. One can ascend the mountain by this couloir and then turn around and ski almost continuously to a base camp at timberline for a vertical descent of 2,500 feet.

Skiers should plan on spending one or two nights at a base camp at or below the snowline, which in early June is generally above 10,500'. From a base camp, the summit lies 2.5 miles to the west. By camping on the north side of the main creek, you can avoid crossing the swollen creek. Further up the valley, above timberline, the creek is solidly bridged with snow and crossing back and forth is not a problem.

From Camp Dick drive, hike or bicycle four miles to the Middle St. Vrain trailhead. From the trailhead it is another two or three miles to the snowline and options for camping. The following day leave camp early and head west keeping to the north side of the creek. Timberline is reached at 10,700' and the valley opens up. Slant to the south side of the snow-covered creek and continue west around the south shore of a small lake at 10,910'. Proceed northwest through a narrows, then up a steep slope to a flat area, and up another steep slope to the uppermost basin, which is actually a depression. To the left is the northernmost St. Vrain Glacier. To the right is Ogalalla Express, the wide slope that leads to the summit ridge. Climb the slope 1,200 vertical feet to its top, drop your skis, and amble 0.2 mile over the rocky tundra to the summit.

The top of the couloir approaches 45 degrees and is prone to sluffing as the sun warms the top layer. Ski back down to the basin. Consider ascending and descending all or part of North St. Vrain Glacier or simply ski back to base camp. During the return a short detour to the southeast starting at 11,000' will bring you to the scenic Gibraltar Lakes and views of the southern St. Vrain Glaciers.

Ogalalla Peak — "Ogalalla Express" is the couloir to the left of the craggy summit ridge. The vertical drop from the saddle to the end of snow shown in the photo is 2,000'.

(12,848')

Elk Tooth

Difficulty/Quality .... Expert / ☺☺
Season .... Late May, early June
Distance .... 17 miles
Starting Elevation ...... 8,638'
Elevation Gain .... 4,200'
Access .... Peaceful Valley/Camp Dick Campground, Page 60

Maps
U.S.G.S. .... *Allenspark, Isolation Peak*
Trails Illustrated .... #102, *Indian Peaks-Gold Hill*
Guidebook .... Pages 187 and 188

Elk Tooth is possibly the oddest looking summit in the Indian Peaks. The signature crag that juts out of the mountain is indeed tooth-shaped. However, it is debatable whether or not any known elk has even one tooth that is so canine in shape. In spite of this misnomer, Elk Tooth is an impressive mountain. Its sheer south face rises two thousand feet above the valley floor.

The eastern edge of Elk Tooth's south face is interrupted by a wide snow slope ("The Snake") that is similar in aspect and appearance to the one described previously for Ogalalla Peak. Unlike the snow slope on Ogalalla, however, the one on Elk Tooth does not put one as close to the summit. Instead, after reaching the top of the slope, the summit is still a 0.4 mile scramble to the west. From the top of The Snake there is an excellent view of massive Mount Copeland (13,176') and the lake studded valley of Cony Creek.

To reach Elk Tooth from a basecamp below timberline, follow the directions for Ogalalla Peak (Route 14) as far as timberline at 10,700' at which point the valley opens wide. The Snake is the obvious slope on your right (northwest). Study the slope and plan your ascent from below. Depending on the locations of runnels, rock outcroppings, and slide debris, you will probably end up snaking back and forth to reach the top. About halfway up the slope another steeper and narrower couloir branches to the west. This couloir usually has a deep runnel that provides a handy excuse for not attempting it. The top of The Snake provides a range of steepness with the west side being the steepest (45 degrees) and the east side less steep (35 degrees).

Having successfully descended The Snake, you should consider taking a short tour across the valley to the Gibraltar Lakes. The northfacing glaciers above the lakes are perfect for some post-lunch or pre-siesta skiing.

"The Snake" on Elk Tooth

(12,400')

Saint Vrain Glaciers Tour

Difficulty/Quality .... Expert / ☺☺☺
Season .... Late May, early June
Distance .... 9 miles (total from basecamp)
Starting Elevation ...... 10,400' (basecamp elevation)
Elevation Gain .... 3,000' - 4,000'
Access .... Peaceful Valley/Camp Dick Campground, Page 60

Maps
U.S.G.S. .... *Allenspark, Isolation Peak*
Trails Illustrated .... #102, *Indian Peaks-Gold Hill*
Guidebook .... Pages 187 and 188

The far west end of Middle St. Vrain Creek contains six pocket glaciers that face north and hold skiable snow for most of the summer. In June, when the snow in the lower portions of the valley has melted, there is still enough snow near and above timberline to connect four of the six glaciers into a ski adventure that promises between 3,000 and 4,000 vertical feet of superb downhill skiing, straightforward routefinding, and gorgeous scenery. To make it easier to follow the route description that follows, we numbered the glaciers from one to six with one being the northernmost glacier below Ogalalla Peak and six the small glacier that lies south of Envy Lake. During this tour you will ascend and descend glaciers 1,2,5, and 6. It isn't necessary to commit to all four glaciers to complete the tour since any one of them may be omitted. However, inclusion in the St. Vrain Glacier Hall of Fame requires that you complete the suggested route.

To start the tour from a basecamp below timberline, follow the directions to the uppermost basin below Ogalalla's southeast face. (See Route 14 - Ogalalla Peak). From the base of the upper bowl climb as far as you wish up Glacier #1, turn around and descend. Climb east out of the unusual depression that forms the base of the upper bowl and ski down 300 vertical feet to the east before turning to the south and climbing up into the narrow bowl that holds Glacier #2. Ascend and descend Glacier #2 back down to elevation 11,400'. Turn east and continue skiing 400 vertical feet down to and past the narrows and the tiny lake at 10,910'. Once past the tiny lake, curve south and uphill to the Gibraltar Lakes. Ascend and descend Glacier #5 and retreat to the north side of the largest

Gibraltar Lake. Turn east and head for an obvious low saddle that divides Gibraltar Lake from Envy Lake. Ski 200+ vertical feet to Envy Lake. Turn south and climb and descend Glacier #6 before returning to Envy Lake. Bushwhack around the west shore of Envy Lake and ski down to the north into Middle St. Vrain Creek. Return to camp and dinner.

Saint Vrain Glacier #5 on the Saint Vrain Glaciers Tour

(12,391')

"Red Deer Mountain"

Difficulty/Quality .... Intermediate / ☺☺
Season .... May
Distance .... 14 miles
Starting Elevation ...... 8,638'
Elevation Gain .... 3,753'
Access .... Peaceful Valley/Camp Dick Campground, Page 60

Maps
U.S.G.S. .... *Allenspark, Isolation Peak*
Trails Illustrated .... #102, *Indian Peaks-Gold Hill*
Guidebook .... Pages 187 and 188

Red Deer Lake at the foot of "Red Deer Mountain" is a popular destination during the snow-free months of summer and fall. Before then it sees few visitors. The lake, which is at 10,372', is set in a peculiar pocket several hundred feet above the main trunk of Middle St. Vrain Creek. The mountain, which we've named "Red Deer Mountain," is the unnamed summit west of the lake. Red Deer Mountain's steep southeast face forms the northern boundary of Buchanan Pass and is taller than its better-known neighbor to the south, Sawtooth Mountain (12,304'). The eastern slope of Red Deer Mountain holds snow through May and allows for a continuous descent from the summit to the lake. The downhill skiing from the lake back down to Middle St. Vrain Creek consists of marginal tree bashing.

The route to the lake and the mountain is long. However, in May, about two-thirds of the jeep road from Camp Dick to the trailhead at 9,583' is snow free and can be hiked in and out at a brisk pace. Park at Camp Dick and hike as far as possible before switching to skis. Use skis for the rest of the approach unless the snow is firm enough to walk on. Cross the bridge at 9,583' and continue up the valley past the Wilderness boundary at 9,800'. One mile past the boundary, at the end of a large clearing that has standing dead timber, there is a bridge and a sign for the Buchanan Pass Trail (9,920'). Cross the bridge, ski northwest about 100 yards to where the Buchanan Pass Trail cuts sharply south. Follow the trail cut for another 100 yards, leave the trail, and cut up through the steep timbered slope that separates the trail from Red Deer Lake. Use a map and compass to orient toward the lake. The lake is surrounded by sparse timber making it easy to spot. Continue around the northeast shore of the lake until you reach a point above the outlet. This is a good place for munching and rehydrating and especially for studying the terrain to the west that leads onto the east slope of Red Deer Mountain. You will need to do some zigging and zagging to reach the summit snowfield and finally the summit, which is just over a mile away. Incidentally, the summit affords an excellent view of the skiable snowslope on Sawtooth Mountain.

View southwest from the summit of Saint Vrain Mountain toward Red Deer Mountain. The broad east snow slope leads down to Red Deer Lake (not visible in photo.)

When the snow on Red Deer Mountain is in top form, you can descend almost 2,000 vertical feet back down to the lake. To return to the Middle St. Vrain road you simply reverse your approach route. In the event that you miss the bridge at 9,920', you should be able to cross the creek on a snow bridge somewhere else and then pick up the main trail nearby. Because of the length of this tour, consider making a basecamp for two nights in the valley of Middle St. Vrain Creek and adding other descents to this one.

(12,304')

Sawtooth Mountain

Difficulty/Quality .... Expert / ☺☺
Season .... Late May, mid June
Distance .... 12 miles
Starting Elevation ...... 9,190'
Elevation Gain .... 3,100'
Access .... Beaver Reservoir / Coney Flats Road, Page 61
Maps
U.S.G.S. .... *Allenspark, Ward*
Trails Illustrated .... #102, *Indian Peaks-Gold Hill*
Guidebook .... Pages 187 and 188

Sawtooth Mountain is one of the most recognizable of the Indian Peaks. One of the best places to view Sawtooth Mountain is from the Peak-to-Peak Highway a few miles south of Peaceful Valley. It is also clearly visible from eastern Boulder County. Its sheer south face and arcing north ridge account for its distinctive sawtooth shape. The northeast face of Sawtooth holds a gem of a snow slope that lasts well into June and is seldom skied. (This is not the snow slope that is usually seen from the vantage points mentioned above. The slope usually seen is on the southeast face.) Even though the summit is some distance from the trailhead, most of the approach to the base of the mountain is a gentle grade. The summit provides close-up views of the northernmost Indian Peaks and Rocky Mountain National Park.

The most direct route to Sawtooth begins on the north end of Beaver Reservoir where a rough and wet 4WD road (gated in the spring) leads east 3.5 miles to the Coney Flats Trailhead at 9,780'. The 4WD road rises gently through a cool forest of mixed aspen and conifers. At 3.5 miles the road crosses Coney Creek and ends in a large clearing with views to the west. The Beaver Creek Trail and the Wilderness Boundary are 150 yards further west. Continue west along the Beaver Creek Trail (may be snow-covered) through open meadows and scrub for 1.5 miles and the Buchanan Pass Trail. Should you lose the trail, head for a high, wide and obvious drift of snow that forms annually at around 10,200'. Surmount this drift and dead reckon (the trail will be buried in snow) toward the wide valley that leads to Buchanan Pass. Once on the north side of Sawtooth at an elevation of 10,800' turn to the southwest and climb the snow slope for 1,400 vertical feet to the flat summit ridge. The summit is a few steps to the south.

While the upper part of the route is between 35 and 40 degrees, most of the descent seldom exceeds 30 degrees. The snow slope may be interrupted by a brief section of talus where the snow has melted. The return from the bottom of the slope retraces the approach.

Sawtooth Mountain (left) from the Buchanan Pass Trail. "Red Deer Mountain" is on the right. The top third and bottom third of the descent route is visible. Wildflowers are abundant in the meadows leading toward Sawtooth Mountain.

(12,162')

Saint Vrain Mountain

Difficulty/Quality .... Intermediate or Advanced / ☺☺
Season .... Late April, early June
Distance .... 7.5 miles
Starting Elevation ...... 8,680'
Elevation Gain .... 3,482'
Access .... Allenspark/Rock Creek Road, Page 60
Maps
U.S.G.S. .... *Allenspark*
Trails Illustrated .... #102, *Indian Peaks-Gold Hill*
Guidebook .... Page 189

St. Vrain Mountain is a relatively short destination that offers solitude, and breathtaking summit views. It makes a fine early season trip while waiting for the snow to stabilize on other higher and steeper routes.

From the parking spot on the northwest side of Rock Creek, ski or walk up the road about two miles. At 10,200' the road turns sharply to the left (south). You can follow the road, which switchbacks a few times, or, if you lack the patience to stay on the road, you can leave the road and bushwhack west through steep timber with Rock Creek never more than a hundred to your right. Try to interconnect a series of small narrow clearings. Eventually the route breaks out into a large clearing (11,200'). Ascend this clearing and veer slightly north until you reach the last of the big timber. The head of Rock Creek is a wide, low angled expanse of krumholz (dwarf spruce) and willow. Soon the wide east ridge (one of the ski descent routes) of St. Vrain Mountain appears. As you ski or walk up this ridge, views of the north faces of Audubon, Paiute, and Sawtooth will supply a needed distraction as well as inspiration for future outings. When you tire of the view south and west, turn your head northward for views of Longs Peak and its brethren peaks rimming beautiful Wild Basin in Rocky Mountain National Park.

The modest summit affords additional generous views of the Middle St. Vrain drainage, the St. Vrain Glaciers, and Wild Basin. Alternatively, the homesick skier can gaze eastward toward the foothills and the high plains.

East Ridge — Intermediate

This descent requires no explanation. It is short enough to allow multiple descents. Keep in mind that the longer you delay your descent, the sloppier the snow will be especially within the steep forest below timberline.

The east ridge descent slope of Saint Vrain Mountain

South Slope — Advanced

Early arrivers in search of a more challenging route may elect to ski the longer and steeper (about 30 degrees) south slope down to timberline, slog back up, then ski the east ridge before heading back down. The wide south slope holds one major and two minor ski routes. The south slope starts a few hundred feet west of the summit. Despite its southerly orientation this snowfield lasts through May and into June. If you don't feel like hiking back to the summit, you can traverse east, then northeast and uphill to the bottom of the east ridge from which you can descend into the trees and retrace the ascent route back to the road and your car.

(13,223')

Mount Audubon

Difficulty/Quality .... Expert / ☺☺☺
Season .... May, mid June
Distance .... 7 miles (*Crooked Couloir*)
8 miles (*Coney Couloirs*)
Starting Elevation ...... 10,500'
Elevation Gain .... 2,700'
4,500' (*Coney Couloirs* without car shuttle)
Access .... Brainard Lake, Page 61
Maps
U.S.G.S. .... *Ward*
Trails Illustrated .... #102, *Indian Peaks-Gold Hill*
Guidebook .... Page 190

Audubon's huge bulk makes it an easy mountain to spot. Its broad gently sloping eastern flank contrasts with the considerably steeper northwest and south faces. The well cairned standard route to the summit is popular during all seasons.

At the Mitchell Lake Trailhead parking area, be sure to locate the Audubon Trailhead, which is on the north side of the parking area, and not the Mitchell Lake Trail, which is on the west side. The Audubon Trail climbs through timber and quickly reaches a narrow clearing (10,820') with a view to the west and a steep snow slope directly in front. Here the trail cuts sharply right (east) angling up and switchbacking twice before reaching a gentler grade. From here the trail swings north then west over tundra and talus before reaching a saddle at 12,600'. From the saddle, rock hop south 0.5 mile to the obvious summit.

The view to the north includes the Longs Peak massif, Wild Basin, St. Vrain Mountain, and the peaks around St. Vrain Glaciers. The range to the northwest is the Never Summer Mountains. To the south lie the other Indian Peaks accessible from Brainard Lake. Neighboring Paiute and Toll are close at hand.

Crooked Couloir

Crooked Couloir is located on the south face of Audubon. It is a terrific line – long and steep. It is overshadowed by the ski descent on Mount Toll, which usurps most of the area's skiing action. This shallow couloir only comes into view along the Blue Lake trail, 0.5 miles east of Blue Lake. It rises more than 1,600 vertical feet above the north shore of Blue Lake.

This couloir can be reached two ways. From the summit walk west along the narrow west ridge for about 200 yards. In May and early June the snow in the couloir extends to the ridge top with just enough bare ground to adjust boots and gather up one's courage. The skiing starts out at a reasonable 35 degrees, but steepens noticeably about one-third of the way down. Two thirds of the way down, the grade relents. Cruise the last few hundred yards to Blue Lake. From Blue Lake hike or ski east on the Blue Lake Trail (usually snowcovered for most of its length), past Mitchell Lake, back to the parking area.

The second, more direct approach to this couloir is to take the snow covered Mitchell Lake Trail (same parking area as before) one mile past Mitchell Lake and another easy mile to Blue Lake. Walk around to the north side of the lake and climb the low angle snow at the base of the couloir. At the point where the snow steepens, you may elect to abandon the snow for the talus on the left (west) side of the couloir. If you have summit fever upon reaching the ridgetop, the top is an obvious 200 yards of talus to the east.

Crooked Couloir faces south, and so an early start is recommended. It melts out by the end of June.

The summit of Mount Audubon is on the right side of the photo.
Crooked Couloir is the prominent slope to the left of the summit in the middle of the photo.

The huge south face of Mount Audubon viewed from Mount Toll. Crooked Couloir is the most prominent couloir left of the summit. Blue Lake is visible in the lower right corner of the photo.

Coney Couloirs

The two Coney Couloirs are embedded in the steep northwest face of Mount Audubon. They are only visible from the Coney Lakes that lie below or from the higher Indian Peaks summits to the north. Viewed from these northern summits, the couloirs appear nearly vertical, and no one in his or her right mind would consider making a descent. But as is so often the case, the couloirs are much more moderate than they appear (they seldom exceed 35 degrees).

The westernmost couloir is the longest and steepest and ends just south of the outlet of Upper Coney Lake. The entrance to the couloir lies at the flat area 250 yards west of the summit. The bottom one-fourth of this couloir may be melted out by the middle of June. When it is in prime condition, one can ski 1,800 vertical feet. The top of the couloir approaches 40 degrees. The easternmost couloir begins at 12,600' just 50 yards northeast of the point where the Mount Audubon Trail curves to the southwest before beginning the final ascent of the summit cone. The top 100-200 feet of this couloir may be melted out by mid-June. The same is true for the bottom. The steepness hovers around 35 degrees.

Persons wishing to ski any of the Coney Couloirs have two options. The first is to start at the Mount Audubon Trailhead (described in the route introduction above), hike up the Mount Audubon Trail, and drop into one of the couloirs from either side of the summit. To return one climbs back up to the Mount Audubon Trail before returning to Brainard Lake. This is not as ridiculous as it seems and is the least complicated and shortest of the two options. The talus slopes adjacent to the couloirs can, for the most part, be climbed by those who find this preferable to kicking steps up the couloir.

The second option, which makes for a full and rewarding day, is to park one vehicle to use as a shuttle at the Beaver Reservoir / Coney Flats Road parking spot (Page 61) and to use the Mount Audubon Trailhead near Brainard Lake as a starting point. After hiking the Mount Audubon Trail to one of the couloirs, descend the couloir and return to the shuttle vehicle via Coney Creek and the Coney Creek 4WD Road. By this route the total distance is around ten miles and involves tricky routefinding and bushwhacking. Persons electing this route should familiarize themselves beforehand with the route to the Coney Lakes from the Coney Flats Trailhead. Be advised that above 10,500' the Coney Lakes valley is floored with an impenetrable mat of dense scrub. The south side of the valley below the couloirs is passable by careful routefinding over talus slopes and small snowfields.

The three Coney Couloirs. The one on the left and the one on the right are the most reasonable descent routes. The central couloir, which starts below the summit is very difficult to access and is not recommended.

(13,088')

Paiute Peak

Difficulty/Quality .... Advanced / ☺☺☺
Season .... May, mid June
Distance .... 7 miles
Starting Elevation ...... 10,500'
Elevation Gain .... 2,600'
Access .... Brainard Lake, Page 61
Maps
U.S.G.S. .... *Ward, Monarch Lake*
Trails Illustrated .... #102, *Indian Peaks-Gold Hill*
Guidebook .... Page 190

Like many of the Indian Peaks, Paiute is a mountain of contrasts. Viewed from Coney Lake the northeast face of Paiute presents a 2,000 foot high obstacle to climbers. This face of Paiute is dark and forbidding. From Blue Lake, however, the south side of Paiute appears sunny, climbable, and especially skiable. Tucked as it is between massive Audubon to the east and Toll to the south, Paiute is usually climbed or skied as an afterthought. There are skiers and snowboarders who ski Toll annually and only eventually get around to investigating Paiute. Take some time to investigate this enjoyable thirteener.

There are two obvious descent routes on Paiute. One is the south-facing run we call Curvaceous Couloir. This couloir is visible from the plains east of Boulder, if you know where to look for it. From Blue Lake and the alpine lake at 11,833', the couloir is easy to spot. It is used for the ascent to the summit as well as the descent. Since it faces south an early start is required to avoid wallowing in knee-deep slush on the descent. Noon is too late. The other descent is the wide snowfield that lies to the west of Curvaceous Couloir.

To reach Paiute start at the Mitchell Lake Trailhead near Brainard Lake. Hike or ski the mostly snowcovered trail for a mile to Mitchell Lake. Continue west for another mile to Blue Lake. The snowcovered trail is difficult to follow because the valley is a patchwork of meadows, rock outcroppings, and impassable dwarf spruce. Avoid skiing over or through the fragile vegetation. Close attention to your map should help. Hiking this trail in late summer and noting key landmarks will help with navigation when the trail is snowcovered. [It is astonishing that this very popular trail is not more clearly marked, signed or cairned. The effects of this lack are evident all over the valley bottom.]

Rest at Blue Lake and marvel at the mind-boggling scenery and descent routes. Visible from left to right are Mount Toll, Paiute Peak, and Crooked Couloir on Mt. Audubon. To reach the base of Curvaceous Couloir or the snowfield to the west, ski to the north side of Blue Lake and ascend north and west along ledgy terrain to the unnamed lake perched at 11,833'. Locate the base of the couloir a bit higher and further west and ascend it. For the snowfield, continue further west from the base of the couloir to reach the base of the snowfield. Ascend the snowfield. If time allows, avoid the temptation to ski immediately, and ascend the south ridge to the summit of Paiute. Careful planning on the way up will enable you to ski 1,500 vertical feet down to Blue Lake.

Note: Early in the season there is a high, wide, and steep snowfield on Paiute's southeast face. This snowfield lies on top of steep, rock slabs. Large, wet snowslides are frequent here. Stay clear of this face.

Paiute Peak viewed from the east bank of Blue Lake. Curvaceous Couloir sweeps downward a few hundred feet to the left of the summit. The wide snowfield described in the last paragraph above is on the right side of the photo.

(12,979')

Mount Toll

Difficulty/Quality .... Expert / ☺☺☺
Season .... May, June
Distance .... 7 miles
Starting Elevation ...... 10,500'
Elevation Gain .... 2,500'
Access .... Brainard Lake, Page 61
Maps
U.S.G.S. .... *Ward, Monarch Lake*
Trails Illustrated .... #102, *Indian Peaks-Gold Hill*
Guidebook .... Page 190

Conjure up an image of the ideal ski descent. It would be esthetic, long, challenging, originate at a summit, and be surrounded by beautiful and rugged scenery. This is a perfect description of Mount Toll. Like its neighbors, Paiute and Audubon, Toll is clearly discernible from points east of Boulder. Travelers in and around Boulder County can monitor its snow condition as summer progresses. Toll is closely watched and frequently skied. For some it is an annual ritual. The route faces south and sees many visitors – two reasons to get an especially early start from the trailhead.

Standing at the east end of Blue Lake and looking up at the snow covered southeast face, one cannot avoid facing the fact that Toll's midsection is steep. One consolation is that the top of the route is much gentler and allows a chance to make a dozen or so warm-up turns before committing to the serious section. Another is that the west edge of the snowy face is slightly less steep. In June it is usually possible to ski continuously from a point just below the summit to the west shore of Blue Lake, a total of 1,600 vertical feet. Another dubious bonus is that on most weekends a crowd of spectators at Blue Lake will be analyzing and discussing your technique.

Mount Toll is reached by hiking or skiing from the Mitchell Lake Trailhead near Brainard Lake. (Follow the directions for Paiute Peak.) After a rest at Blue Lake, hike northwest around the lake, then traverse west and uphill to a broad bench (11,400') west of the lake. From the bench continue west and southwest up a snow slope for 600 vertical feet to another broad bench (12,000'). From here head west up a long steep slope to the obvious saddle between Pawnee Peak and Toll. From the saddle, turn north and hike to the summit. Easily visible from the summit are the surrounding Indian Peaks as well as the peaks and side valleys of upper Cascade Creek. There is also an impressive view of Fair Glacier west of Apache Peak. A few steps back down bring you to the start of the descent. With views this great you'll be in no rush to start your descent.

After skiing the long steep section of the southeast face, start curving to the east and then northeast on fairly wide slopes and flats that lead back to the northwest corner of Blue Lake.

Mt. Toll from Blue Lake. Photo taken early June. Blue Lake remains ice-covered for most of June. This is one of the most beautiful alpine settings in the Front Range. Below: *Skiing Toll, end of June.*

Owen Lunz

...skiing Toll end of June...again.

(12,943')

Pawnee Peak

Difficulty/Quality .... Intermediate, Advanced or Expert / ☺☺☺
Season .... May, mid June
Distance .... 7.5 miles
Starting Elevation ...... 10,500'
Elevation Gain .... 2,450'
Access .... Brainard Lake, Page 61
Maps
U.S.G.S. .... *Ward, Monarch Lake*
Trails Illustrated .... #102, *Indian Peaks-Gold Hill*
Guidebook .... Page 191

Unlike its neighbors to the north and south, Pawnee Peak is a difficult mountain to spot from the plains or from Brainard Lake where only a bit of its summit is visible. The best view of the peak and its snowy southeast slope is from the Brainard Lake Road roughly a mile before reaching the lake. More easily identified is Pawnee Pass, which is south of the peak and accessible by a trail. This pass is an important route for crossing the Continental Divide from east to west into the remote valleys that dissect the western slope of the Indian Peaks (See Route 25: "Indian Peaks Super Tour").

In addition to the obvious (and short) intermediate snowfield that stretches from the summit and down the southeast slope of Pawnee Peak, there are several varied descents in the vicinity of the peak that make a trip to Pawnee worthwhile. The summit can be skied from late April until mid-June. The steeper routes ("The Keyholes") below the summit snowfield should only be skied later in the season (usually June) when the snow has consolidated.

Southeast Slope — Intermediate

This is a route that you will want to ski, reclimb, and ski again. It is high, wide, and skiable from the summit. To reach Pawnee Peak, start at the Long Lake Trailhead near Brainard Lake and follow the trail 0.25 mile to Long Lake. Continue west along the trail, pass Long Lake on its north side, and continue up to Lake Isabelle, two miles from the trailhead. Lake Isabelle is an extremely popular Indian Peaks destination — a fact requiring no explanation.

A sign slightly past the east end of Lake Isabelle points the way to the Pawnee Pass Trail, which heads north and then west 0.75 mile into a small, rocky, and obscure basin (11,200') due east of Pawnee Pass. (The trail from Lake Isabelle is incorrectly marked on the U.S.G.S. Ward quadrangle.) At the west end of this basin, admire the three steep rock-walled couloirs, the "Keyholes," with a tiny pond (11,320') at the foot of the rightmost couloir. If you would like to attempt one of them on the return, make careful note of their locations with respect to the surroundings.

From the little basin angle up and southwest to gain the flat spot (11,800') on the ridge that juts southeasterly from Pawnee Pass. Climb steeply up this ridge to Pawnee Pass. From the broad pass, the route north to the summit is obvious. The big cirque that stretches between Pawnee Pass and Shoshoni Peak is "Shoshoni Bowl." Point 12,878', which is south of the pass, is "Pawshoni" and is another enjoyable descent (see below) that can be combined with Pawnee Peak.

From the summit, ski the southeast slope of Pawnee retracing your steps back to the flat spot at 11,800'.

The Keyholes — Expert

The Keyholes are steep couloirs that drop due east of Pawnee Pass into the little basin described above in the approach to Pawnee Peak. Combined with the Southeast Slope route, it is often possible in May and early June to ski from the summit, down one of the couloirs, and down the drainage to the east end of Lake Isabelle, a vertical descent of 2,300'. The first (left) couloir is the longest and steepest. The third (right) couloir is shorter and is only steep at its very top

Shoshoni Bowl and Shoshoni Peak's North Face — Advanced

The broad cirque ("Shoshoni Bowl") between Pawnee Pass and Shoshoni Peak is obvious during the ascent of Pawnee. Shoshoni Bowl can be skied a variety of ways. The central portion tends to melt out first but the bowl's north and south sides (especially the north face of Shoshoni Peak) hold snow into June and provide a variety of skiing terrain. The bottom of the cirque funnels into a steep, rocky gully that opens onto the west end of Lake Isabelle. This is not a safe way to exit the bowl. The preferred exit is to walk north to the Pawnee Pass Trail and retrace the approach.

"Pawshoni" 12,878' — Advanced

"Pawshoni" lies just south of Pawnee Pass and makes a great addition to a descent of Pawnee Peak. It is a short climb from the pass to the summit of Pawshoni. From the summit there is a view of Pawnee Lake on the west side of the Divide. One can ski directly east from the summit to the base of Shoshoni Bowl (see above), take a break, and then ascend a short distance to the Keyholes for a dramatic final descent. Regardless of one's choice, the return route is only a few hundred yards to the north.

North Face — Advanced

For those who prefer to make a circuit route out of a trip to Pawnee, this is a variation, which isn't done very often. From the summit walk a few hundred feet to the west and drop down (north) to the obvious snow slope that leads into the bowl between Mt. Toll and Pawnee Peak. Continue skiing to the west shore of Blue Lake as described above for Mt. Toll. Return via Blue and Mitchell Lakes and the Mitchell Lake Trail. The Mitchell Lake Trailhead is a short walk from the Long Lake Trailhead. See the map on page 190.

Pawnee Peak from the snowcovered Pawnee Pass Trail. The Southeast Slope route forms the skyline left of the summit. The Keyholes are the two snowfilled gullies on the left side of the photo.

(13,441')

Apache Peak

Difficulty/Quality .... Expert / ☺☺☺
Season .... Mid May, June
Distance .... 9 miles
Starting Elevation ...... 10,500'
Elevation Gain .... 2,940'
Access .... Brainard Lake, Page 61
Maps
U.S.G.S. .... *Ward, Monarch Lake*
Trails Illustrated .... #102, *Indian Peaks-Gold Hill*
Guidebook .... Page 191

As the second highest Indian Peak and with steep slopes on all sides, Apache looms large when viewed from all points of the compass. Any attempt to ski Apache should include a trip to the summit. The view is tremendous. There are views of the intricate north face of North Arapaho, rarely-seen Triangle Lake below Fair Glacier, and the entire Cascade Creek drainage to the northwest.

Clearly visible from Brainard Lake are two couloirs that attract climbers and skiers once the snow has consolidated. Both of these couloirs hold snow through July, and snow lingers in their lower portions through the summer. However, unlike wine, as the snow ages it becomes *less* mellow as icy patches, rough spots, footsteps, and grit accumulate. For maximum enjoyment ski these in late May or June.

To reach the base of Apache Peak from Brainard Lake follow directions to Lake Isabelle as described under Pawnee Peak (Route 23). Continue hiking west on the unsigned Isabelle Glacier Trail along the north shore of the lake, then ascend a snow slope to a lovely hanging valley at 11,260'. Follow cairns and a wet trail around the southern rim of this valley and ascend again to an unnamed lake at 11,420'. Climb the snow slope at the west end of this lake to flatter ground at 11,900'. Isabelle Glacier and the bottom of Queen's Way lie to the northwest. For Apache Couloir, turn southwest and hike up to a basin (12,120'). From below the descent route will be obvious.

Apache Couloir

Highly recommended. This couloir appears as a mirror-image of Queen's Way when Apache is viewed from the east. It is steeper and more intimidating than Queen's Way. Early in the season, the top of the couloir blends into a large, lower angled snowfield that allows you to crank lots of "practice" turns before dropping into the couloir. The top of the snowfield reaches a point on the south ridge about 100 yards from the summit, which is reached by climbing talus. Reverse your route for the descent. Energetic skiers may elect to ascend and ski Navajo Snowfield or Airplane Gully on Navajo before pointing their skis toward Brainard Lake.

Apache Couloir is a popular ascent and descent route for people climbing Apache especially during summer weekends. The couloir, which faces east, catches early morning sun. For these two reasons plan on an especially early start and keep an eye out for others in the couloir.

Queen's Way

This snowy ramp is a steep extension of Isabelle Glacier. It is located along the south edge of the small northeast face of Apache. It does not extend, as one would hope, to the summit of Apache.

From the southwest corner of the glacier, climb the ramp to its top. Here the summit is hidden from view. To reach the summit traverse over mixed snow and boulders 300-400 yards southwest to the summit. Reverse your route for the descent. Depending on conditions, it may be possible to ski as far as the west end of Lake Isabelle.

View west from Lake Isabelle. The mountain in the center of the photo is Apache. The Y-shaped snow slope left of the summit is Apache Couloir. Queens Way is the C-shaped slope to the right of Apache Couloir. The conical summit toward the left is Navajo with Navajo Snowfield on its right. The imposing mass on the right is Shoshone, which appears highest because it is closer.

(13,240')

Indian Peaks Super Tour

Difficulty/Quality .... Expert / ☺☺☺
Season .... End May, mid June
Distance .... 20 miles
Starting Elevation ...... 10,500'
Elevation Gain .... 5,800'
Access .... Brainard Lake, Page 61
Maps
U.S.G.S. .... *Ward, Monarch Lake*
Trails Illustrated .... #102, *Indian Peaks-Gold Hill*
Guidebook .... Pages 191 and 192

If hiking a few miles, taking a break, climbing and skiing a peak, and getting home early is *not* your idea of a backcountry challenge, this is the tour for you. This tour includes steep snow climbing, a ski descent of Fair Glacier and Pawnee Peak, plus a tour through some of the wildest mountain scenery along the Front Range.

Get an early start from the Long Lake trailhead near Brainard Lake. Follow the directions to Apache Couloir (See Apache Peak, Route 24). From the top of the couloir, continue west to Apache's south ridge (13,240'). From the ridge, you can hike north to the summit, if you wish. From the south ridge traverse across the south face to the southwest ridge (13,200') of Apache. Follow the southwest ridge downhill to 12,700'. At this point you will be slightly below the saddle between Point 12,876' and the southwest ridge. Getting to this saddle is the key to reaching Fair Glacier and upper Cascade Creek. From 12,700' on the ridge, drop down slightly west until you are a short distance below and south of the saddle. Hike uphill (north) to the saddle.

From the saddle, ski Fair Glacier to Triangle Lake. Curve around the northwest bank of the lake and follow the outlet (hidden beneath large boulders) to the snowcovered floor of the valley below. Double pole along the west side of the valley amid incredible surroundings past the outlet of Crater Lake. One hundred yards past the outlet, a primitive bridge crosses Cascade Creek to the east side of the creek. Continue for 0.75 mile along the Cascade Creek Trail (probably snow-covered) to the junction with the Pawnee Pass Trail. A single log bridge crosses the rushing creek that pours out of Pawnee Lake.

Follow the Pawnee Pass Trail uphill to the east and eventually into the Pawnee Lake basin. Continue along the Pawnee Pass Trail, passing Pawnee Lake along its east bank, to the base of the steep headwall that leads to Pawnee Pass. Switchback endlessly up the headwall to Pawnee Pass (12,541'). From the Pass, hike to the summit of Pawnee Peak. Ski the peak or any of the surrounding features (see Pawnee Peak, Route 23) and return to the trailhead via the Pawnee Pass Trail, Lake Isabelle, and Long Lake. Have a beer.

View south from the outlet of Triangle Lake toward Fair Glacier. Apache Peak is on the left edge of the photo. Mount George is on the right.

Ascending Apache Couloir. Lake Isabelle is visible in the upper right corner of the photo.

(13,409')

Navajo Peak

Difficulty/Quality .... Expert / ☺☺
Season .... Mid May, June
Distance .... 9 miles
Starting Elevation ...... 10,500'
Elevation Gain .... 2,900'
Access .... Brainard Lake, Page 61
Maps
U.S.G.S. .... *Ward, Monarch Lake*
Trails Illustrated .... #102, *Indian Peaks-Gold Hill*
Guidebook .... Page 191

Navajo Peak is the alpine culmination of Niwot Ridge, the huge ridge that stretches seven miles from the Peak-To-Peak Highway to the Continental Divide. Niwot Ridge is the site of the University of Colorado's renowned Mountain Research Station. The climate, flora, and fauna of the ridgetop resemble those found at arctic latitudes making Niwot Ridge an excellent site for studying alpine environments.

Navajo's summit is a distinctive cone with a large, steep snowfield ("Navajo Snowfield") on its north side. From the top of Navajo Snowfield, the route to the summit is Class 4 and requires a rope. Most people are content to ski the snowfield and to forgo the summit. (An easier route for summit-seekers is "Airplane Gully"* (Class 3) which lies 200 yards east of Navajo Snowfield.)

A curious feature of Navajo is the easily recognized 75 foot pinnacle jutting from the ridge between Navajo and Apache. Its name is "Dicker's Peck."(hmmm) It's only usefulness, aside from titillating the mountaineer's sophomoric imagination, is that it serves as a handy gauge of one's progress up the snowfield, for when you've reached Dicker's Peck, you've reached the top!

To reach Navajo Snowfield follow directions to the base of Apache Couloir and Navajo Snowfield (see Pawnee Peak, Route 23 and Apache Peak, Route 24). If you're lucky, some fellow climbers will have already kicked steps up the steep snowfield. The top of the snowfield is at 13,100'. The view south into Wheeler Basin is dizzying. This is the best place to study the north face of North Arapaho. Take a moment to contemplate a future ski descent of this face (Route 27).

Now back to Navajo Snowfield. The descent is steep, sustained and satisfying. As with the other nearby descents, it is usually possible to ski to the west end of Lake Isabelle, a vertical drop of 2,200'.

**From the flat basin below Navajo Snowfield, two similar-looking couloirs are visible slicing into Navajo's north face. The one on the climber's left is "Airplane Gully," so named because in 1948 a Civil Aeronautics Authority plane crashed during a snowstorm into the top of the couloir killing three airmen. Pieces of the wreckage litter the couloir and the rocky outwash from the couloir. Although we have never skied this couloir, it may be possible to do so.*

The top of Navajo Snowfield from the top of the Airplane Gully route. The entire snowfield is a uniform steepness of around 45 degrees. Because it faces north, it is skiable in the afternoon.

(13,502')

North Arapaho Peak

Difficulty/Quality	Northstar - Expert / ☺☺
	North Face - Expert / ☺
Season	Mid May, mid June
Distance	Northstar - 7 miles
	North Face - 16 miles
Starting Elevation	10,130'
Elevation Gain	3,370'
Access	Fourth of July Trailhead, Page 62
Maps	
U.S.G.S.	*Monarch Lake*
Trails Illustrated	#102, *Indian Peaks-Gold Hill*
Guidebook	Page 193

North Arapaho is the highest of the Indian Peaks. In conjunction with South Arapaho Peak, it forms one of the most recognizable massifs along the Front Range especially when viewed from the city of Boulder and east Boulder County. The small glacier that lies to the east of the Arapaho Peaks is part of Boulder's water supply. Skiing on this glacier is forbidden. Hikers usually include N. Arapaho with a hike to the summit of S. Arapaho, which is reachable by a popular trail. It is possible to reach the two routes described below by summiting N. Arapaho and poking around for the top of either descent route. However, it is safer and more interesting to approach these routes via the routes described below, even though doing so makes for a longer day.

Northstar Couloir — Expert

Northstar Couloir is located near the middle of N. Arapaho's complex west face. It is a lonely place that sees only an occasional group of snow climbers on weekends. This is one of the most spectacular settings for a ski descent and is well worth the effort. From the Fourth of July Trailhead hike along the gently graded Arapaho Pass Trail two miles to the Fourth of July mine site, an area littered with rusty mining equipment. From the mine site leave the trail and head north, along the path of least resistance, toward a pocket cirque on the west side of S. Arapaho's south face. Hike or ski up this cirque to a cozy saddle. Drop down the west side of the saddle for 200 vertical feet and begin a traverse northwards across alternating snowfields and talus. An ice axe is recommended when crossing these snow slopes as they are likely to be frozen solid. Try to maintain your traverse along as high an elevation as possible (11,400'). After about 800 yards the prominent couloir will come into view on the right. Climb the couloir as far as there is snow. In early June, the top few hundred feet of snow will have melted. You can drop your skis and continue climbing to the northwest ridge, which eventually leads 300 yards to the summit. After returning to the top of the couloir, you can ski as much as 1,600 vertical feet from the high point of the snow. The return retraces the ascent.

View north toward North Arapaho.
"Northstar" is the continuous couloir that begins to the left of the summit.

North Face — Expert

The remote, snow-streaked north face of North Arapaho is clearly visible from the summits of Navajo and Apache, which lie to the north. Anyone planning to ski the north face should be prepared to spend two or three days. The north face is located on the west side of the Divide above the upper reach of Wheeler Basin, an obscure and seldom-traveled valley. Wheeler Basin is a side branch of Arapaho Creek. Arapaho Creek forms a beautiful forested canyon stretching seven miles from Caribou Lake (11,147') to Monarch Lake. You have the option of reaching Wheeler Basin via the Arapaho Creek Trail, which originates at Monarch Lake, or via the Fourth of July Trailhead and the Arapaho Pass Trail on the east side of the Divide. We suggest the latter route.

From the Fourth of July Trailhead hike along the Arapaho Pass Trail to Arapaho Pass (11,906'). From the Pass, the trail switchbacks downhill into the Caribou Lake basin. Coyote Park is a large clearing in the valley directly to the north. Leave the trail and make an angling descent slightly east of north along snowfields into the thinly forested area that eventually opens into Coyote Park. Camp overnight along the east edge of Coyote Park at about elevation 10,360'. Because of the length of the return route from the north face back to the trailhead, consider camping for two nights at Coyote Park.

To reach Wheeler Basin from Coyote Park head north along the east edge of the Park and aim for a timbered bench above elevation 10,480'. A gradual ascent will deposit you on the flatter (but still quite rugged) south side of Wheeler Basin clear of the steep, cliffy terrain that lies to the west. Angle northeasterly until you reach the creek. There is a good trail (which may be snowcovered) on the north side of the creek. Reaching this involves an easy but wet crossing of Wheeler Creek at around 10,500'. Whether or not you cross the creek, battle your way along the drainage for a half-mile at which point the basin opens into an astonishingly beautiful high valley. At the last moment the north face will come into view. The two best ski routes lie on the right (west) side of the face. While neither of the two actually extends to the summit itself, they both reach the northwest ridge. The closest one can get to the summit is to climb the couloir that leads to a U-shaped platform at the base of a prominent pillar. From the platform turn left (southeast) along a lower angled snow ramp that leads to the top of the northwest ridge (13,040'). Drop skis and scramble a quarter mile to the broad summit or forgo the summit and descend along the ascent route. When snow is plentiful on the face and in the bowl, one can earn 2,000 vertical feet of skiing. All the couloirs and snowfields on the north face approach 45 degrees and should be skied cautiously. The return retraces the approach.

View south from Navajo Peak toward N. Arapaho's north face.

North Face of North Arapaho

(13,397')

South Arapaho Peak

Difficulty/Quality .... Expert / ☺☺
Season .... Mid May, mid June
Distance .... 4.5 miles
Starting Elevation ...... 10,130'
Elevation Gain .... 3,270' to summit
3,000' to top of couloir
Access .... Fourth of July Trailhead, Page 62
Maps
U.S.G.S. .... *Monarch Lake*
Trails Illustrated .... #102, *Indian Peaks-Gold Hill*
Guidebook .... Page 193

Skywalker Couloir on the south face of South Arapaho is one of the most accessible Indian Peak descents. When viewed from the Fourth of July mine site, the couloir appears intimidating. The top of the couloir pushes 50 degrees. The route is often used as a technical alternative to the Arapaho Glacier Trail route for climbing S. Arapaho. The condition and amount of snow in the couloir varies from year to year especially near the steep top of the route. We suggest that the route be studied, ideally with binoculars, before attempting a descent. We recommend that a climbing helmet be worn while in the couloir due to the inset nature of the route and the potential for rockfall.

The top half of the couloir is bounded on the east by a rock wall that shades the couloir until mid morning. For this reason the snow in the couloir, which faces south, does not experience the softening effects of the sun until later in the morning. Take this into account when timing your approach, since starting out too early will make ascending the couloir dangerous when the snow is hard unless you choose to wear crampons. This is one of the few exceptions to the "get an early start" rule. An involuntary glissade down this couloir poses two risks: first is the risk of bodily injury; second is the risk of humiliation since your descent will be witnessed by the hordes headed for Arapaho Pass.

To reach Skywalker, hike from the Fourth of July trailhead toward Arapaho Pass. At the obvious Fourth of July mine site (1.5 miles from the start), turn north along the signed Arapaho Glacier Trail for about 100 yards. Turn off the trail and head directly toward the couloir. Climb the couloir to the top. At this point a decision must be made whether to climb to the summit. The most sensible route to the summit ridge is to exit left (west) near the top of Skywalker and enter a steep, narrow couloir. At the top of this slot, follow the talus north a short distance to the summit ridge. The summit lies 100 yards to the east. This route is a questionable undertaking unless one is suitably equipped and experienced. Alternatively you may choose to forgo the summit and ski the couloir directly. The total descent is between 1,000 and 1,500 vertical feet depending on how high you climb and on how much snow has melted along the runout of the couloir. Since this route is popular among early season snow climbers and glissaders, a deep runnel may develop that obviously must be avoided. The return to the trailhead is the reverse of the approach.

Skywalker Couloir on the south face of South Arapaho. View is from the Fourth of July mine site.

Crater Lake and Lone Eagle Cirque

Difficulty/Quality .... Advanced or Expert / ☺☺☺
Season .... End May, June
Distances .... 16 mi. RT to basecamp near Crater Lake
2.5 mi. RT from base camp to Peck Glacier
3.5 mi. RT from basecamp to Fair Glacier
Starting Elevation ...... 8,346'
Elevation Gain .... 1,900' to basecamp
Access .... Monarch Lake Trailhead, Page 63
Maps
U.S.G.S. .... *Monarch Lake*
Trails Illustrated .... #102, *Indian Peaks-Gold Hill*
Guidebook .... Page 192

An overnight trip to the upper reaches of Cascade Creek on the west side of the Continental Divide is a complete ski mountaineering experience. Steep-sided valleys, tall timber, thundering waterfalls, emerging wildflowers, and sunlit meadows are preludes to the area's centerpiece, Lone Eagle Peak. This polished pinnacle and the two great cirques that flank it constitute the most breathtaking scenery in the Indian Peaks. For the skier or snowboarder who is willing to pack in provisions and gear for a couple of nights, the rewards are solitude, great scenery, and two fine ski descents. Plan to devote a full and satisfying day just to hiking in.

From the Monarch Lake parking area, follow the Cascade Creek Trail along the north shore of the lake for a mile and enter the forest. Pass junctions, first with the Arapaho Pass Trail and, later, with the Buchanan Pass Trail, as you ascend to the meadows at the foot of Cascade Falls (9,200'). Passing the tremendous waterfall, the trail steepens with tantalizing glimpses of the high country that lies ahead. Further along, crossing the wide, gushing outlet of Pawnee Lake (10,000') may be problematic. Soon after the crossing, a junction with the Crater Lake trail and the Pawnee Pass Trail, which branches left toward Pawnee Pass, is reached. Continue straight ahead on the Crater Lake trail. At the beginning of June during an "average" snow year, the snowline is just above 10,000 feet. Consider donning skis and skins or else brace yourself for a mile of agonizing postholing. Map in hand, watch for a meadow (10,200') just north of and across from the Mirror Lake outlet. There is a log bridge in this area, but it could be snow covered. With luck you may find a dry campsite nearby. Dry campsites are even scarcer around Crater Lake, where summer visitors usually camp. From this meadow it is an easy and obvious hop to Mirror and Crater Lakes.

Cascade Falls. The foot of the falls is carpeted with wildflowers.

"Lone Rabbit" (11,800') — Advanced (Expert at the top)

Between Mount Achonee and Lone Eagle there is a large basin with Crater Lake at its foot. Tucked into the southeast corner of this basin is tiny Peck Glacier, a mere shred of the alpine glacier that once filled the basin and the whole of upper Cascade Creek.

Stand on the northeast shore of Crater Lake and locate Peck Glacier just right of Lone Eagle. The upper reach of the glacier is a cornice-capped hourglass couloir that extends to the ridgetop. "Lone Rabbit" starts along the horizontal line of snow to the left of this couloir and runs continuously for 1,600 vertical feet to the southeast shore of Crater Lake. The top of the run is steep (Expert) but very short and quickly moderates to a more comfortable grade (30-35 degrees).

To reach Peck Glacier and "Lone Rabbit," walk to the outlet of Crater Lake and cross the outlet on a logjam. Head south out of the trees and angle up toward the base of Lone Eagle on a line that intersects "Lone Rabbit" at 10,600'. Here the terrain flattens for 100 yards before ascending steeply up a second long snow pitch. (Keep an eye out for the Rabbit. He's watching the Eagle.) This second snow pitch tops out at the base of Peck Glacier. Continue as far up the glacier's headwall as you like before putting on skis and taking the plunge. Stay clear of the runout zone beneath the aforementioned couloir in the even that the cornice breaks.

Fair Glacier (12,400') — Expert

To travel into the stark bastion of Fair Glacier is an otherworldly experience. Towering at the head of a narrow cirque east of Lone Eagle, Fair Glacier defies descent. But for ski mountaineers with the drive to reach its base and the energy to climb it, Fair Glacier belies its name — in reality it's excellent. As is so often the case when viewing snow slopes head on, it's not as steep as it looks. The lower half is 30-35 degrees up to 12,200' and 40-45 degrees to the top. The total descent from the top of the glacier to Triangle Lake is 1,400 vertical feet.

To reach Fair Glacier from a 10,200' camp below Mirror Lake, cross Cascade Creek on a log bridge and head upstream to the Mirror Lake outlet stream. Cross the outlet stream wherever feasible and continue upstream along Cascade Creek and cross back to the east side on a snow bridge as soon as possible. (This circuitous route avoids the maze of house-sized boulders on the east bank of Cascade Creek.) Once you are back on the east side of the creek, climb a few steps to higher ground eventually leading into the beautiful park-like valley. Note the puppet-like rock formations on the ridgetop to the left. At the end of this flat valley, turn right and clamber up the big talus that entombs the outlet of Triangle Lake. Catch your breath at the lake (10,980').

From here head around the west end of the lake and the rest of the route is an obvious steep snow climb. From the top of the glacier, one can drop skis and scramble west 200 yards to the unimposing summit of Mount George (12,876'). The sheer-sided 12,799' summit located two-thirds of a mile northwest is nicknamed "Iroquois."

Early in June it is possible to ski back down to Triangle Lake. There are two precautions. First, the snow near the top of the glacier may not be sufficiently consolidated in early June to be skied safely or enjoyably. Second, a crevasse lurks below the snow at 12,200' but is likely to be solidly bridged in June. This crevasse opens up later in the summer when the snow overlying the glacier has melted away exposing the ice.

You'll be pleased to learn that the horizontal distance from the lake to the glacier's base appears foreshortened when viewed from the lake. Actually there's a terrific stretch of low angle cruising once you're off the glacier itself. Regardless of how much of the glacier you choose to ski, you won't regret your attempt. You can squeeze 300 more vertical feet of skiing out of your return trip by skirting the big talus below the lake. Instead of descending the talus, veer right (east) onto a boulder-strewn bench that leads north to a snow slope that faces directly down the valley. Crank out a few more turns before gliding back to camp.

Lone Eagle from elevation 10,000' on the Cascade Creek Trail, near Mirror and Crater Lakes.

Lone Rabbit and Peck Glacier from Crater Lake. Lone Eagle is the monolith on the left.

(12,814')

Mount Neva and North Fork Lakes Bowl

Difficulty/Quality	Northeast or Southeast Face - Expert / ☺ North Fork Lakes - Advanced / ☺☺
Season	May, mid June
Distance	7.5 miles
Starting Elevation	10,130'
Elevation Gain	3,300', Neva summit; 2,500' N. Fork Bowl
Access	Fourth of July Trailhead, Page 62
Maps	
U.S.G.S.	*Monarch Lake, East Portal*
Trails Illustrated	#102, *Indian Peaks-Gold Hill*
Guidebook	Page 194

Mount Neva is a prominent, easily recognizable peak located a mile southwest of Arapaho Pass. Because of its accessibility and its proximity to the pass and lovely Lake Dorothy, it is climbed often. Mount Neva is a snap to get to from the Fourth of July Trailhead. Hike three miles west to Arapaho Pass along the well-maintained Arapaho Pass Trail. At the pass the trail continues west on flat tundra 0.3 mile to Lake Dorothy, an alpine lake in a beautiful setting. Rock hop around the east shore of the lake and pick your way toward the center of the northeast face.

Northeast Face — Expert

The wide bowl at the base of the northeast face is short and steep. Above the bowl there are several steep couloirs (40+ degrees). In May it is possible to ski from the summit, down one of these couloirs, down the bowl and out onto flatter terrain at 11,500' east of the peak - a total of 1,300 vertical feet. There are four obvious couloirs that empty into the bowl. These are described from east to west (climber's left to right). The eastmost couloir is short, wide, and and has no cornice. The next couloir has no cornice, but its top is quite steep (50 degrees). The third one has a truck-sized, overhanging cornice topping its right side. It is as steep as the second and is obviously less safe. At the north end of the bowl there is a wider couloir. It is a bit longer than the others and has a more benign cornice. The cornice is avoidable by keeping to the right as you climb. With the exception of the first couloir, they all lead to the summit ridge, the summit being a short, pleasant walk away. The summit provides great views of the Arapaho Peaks, the 2,000' high west faces of Arikaree, Navajo, Apache and the peaks surrounding Lone Eagle Cirque.

Having skied the route of your choice, you can exit the bowl one of two ways. Either return back to Lake Dorothy and the Arapaho Pass Trail or ski down and out of the bowl from its east side to the boggy flat area east of the Pass. If you choose the latter, turn northeast when you reach the flats, cross alternating talus, tundra, and snowfields for 0.25 mile, then turn north and uphill to reach the Arapaho Pass Trail.

Southeast Face — Expert and North Fork Lakes Bowl — Advanced

The large bowl on the south side of Neva cradles two unnamed lakes. There is good skiing in the bowl that surrounds these lakes. The lakes comprise the headwaters of the North Fork of Middle Boulder Creek. Frankly, they deserve to have names. The steep southeast face of Neva rises above the lower lake and provides a short but challenging ski descent. The less steep northwest face of "Jasper Peak" (Point 12,923') rises above the upper lake. There are other skiable lines within this beautiful bowl.

To reach the lakes and the bowl, leave the trail at the Fourth of July mine site and walk downhill and southwest to Middle Boulder Creek and cross the creek on a snow bridge. Continue southwest above the left (south) bank of the creek for just over a mile until you reach the lakes. From the lakes, the descent routes mentioned above will be obvious. To return to the Fourth of July mine site, retrace the approach route.

Mount Neva from the Fourth of July Mine along the Arapaho Pass Trail. The Northeast Face lies to the right of the summit. The Southeast Face lies to the left. North Fork Lakes Bowl is out of the left side of the photo.

(12,923')

"Jasper Peak"

Difficulty/Quality .... Expert / ☺
Season .... May, mid June
Distance .... 8.5 miles
Starting Elevation ...... 10,130'
Elevation Gain .... 2,800'
Access .... Fourth of July Trailhead, Page 62
Maps
U.S.G.S. .... *Monarch Lake, East Portal*
Trails Illustrated .... #102, *Indian Peaks-Gold Hill*
Guidebook .... Page 194

Jasper Peak is the next major mountain south from Mount Neva along the Continental Divide. From its summit, there is a short and steep snow slope called "Snow Lion" that plunges down the southeast cirque above Upper Diamond Lake. Its steepest section, which is short, approaches 45 degrees. There is no cornice at its top although a large cornice lurks to the climber's right. Because it faces east, it should be climbed and skied early in the day. Previous sloughing and cornice breakage from neighboring gullies may roughen portions of the route. From the bridge crossing of Middle Boulder Creek (see below), the route is mostly a snow-covered trail and routefinding to the Diamond Lakes and beyond to Snow Lion can be tricky.

From the Fourth of July Trailhead, follow the Arapaho Pass Trail one mile uphill to the signed junction with the Diamond Lake Trail. Descend the Diamond Lake Trail 0.5 mile to the bridge crossing of Middle Boulder Creek. (The Diamond Lake Trail has been rerouted west and north of the purple trail shown on the U.S.G.S. East Portal map.) The south bank of Middle Boulder Creek is usually snow-covered in May and early June. As a result, following the trail (one mile) to Diamond Lake requires vigilance. Keep map and compass handy. The Diamond Lakes are set in a long, broad-mouthed hanging valley that is hard to miss. When you reach the lake stay above the northwest bank of the lake. The flat terrain north and west of the lake is marshy, willowy, and spongy and should be avoided. Stay north of the main drainage, and, map in hand, look around for a mostly snow-covered high route that leads up the valley. Pass just north of an unnamed small lake at 11,350', then beeline for the outlet of Upper Diamond Lake. Travel along the north side of the lake and into the southeast cirque. Snow Lion should be obvious, topping out just right of the summit. From the lower Diamond Lake to the Upper Lake is 1.5 miles; from the Upper Lake to the summit is 0.75 mile.

As you enter the cirque and begin your ascent, beware of the huge overhanging cornice east of Snow Lion. Ascend Snow Lion directly, reveling in your proximity to the summit when you kick your last step. From the summit you can spot James Peak to the south. Mount Neva, the Arapaho Peaks, Navajo, Apache and others are visible to the north. When your eyes are full, return to the top of Snow Lion and ponder your first turn. After descending the couloir ski past the upper lake on its south side this time. With a good snowpack and advance planning, you can catch a few more skiable pitches down to a point below lower Diamond Lake – 2,000 vertical feet in all. Recross the bridge and bask in the sunshine on the north side of the creek. Don't forget to stop to admire the waterfall 200 feet west of the bridge along with the June wildflowers, especially the blue columbine and Indian paintbrush.

"Snow Lion" is on the right side of this large bowl below the summit of "Jasper Peak." Upper Diamond Lake is visible in the lower right of the photo.

(12,500')

Upper Jasper Creek: Challenger Glacier and Storm Lakes Bowl

Difficulty/Quality	Intermediate, Advanced or Expert / ☺☺
Season	Late May, June
Distance	9 miles RT to camp at Jasper Reservoir 4.5 miles RT from camp to Challenger Gl. 4 miles RT, camp to Storm Lakes Bowl
Starting Elevation	9,000'
Elevation Gain	1,800' Hessie to basecamp 1,300' - 1,800' camp to descent routes
Access	Hessie Trailhead, Page 62
Maps	
U.S.G.S.	*Nederland, East Portal*
Trails Illustrated	#102, *Indian Peaks-Gold Hill*
Guidebook	Page 195

In late May and June the two huge bowls at the head of Jasper Creek offer fine skiing opportunities in an uncrowded and isolated setting. It is possible to reach these bowls from Rollins Pass to the south by hiking 2.5 to 4 miles along the Corona Trail that runs near the crest of the Continental Divide. We prefer the longer route from the Hessie town site and trailhead a few miles west of Nederland. It is worth camping overnight at Jasper Lake (a.k.a. "Reservoir") near the head of the valley and spending two days skiing.

The route up Jasper Creek begins at the vacated town site of Hessie. From the Hessie Trailhead walk a quarter mile to a bridge crossing of the North Fork of Middle Boulder Creek. Cross the creek and follow the old winding jeep road uphill for a mile to the next large bridge. A few feet before this bridge there is a sign on the right for Jasper Reservoir. This is the start of the Devil's Thumb bypass trail. This trail is not shown on the U.S.G.S. East Portal map but is shown on the Trails Illustrated map. Take this trail.

When it is free of snow, the Devil's Thumb bypass trail provides a more direct and scenic route up the valley than does the main trail which continues straight ahead across the bridge. Steep at first, the bypass trail crosses a large meadow, before eventually climbing into the Jasper Creek drainage. From here the trail follows an old road that slants gradually up the hillside on the north side of the valley, and eventually reaches the outlet of Jasper Reservoir about 4.5 miles from Hessie. There are campsites along the west and east shores of the reservoir. A permit to camp is required after June 1.

Storm Lakes Bowl — Advanced

Above the north end of Jasper Reservoir there is a large, seldom-visited bowl that contains Upper and Lower Storm Lakes. No official trail accesses these gems. Even in June there is abundant snow in the left (west) side of this bowl.

To reach the bowl, hike or ski around the west shore of the reservoir and locate the inlet stream. Follow close to this stream steeply uphill through breaks in the trees to 11,000' and timberline. The first lake is reached at 11,400'. Ski along the east and north edge of the lake, then turn west and head directly up the snowcovered west side of the bowl. Choose a slope that suits your ability. There is a continuous run down from the unmarked point (elevation 12,650') due west of lower Storm Lake. At the end of May you can usually ski continuously 1,800 vertical feet to Jasper Reservoir.

View northwest into the Storm Lakes Basin. Jasper Reservoir is at the bottom of the photo.

Challenger Glacier and Bowl — Expert

From Jasper Reservoir, continue about a mile further along the trail to beautiful Devil's Thumb Lake located at timberline. From the lake you can get a close-up view of the Devil's Thumb, a prominent landmark northwest of the lake. The lake is a great place to refuel and to survey the surrounding bowls. Challenger Glacier, one of the steepest descents in the Indian Peaks, is located in the southwest corner of the valley. It is set in a northeast-facing pocket due west of "Skyscraper Peak" (Point 12,383'). A couple of other ski descents are located to the right (north) of Challenger Glacier.

The easiest way to reach Challenger Glacier and other descent routes is to continue along the trail (probably snow covered). The trail to the pass shown on the U.S.G.S. map has been rerouted to the south where it now accesses the Divide via the spur just southwest of the tarn at 11,250'. Just as the trail starts to climb the spur, leave the trail and hike south cross-country into the bowl below the glacier. The route to the descent of your choice will obvious from here.

The map of this area in the back of this book shows the location of Challenger Glacier. Be aware that the uppermost portion of this tiny glacier, which is separated from the cornice above by a crevasse, reaches 50 degrees. The condition of the snow, which may be roughened by debris from broken cornices and wet sluffs, and the large cornice should be studied carefully before climbing and skiing this route. The snow filled bowl at the base of the glacier is a fine place for intermediate skiers to play between bouts of sunbathing. (Neither Challenger Glacier nor its sister glacier to the south, "Skyscraper Glacier," are drawn on the U.S.G.S. East Portal map.)

Challenger Glacier is tucked into the southwest corner of the Upper Jasper Creek drainage. This viewpoint is near the summit of "Skyscraper Peak," Point 12,383'.

Region 4

Approaching "Radiobeacon" Mountain

ROLLINS PASS

This region is bounded by "Skyscraper Peak" (Point 12,383') on the north and the Arapaho Lakes on the south. The summits in this area are atypical as compared with the other mountains in this guidebook. Instead of isolated peaks separated by conspicuous and deep saddles, the summits are gentle 12,000' feet bumps rising short distances above the Continental Divide. This explains why none of the summits have official names. The names used in this book to identify the various summits were conjured up by local climbers. The vertical drops range between 600 and 1000 feet. Since the heads of the various valleys contain two or three snow-filled cirques, one can ski or snowboard several snowfields or couloirs in a day.

Depending on how early or late you choose to ski a route and depending on the height of the snowpack, there are three ways to access these peaks and bowls. When the Rollins Pass Road from Winter Park (on the west side of the Divide) is snow-free, you can drive to Rollins Pass and hike north or south along the Divide to access particular routes. If you want to avoid the long drive to Winter Park and up to Rollins Pass, or if the Pass road is impassable on the west side, you might want to drive along the Rollins Pass Road from the east side as far as you can, then park and hike the rest of the way to the Divide. For Forest Lakes Bowl and Couloirs, "Radiobeacon Mountain," and "Frosty Mountain" a third option is to park at East Portal and hike along the South Boulder Creek and then the Arapaho Creek Trail.

Parking and Trailheads

The Rollins Pass Road is a 2WD dirt road that used to make it possible to drive from Boulder County to Winter Park. The road crosses the open tundra of the Continental Divide at Rollins Pass (elevation 11,671'). The road was once a railroad grade and so it contours extensively at a grade never exceeding 5%. You can find out the condition of the Rollins Pass Road by checking with the Arapaho-Roosevelt National Forest. (See page 216 of the Appendix.)

Rollins Pass (11,671') — via road on the west side

To reach Rollins Pass from the west, drive to Winter Park via U.S. 40 over Berthoud Pass. Look for the sign for the Rollins Pass Road on the right side of the highway. It is 14 miles to Rollins Pass from Winter Park. Parking at the pass allows the shortest access to all of the ski descents in this region.

Rollins Pass Road — East side (elevation may vary)

It is no longer possible by car to reach Rollins Pass from the east. The Needle's Eye Tunnel, situated above Yankee Doodle Lake about 1.5 miles before the Pass, has been closed due to rock fall. Another problem is snow closure. In the spring there are two spots where major amounts of snow can block the road. The first is the rock cut (9,900'), 5.5 miles from the start of the road. The second is just past Yankee Doodle Lake (10,711'), ten miles from the start of the road. These snowbanks are plowed eventually by early June. Because of the possibility of snow closure, we included more than one parking spot for the route descriptions in this region. These different parking spots are also shown on the maps on Pages 196 and 197.

From the traffic circle in Nederland drive south on the Peak-To-Peak Highway (Route 119) for five miles to Rollinsville. Turn right (west) onto a 2WD dirt road. This road shares the broad valley of South Boulder Creek with the Denver & Rio Grand Railroad. At 7.6 miles the signed Rollins Pass Road turns right off the main road.

Drive as far as you can with your map close at hand. For Skyscraper Peak etc. (Route 33) Yankee Doodle Lake is the best place to park when approaching from the east. For Forest Lakes (Route 34) and Radiobeacon Mountain (Route 35) the Forest Lakes Trailhead is ideal. But, if the F.L. Trailhead isn't accessible, another good place to park is at elevation 10,457' where the road takes a sharp right across a creek.

Reaching Rollins Pass from Yankee Doodle Lake is easy. From the lake hike to the top of the steep slope above the north bank of the lake. Turn left (west) to reach the road (this bypasses the tunnel). Walk the scenic remainder of the road to the Pass. The view north toward the wide alpine basin that surrounds King, Bob and Betty Lakes is perfect for assessing snow conditions and planning a descent.

East Portal (9,211')

Follow the directions above to where the Rollins Pass Road turns right from the main road. Continue on the main dirt road 0.75 mile to the road's end and park on the left, 150 yards from the sooty maw of the Moffat Tunnel. This improbable edifice is the eastern portal of a tunnel that pierces the Continental Divide for a distance of six miles, connecting Winter Park and the Fraser Valley with the eastern slope. If you're lucky, the tunnel will disgorge a train as you fiddle with your gear. To reach the South Boulder Creek trailhead, walk toward the tunnel, turn left across the tracks, cross the creek on a bridge and turn west on the obvious wide trail into the woods. Use this trailhead to access Arapaho Lakes, Forest Lakes, and "Radiobeacon Mountain" when there is a heavy snowpack and the Rollins Pass Road is impassable on either the west or east side of the Pass.

James Peak Lake Trailhead (11,600')

This is an underutilized, high elevation trailhead that provides access to James Peak Lake and the spectacular east face of James Peak. A high clearance 4WD vehicle is needed to reach it. It is an alternative to the St. Mary's Glacier trailhead described under Interstate 70 Region. Head west from Rollinsville (see above) on the 2WD dirt road for five miles to Tolland. Just past Tolland turn left onto FR 176 (4WD), which climbs into Mammoth Gulch and becomes FR 353. The road climbs steadily along the south rim of Mammoth Gulch across gently sloping meadows and some clear cuts. There are views of the east face of James Peak as well as the peaks above East Portal.

The condition of the road worsens the higher one goes. In June, at about mile 5 from Tolland (11,000') the road is likely to be blocked by intermittent snowdrifts. If the road is passable at this point, bounce along toward the signed James Peak Lake Trailhead at 6.5 miles and park. If the road isn't passable, find a pullout, park, and walk the easy mile or two to the trailhead. Considering the poor condition of the road above 11,000', you won't waste much time by hiking instead of driving, and besides, the scenery is terrific. It takes about 45 minutes to drive from Tolland to the trailhead, so an especially early start is needed to account for this portion of the trip.

You can use this trailhead as an alternative way to access the "Starlight Couloir" and "Bailout" that drop down from the east shoulder of James Peak (described under "Interstate 70 Region.")

(12,383')

"Skyscraper Peak" "Skyscraper Glacier" and King Lake Bowl

Difficulty/Quality .... Intermediate to Expert / ☺
Season .... Late May, June
Distance .... 0.1 to 6 miles from Rollins Pass
Starting Elevation ...... 11,671', Rollins Pass
Elevation Gain .... 800' to 1,600'
Access .... Rollins Pass Rd.— west side, or
Rollins Pass Rd.— east side, Page 114
Maps
U.S.G.S. .... *East Portal*
Trails Illustrated .... #102, *Indian Peaks-Gold Hill*
Guidebook .... Page 196

In late May, when the Rollins Pass Road from Winter Park is free of snow, you can drive to Rollins Pass and access the large bowl that surrounds King Lake, Bob Lake and Betty Lake. Their proximity to Rollins Pass makes these lakes some of the most visited lakes in the Indian Peaks. All this attention is justified since they are situated in beautiful surroundings near or above timberline. The high steep bowls above the lakes have attracted alpine skiers and snowboarders for years. The runs here are short, but some are steep enough to test one's skills and nerve. If you prefer to reach Rollins Pass from the east, realize that you will need to hike an additional 2 miles from Yankee Doodle Lake. The descent routes described below are listed from north to south.

"Skyscraper Peak" (Point 12,383') — Intermediate

From the Pass hike north along the Corona Trail for two miles. When Point 12,307' is directly to your right (east), leave the trail and wander northeast and east off the trail and head across the tundra for the rocky ridge that leads to the knobby summit of "Skyscraper Peak." Continue east past the summit for a few hundred yards to a bench at 12,100'. From this bench a south-facing snow slope drops 700 vertical feet to the north bank of Skyscraper Reservoir. To return to the Pass, follow the cross-country route suggested in the map on page 196. This route melts out earlier than the others described in this section.

"Skyscraper Glacier" — Expert

"Skyscraper Glacier" is not identified on the U.S.G.S. East Portal map. It is located on the steep slope northwest of Bob Lake. Short and steep, the glacier can be skied along with other nearby descents without a major expenditure of time or energy. The walk to Skyscraper Glacier or Peak from Rollins Pass via the Corona Trail is gorgeous. There are wildflowers in profusion, marmots bustling, and birds calling which contrasts markedly with the rawness and icy sterility of the Divide in winter.

From the pass, follow the directions above for Skyscraper Peak. About 300 yards after leaving the Corona Trail, locate the drop-off and cornice of the glacier on your right. It is unlikely that you will be able (or want) to access the top of the glacier via its corniced top. Instead pass by the top of the glacier and locate a grassy, southwest-facing slope that lies along the east edge of the glacier. It is more reasonable to descend this slope a bit and then traverse out onto the middle of the glacier, which can be climbed from this point.

After skiing the glacier, proceed around the west side of Bob Lake and continue along a terrace that leads past over-camped patches of bare ground by the outlet of Betty Lake. Cross the outlet (wet) and locate the poorly marked trail leading from Betty Lake. Follow it down to the King Lake Trail and ascend the King Lake Trail back to Rollins Pass.

King Lake Bowl is on the left. Point 12,100' is in the center. "Skyscraper" Glacier is on the right.

King Lake Bowl — Advanced

The two best descents are located in a small cirque above and northwest of King Lake. There is an unnamed sausage-shaped tarn at the base of this cirque. The precise locations of these two runs can be pinpointed by hiking east away from the Pass on the Rollins Pass Road for a few hundred yards.

From Rollins Pass, start out heading north on the Corona Trail. After about a mile, veer east to the edge of the tundra and locate the top of either the first or second descent route. Having skied one route, the second can be climbed and skied. To exit, head southeast to a slope that drops down to the north edge of King Lake, cross the outlet, and find the King Lake Trail a few yards from the crossing. Ascend the trail back to Rollins Pass.

Rollins Pass Runs — Intermediate

There are two parallel ski slopes that extend north-northeastward from the east edge of Rollins Pass. They both hold reliable snow through May and June and provide a training ground for skiers who prefer to practice their turns without the drudgery of a long approach.

(12,000')

Forest Lakes Bowls and Couloir

Difficulty/Quality .... Advanced or Expert / ☺☺
Season .... Mid May, mid June
Distances .... 3 miles from Rollins Pass or
4.6 mi. Rollins Pass Rd.— East. Elev. 10,457'
Starting Elevation ...... 11,671' (Rollins Pass) or 10,457' (East side)
Elevation Gain .... 1,700' (Roll. Pass) or 2,000' (Elev. 10,457')
Access .... Rollins Pass or Rollins Pass Rd., Page 114
Maps
U.S.G.S. .... *East Portal*
Trails Illustrated .... #102, *Indian Peaks-Gold Hill* or
#103, *Winter Park, Central City, Rollins Pass*
Guidebook .... Page 197

The routes described below lie within two steep-walled cirques north of "Radiobeacon Mountain" (Point 12,072'). These bowls can be reached from Rollins Pass when the road from Winter Park is open. They can also be reached from the Rollins Pass Road. Where you park along the road depends on where it's blocked by snow (See page 114). Suggested parking spots and shortcuts are shown on the map on page 197.

The first bowl lies due west of the Forest Lakes Trailhed on the Rollins Pass Road and drops from the Divide to a tarn. The second bowl is due west of the upper Forest Lake and also drops from the Divide to a tarn. The third is, in fact, a couloir set into the northeast face of "Radiobeacon Mountain." This couloir is very steep and narrow, and skiing it is serious business.

The easiest way to reach the first bowl (advanced) is to drive as far as possible along the road until you are blocked by snow. Use the map in the back of this book (page 197) to navigate west and south onto the Divide via the easterly ridge southwest of Jenny Lake. Ascend the north side of this easterly ridge. From the top of the ridge hike west a short distance to the Divide and then south for a few hundred yards to the top of the bowl. Ski the bowl to the tarn at its base. To return to the trailhead hike southwest uphill past a knoll, then ski down into the bottom of the next small bowl, where there is another tarn. Pass the tarn on its north side and hike or ski down a steep slope to the upper Forest Lake. The trail back to the trailhead is on the north side of the lake 200 vertical feet below the Forest Lakes Trailhead. If you choose to reach the first bowl via Rollins Pass, simply hike south for a half mile to the top of the bowl and drop in. To return to the Pass from the Forest Lakes Trailhead, regain the Divide (see beginning of this paragraph) and hike back to the Pass.

The second bowl (expert), which is further south, has a cornice at its top that makes an approach from below easier than launching off the cornice. To reach the bowl from below, hike downhill from the Forest Lakes Trailhead to the upper Forest Lake. Hike around the north and west sides of the lake and hike southwest up a short steep slope to a tarn at 11,030'. Turn north and hike to the base of the snow slope and ascend it.

The third descent is the couloir (expert+) on the northeast side of Radiobeacon Mountain. Because of its steepness and the potential for poor conditions, it definitely should be approached from below. You can reach the base of the couloir by hiking to upper Forest Lake (see above) and climbing southwest up a short slope to the base of the couloir. The couloir itself is 800 vertical feet.

View north into Forest Lakes Bowls from the northeast slope of "Radiobeacon" Mountain.

This spectacular couloir is located on the northeast face of "Radiobeacon" Mountain (summit shown in photo) and overlooks Upper Forest Lake.

(12,072')

"Radiobeacon Mountain"

Difficulty/Quality .... Advanced / ☺☺☺
Season .... May, mid June
Distances .... 4 mi. (Rollins Pass) or 5 mi (East side)
Starting Elevation ...... 11,671' (Rollins Pass) or 10,457' (East side)
Elevation Gain .... 1,500' (Rollins Pass) or 2,000' (East side)
Access .... Rollins Pass or Rollins Pass Road, Page 114
Maps
U.S.G.S. .... *East Portal*
Trails Illustrated .... #102, *Indian Peaks-Gold Hill* or
#103, *Winter Park, Central City, Rollins Pass*
Guidebook .... Page 197

Don't be surprised if a descent down the northeast slope of "Radiobeacon Mountain" becomes a late spring ritual. This modest mountain rises above Forest Lakes and is a gem to ski.

If you are driving from Rollinsville on the east side of the Divide, examine the snowy skyline above the dirt road when you are about a mile and a half from East Portal. The mountain at the extreme right with the broad snow slope originating at the summit and running down its east-northeast face is Radiobeacon Mountain. It isn't named on the U.S.G.S. East Portal map. We named it "Radiobeacon" because the U.S.G.S. map indicates that there is a radiobeacon on its summit. All that is left of this structure is a 10 feet by 10 feet concrete pad that lies a stone's throw from the summit.

Radiobeacon can also be reached by driving from Winter Park to Rollins Pass and hiking south from the Pass along the Divide for just over a mile to the summit. We prefer the approach from the east via the Rollins Pass Road. Follow the directions for reaching the Divide given under Route 34, Forest Lakes Bowl. Upon reaching the Divide, hike south for roughly a mile to the summit of Radiobeacon.

From the summit you can see the crest of the Divide stretching from James Peak (looking south) to the Arapaho Peaks (looking north). Other interesting sights include the Winter Park Ski Area and the Williams Fork Mountains to the west, Fraser Valley to the northwest, Rollins Pass to the north, and the Needle Eye Tunnel along the Rollins Pass Road to the northeast.

You can begin your descent almost from the summit. The slope is 35 degrees at first but moderates to 25 degrees. Another exciting choice is to hug the north edge of the snow slope, eventually veering north down a steep slope into the bowl on the north side of the mountain.

The easiest way to return to the Rollins Pass road is to ski or walk to the upper Forest Lake. On the northeast corner of the lake there is a short trail (usually snowcovered) that leads north and uphill to the Forest Lakes Trailhead. From the trailhead, you can walk back to your vehicle, unless you were lucky enough to park at the trailhead.

If you parked at Rollins Pass then you need to reach the Divide from the Forest Lakes Trailhead. To do this follow directions given under Route 34.

"Radiobeacon" Mountain from the north. James Peak in the distance. The steep couloir facing the camera in the center of this photo is an alternate, steeper descent that also shortens the return to the Forest Lakes Trailhead. This alternative is not shown on the map on Page 197.

(11,960')

Arapaho Lakes and "Frosty Mountain"

Difficulty/Quality .... Intermediate / Advanced / ☺☺
Season .... May, mid June
Distance .... 8 miles
Starting Elevation ...... 9,211'
Elevation Gain .... 3000'
Access .... East Portal, Page 115
Maps
U.S.G.S. .... *East Portal*
Trails Illustrated .... #103, *Winter Park, Central City, Rollins Pass*
Guidebook .... Page 197

Frosty Mountain is a big bump on the Continental Divide, 0.4 mile south of "Radiobeacon Mountain" (Route 35). It is neither named nor numbered on the U.S.G.S. map. It sits at the head of the mile wide cirque ("Frosty Bowl") that cradles the Arapaho Lakes. It is easy to spot from the 2WD dirt access road one mile west of East Portal, where the road crosses the railroad tracks. Look for a symmetrical, snowcovered pyramid to the left (south) of Radiobeacon Mountain.

Frosty Mountain offers an enjoyable descent in a large bowl that otherwise is threatened by steep headwalls and menacing cornices. Except for the 100 feet below the summit, the descent along the east slope of the mountain is between 25 and 30 degrees. There is usually snow on the mountain and in Frosty Bowl through June.

To reach "Frosty" hike west along the South Boulder Creek Trail for a mile to a long meadow. Upon entering this meadow (marked "Grave" on the U.S.G.S. map) turn right (north) and locate the start of the Forest Lakes Trail (unsigned) that turns sharply right and uphill along a wide path. Hike or ski along this trail for 1.5 miles. When you reach the large meadow (10,280') that marks the confluence of Arapaho Creek and the creek from the Forest Lakes, turn left (southwest) cross the creek on a snow bridge or primitive wood bridge and ascend a steep timbered slope for about 400 vertical feet. Try to locate a swath through the trees that will deposit you near the pond at 10,780'. Locating this swath will make the descent easier as it is wide enough to make turns.

As the grade eases continue west along Arapaho Creek. Frosty Mountain lies dead ahead. The mountain to the north is Radiobeacon Mountain (12,072'); to the south is "Sprint Peak" (12,110'). Plot a route to the base of Frosty's east slope. Ascend the slope and final steep section to the summit.

Descend the same way you ascended. In May, conditions permitting, it should be possible to ski continuously to the start of the Forest Lakes Trail. There are other obvious lines in Frosty Bowl (not drawn in the map on page 197).

"Frosty Mountain" from the east.
The mountain on the right that is partially cut off is "Radiobeacon."

Region 5

Foggy day in May on Squaretop Mountain

Interstate 70

Interstate 70 is the highway that Colorado skiers love to hate. On winter weekends hordes of Front Range skiers, frantically bent on reaching the resorts of Summit, Grand, and Eagle Counties, converge on I-70. By April the number of skiers on the highway drops considerably. During May and June spring ski mountaineers can enjoy a leisurely drive up the Interstate to some of the best corn snow that the Front Range has to offer.

Visitors who live outside the Fort Collins, Denver, Colorado Springs corridor should consult a Colorado road map to locate Interstate 70. Directions to the various parking areas and trailheads have been written assuming one is driving west from the direction of Denver.

Most of the mountains between Berthoud Pass (left edge) and James Peak (right) are visible from this high point along Interstate 70. This is a perfect place to judge the snow conditons in the high country.

Parking and Trailheads

Fall River Road: St. Mary's Glacier Trailhead (10,400')

Take I-70 west toward Idaho Springs. One mile past the last Idaho Springs exit, leave the highway at Exit #238 ("Fall River Road"). Drive 8.6 miles from the start of the Fall River Road. There is a parking turnout on the left for St. Mary's Glacier. A few hundred feet before the turnout, on the left, there is a sign that reads "Glacier Hike." This is one of the starting points for routes on James Peak. Walk up the rocky jeep road for three quarters of a mile past St. Mary's Lake to the toe of St. Mary's Glacier.

Fall River Road: Alice (10,400' or higher)

As described above, take Exit #238 ("Fall River Road"). Turn right onto Fall River Road. The subdivision known as "Alice" is located 8.0 miles from the start of Fall River Road. At the 8.0 mile point on Fall River Road, locate the dirt RD 275. Turn left and continue 0.9 mile uphill to Stewart Road, which forks right at 10,400'. Continue 0.4 miles to a pullout on the right besides a huge tailings pile. With a suitable vehicle, you can continue farther up Stewart Road (a 4WD road that gets rougher). The road eventually leads to Loch Lomond (11,200'), which lies at the foot of Mount Bancroft, south of James Peak.

Fall River Road: Fall River Reservoir Rd. (10,700' or lower)

As described above, take Exit #238 ("Fall River Road"). Turn right onto Fall River Road. After 6.7 miles from the start of the Fall River Road, there is a hairpin where the paved main road turns right. The dirt Fall River Reservoir Road (unmarked) continues straight ahead. Drive as far as possible on this road. Where you park will be determined by the time of the year and by the extent of the spring snowpack. In June it is usually possible to drive three miles from the hairpin, almost to Fall River Reservoir. From reservoir dam, you can reach Parry Peak, Mount Eva, and Witter Peak.

Stanley Slide Path Parking (11,000')

Leave the interstate at Exit #232 ("U.S. 40W, Empire, Granby") and drive west on U.S. 40 two miles to the town of Empire. From Empire continue west on U.S. 40 for about 7 miles to the first switchback (turns right) heading toward Berthoud Pass. The bottom of the Stanley Slide path is one mile from this first switchback. Consider parking a vehicle here on the wide right side (south) shoulder to facilitate a return to the upper parking spot. Count four more switchbacks. At the fourth switchback (turns right) at 11,000', park on the inside of the hairpin. Cross the road to begin the tour to the Stanley slide path.

Bard Creek Trailhead (10,200')

Exit the highway at Exit #232 ("40W, Empire, Granby") and drive west on U.S. 40 two miles to the town of Empire. In the center of Empire turn left (south) onto Bard Creek Road (2WD dirt). At 2.4 miles there is a parking area on the right. Park here only if you do not have a high-clearance 4WD vehicle and you don't mind an extra leg-pounding two miles of hiking each way. The next two miles to the trailhead consist of a rough and steep 4WD road. The trailhead is located where the road makes a sharp right turn uphill. There is no official parking, so be sure to park as close to the side of the road as possible in order to not obstruct other vehicles. From the parking spot at the turn in the road, a rocky trail heads west above the north bank of Bard Creek.

Guanella Pass Parking (11,669')

Exit the highway at Exit #228 ("Georgetown"). From the exit turn left. Drive under the highway overpass and turn right at the next intersection onto Argentine Street. Drive 0.7 mile to Sixth St. and make a left and then make a right on Rose St. There are small signs for "Guanella Pass" along this route. The road to the pass is initially paved, then changes to 2WD dirt. There is a campground 8.7 miles from Georgetown. The parking area is 12 miles from Georgetown on the left (east) side of the road. The South Park Trail to Squaretop Mountain begins on the opposite side of the road.

Kelso Mountain Parking (10,800')

Exit the highway at Exit #221 ("Bakerville"). From the exit turn left and drive over the highway overpass. Continue about 100 yards to a Forest Service sign that reads "Grays Peak." The dirt road (steep and rough 2WD) turns left and heads uphill through the forest. After one to two miles, the road is often blocked with snow. Park on the right side. The tour to Kelso Mountain begins two miles from I-70 immediately after a rust-colored, two story abandoned building on the right.

Grizzly Gulch Parking (10,340')

Exit the highway at Exit #221 ("Bakerville"). From the "Grays Peak" sign (see Kelso Mountain above) drive up the dirt road (steep, rough 2WD) for one mile and turn right onto a flatter, smoother road that heads up Grizzly Gulch. After 0.3 mile on this road, you'll cross a large culvert and see several abandoned buildings. Park on left side of the road, but don't block traffic. There is no official parking spot. Just past the culvert and the 2WD vehicle parking spot, there is a rough 4WD road (#189.1C) that turns off the 2WD road. This is the jeep road into Grizzly Gulch. With a high clearance 4WD vehicle, you can continue into Grizzly Gulch on this jeep road until blocked by snow or rough road conditions.

Stevens Gulch Parking (11,300')

Exit the highway at Exit #221 ("Bakerville"). From the "Grays Peak" sign (see Kelso Mountain above) drive three miles and park on the left side of the road in an official parking area that has a restroom. The custom-made trail to Grays Peak begins across the road at a steel bridge.

Herman Gulch Parking (10,300')

Exit the highway at Exit #218 (unnamed). From the exit make a sharp right directly into the large parking lot. There is a restroom. The trail leading into Herman Gulch and Pettingell Peak begins directly from the restroom.

Dry Gulch Parking (10,600')

Exit the highway at Exit #216 ("6W, Loveland Pass"). At the first opportunity make a hard right onto a narrow, unsigned dirt road (2WD) that heads east parallel to the exit ramp that you were just on. Drive 0.6 mile east to a gate and park on the left side. The tour into Dry Gulch, Hagar Mountain and "Citadel" begins on the other side of the gate on a continuation of the dirt road.

Loveland Pass (11,990')

Exit the highway at Exit #216 ("6W, Loveland Pass"). Drive past the Loveland Basin ski area along U.S. 6 west to Loveland Pass. The pass is 4.5 miles from Exit #216. Park on the left (east) side of the road by the sign for the pass. The small parking area has no restrooms. All the ski runs in the vicinity of the pass can be accessed from the parking area. This is windy place with outstanding scenery in all directions.

Summit fever

(13,294')

James Peak

Southeast Slope Route

Difficulty/Quality .... Intermediate / ☺☺
Season .... Late April, May
Distance .... 8 miles
Starting Elevation ...... 10,400'
Elevation Gain .... 2,900'
Access .... Fall River Road: St. Mary's Glacier, Page 128
Maps
U.S.G.S. .... *Empire*
Trails Illustrated .... #103, *Winter Park, Central City, Rollins Pass*
Guidebook .... Page 198

"Starlight Couloir"

Difficulty/Quality .... Expert / ☺☺
Season .... Mid May, mid June
Distance .... 4.5 miles
Starting Elevation ...... 11,600'
Elevation Gain .... 2,100'
Access .... James Peak Lake Trailhead, Page 115
Maps
Same as above

"Bailout"

Difficulty/Quality .... Advanced / ☺☺
Season .... Mid May, mid June
Distance .... 4.5 miles
Starting Elevation ...... 11,600'
Elevation Gain .... 2,000'
Access .... James Peak Lake Trailhead, Page 115
Maps
Same as above

In the spring, as you drive west on Interstate 70 out of Denver, the highway eventually reaches the top of the long grade up Mount Vernon Canyon. At this high point a mesmerizing view of seven mountains from Berthoud Pass to James Peak suddenly pops into view. The mountain on the north end of the chain is James Peak, identifiable by its broad southeast shoulder. Among local skiers, James Peak is well known for an easily accessible and long ski route on this snow covered shoulder. This popular, intermediate route is approached from St. Mary's Glacier.

In addition to the southeast slope route, there are two additional ski descent routes on James—Starlight Couloir and Bailout – that drop down the much steeper north side of the massive southeast ridge. These two routes can be accessed from St. Mary's Glacier also, but, for a more complete mountaineering experience, we suggest an approach from the James Peak Lake Trailhead above Mammoth Gulch (page 115). This latter trailhead is higher and shortens the trip distance, but it requires the use of a high-clearance 4WD vehicle. In addition, the high, rough road that leads to this trailhead may be blocked by snow one or two miles before the trailhead. St. Mary's Glacier or the James Peak Trailhead? The choice is yours.

Southeast Slope Route — Intermediate

The southeast slope route is the one most commonly skied from the summit of James Peak. The lower portion is pleasantly angled and is a beautiful place for budding skiers and snowboarders to sharpen their turning skills. The short, south-facing drop from the summit has enough steepness to push intermediate skiers.

From the St. Mary's Glacier trailhead walk up the steep, rocky and/or snow covered jeep road to St. Mary's Lake. From the lake head north and walk a short distance to the glacier. Foot and ski tracks abound. Walk or ski east up the glacier to the immense, low-angled east ridge of James Peak (11,600'). Stroll westward for a mile to obvious steeper ground and follow the southeast ridge to the summit.

The descent is as obvious as the ascent. The summit provides close-up views to the south of Bancroft, Parry and Eva. All of these peaks have fine ski descents. The view to the north extends to Rocky Mountain National Park.

The run from the summit to the flat area is a mile long and 1,300 vertical feet. After skiing down to the flat area, there is an additional 400 vertical feet of skiing down St. Mary's Glacier.

"Starlight" Couloir — Expert

The majestic east face of James Peak can only be seen closely and in its entirety from the Mammoth Gulch Road south of East Portal. The face is 1,000' high and is penetrated by several very steep, snow-filled couloirs (the "Star" couloirs). These couloirs are documented snow-climbing routes. The more moderate "Starlight" couloir slices through the north-facing section of the east face, and for this reason, is not visible unless one is standing at the base of the east face or looking down onto it from the southeast ridge.

Sometime after June 1, the road to the James Peak Lake Trailhead is sufficiently free of snow that you can drive within a mile or two of the airy James Peak Lake Trailhead at 11,600'. This road and trailhead are one of the more scenic starts to an outing. Standing at the trailhead one's inclination is to walk a mile downhill to James Peak Lake, climb up to the base of the east face, locate the "Starlight" couloir, climb it and ski it. This is certainly an option. However, we suggest the following circuit route that takes advantage of the trailhead's high elevation.

From the trailhead hike uphill cross-country in a south-southwesterly direction along a ridge to 12,000' to reach the east shoulder of James Peak. Turn right (west), drop a bit passing Point 11,887', and then continue west toward the northern edge of the east slope where the east face drops off. Upon reaching 12,800' on the east ridge, the next step is to locate the top of the couloir which is only 20 feet wide at its top, faces north, has no cornice, and is walled in by rock. You must be standing at the top of it looking down to see it. The solution is to inspect every couloir you pass. If a couloir looks as though you would need a rappel to get into it, it is not the right couloir! The top of "Starlight" is located at around 12,930' and the very top may be melted out or icy. A few feet of easy scrambling down is needed to reach the snow.

Once you've located the couloir, you can drop your skis to mark the couloir and head the rest of the 0.3-mile to the summit. Or you can just ski the couloir and forget the summit. The maximum steepness is 40 degrees and it widens fairly soon. The vertical drop into the east face basin is 700 feet. Watch out for rocks that have fallen into the couloir from the adjacent rock walls. If after seeing the couloir, you decide that it is too intimidating to ski, relax. There is a kinder, gentler slope ("Bailout," described below) farther east along the ridge that leads down toward James Peak Lake.

Having successfully descended the couloir, ski northeast through the bowl below the east face for 800 hundred yards before turning east and passing 50 yards south of the tiny 11,800' depression that is the bowl's low point. Boulder hop east across the moraine until you see an opening onto the wide snow slope that rises above the northwest side of the lake. Ski down to the edge of the lake and locate the tiny cabin that sits above the lake's outlet. Hike around the south shore of the lake to the cabin. The trail back to the trailhead begins at the cabin. Portions may be snowcovered, but it is generally easy to follow. The trailhead is a mile from the lake and 400 feet above the trail's low point.

"Bailout"—Advanced

Follow the description above for Starlight Couloir. Once on the east ridge, you can see the top of the route. Hug the edge of the east ridge, and once you've passed the 12,800' top of the steeper section, the ridge flattens noticeably and Bailout is visible on your right. Continue a bit further uphill to the top of the snow slope.

Bailout curves down 1,900 vertical feet to the south shore of James Peak Lake. To return to the trailhead from the lake, again follow the description for Starlight Couloir. If you chose to access Bailout from St. Mary's Glacier (page 128), then the "easiest" exit is to climb the steep, talused slope that lies east of the descent route back to the broad plateau at 11,280'. Hang a left (east) and return to the glacier and your car.

The broad east slope of James Peak. Part of the steep east face is visible below the summit.

Starlight Couloir from the bowl below the east face of James Peak

(13,250')

Mount Bancroft

Difficulty/Quality .... Advanced / ☺☺☺
Season .... Mid May, mid June
Distance .... 6.5 miles
Starting Elevation ...... 10,400' or higher
Elevation Gain .... 2,800' or less
Access .... Fall River Road: Alice, Page 128
Maps
U.S.G.S. .... *Empire*
Trails Illustrated .... #103, *Winter Park, Central City, Rollins Pass*
Guidebook .... Page 199

Some of the best spring skiing and snowboarding in the Front Range can be found from Mount Bancroft south to Mount Eva. Mount Bancroft is the first mountain south of James Peak. Overshadowed by the sprawling mass of James Peak, Bancroft and its southerly neighbors see relatively few visitors even on a day when James Peak and St. Mary's Glacier are hosting throngs of climbers and "sliders." The two alpine basins on the east side of Bancroft contain six beautiful lakes, the first of which, Loch Lomond, is a reservoir that is accessible in June by a rough 4WD road. Easy access, a scenic approach and fine skiing combine to make Bancroft a "must do" peak for backcountry skiers and snowboarders.

To reach the bowl on the east side of the mountain and the summit, drive west from the Alice subdivision on Stewart Road until the road becomes impassable due to snow or rocks. The first one-third mile of Stewart Road is 2WD but turns into 4WD near a huge tailings pile at 10,400'. Park and then ski or hike toward Loch Lomond along the remainder of this scenic road. Drivers of high clearance 4WD vehicles may be able to continue along the rocky and steep road, assuming it is free of snow, to a clearing just before the Loch Lomond dam.

Whether you drive, hike or ski, about 200 yards before the Loch Lomond dam, veer left (west) and then southwest and head up into Bancroft Bowl via a snowcovered jeep road (if you can find it). Pass about 100 yards north of the rocky nubbin, Point 11,942'. From here two routes to the summit are possible. You can head on snow directly west up the bowl and then slant left to reach the

Mount Bancroft from the northeast

southeast ridge at elevation 12,600'. However, a more scenic and breezier route involves climbing onto the snow-free southeast ridge soon after passing the rocky nubbin. Once on the southeast ridge follow it to the summit.

To reach the bowl from the summit, ski about 150 yards northeast along the summit ridge to the top of the bowl. From here you can descend over 1,000 vertical feet to the west end of Lake Caroline. The slope isn't as steep as it looks. From the west end of Lake Caroline, ski around the south shore, and then continue downhill another 600 vertical feet to the west shore of Loch Lomond. Ski south past the dam about one-third mile and pick up the approach route and reverse it back to your car.

(13,391')

Parry Peak

Difficulty/Quality .... Advanced / ☺☺☺
Season .... May, mid June
Distance .... 4.5 miles or more
Starting Elevation ...... 10,700' or lower
Elevation Gain .... 2,700' or more
Access .... Fall River Reservoir Road, Page 128
Maps
U.S.G.S. .... *Empire*
Trails Illustrated .... #103, *Winter Park, Central City, Rollins Pass*
Guidebook .... Page 199

Many people drive to Fall River Reservoir and nearby Chinns Lake, to fish and view the surrounding peaks. Fewer people continue above these lakes to climb and ski. Of the peaks that stretch south from James Peak to Berthoud Pass, Parry is the tallest. When viewed from the valley below, the snow covered southeast face of Parry Peak appears to be a daunting line to ski. In truth advanced skiers will find both the climb and the descent of Parry Peak within their abilities.

Drive as far as possible along the dirt road that leads toward Fall River Reservoir from the paved Fall River Road. The road is in relatively good condition as far as the mill site at elevation 10,225' just past the bridge across Fall River. Beyond this point snow banks and meltwater may be present in May or early June. There is little value in pushing your luck further up valley, so park, heave your gear on your back and head along the road to the reservoir which sits 1.5 miles farther.

At the reservoir, stand on the south end of the dam and check your map. It might appear that to reach the upper valley you should skirt the reservoir and climb the steep slope at its west end. Actually a better route is to walk north along the dam, head north uphill through a slot in the trees to around 11,000', then veer northwest and eventually west along open slopes that will deposit you on the north side of the basin at 11,300'. Proceed west for a third of a mile to the base of Parry's obvious southeast snow slope. This is where the real climbing begins. Slog up the slope for 1,400 vertical feet until you reach a small saddle at Point 12,997'. The summit lies to the west, an easier 400 vertical feet more of climbing. The descent retraces the ascent. With a healthy snowpack it is possible to ski a total of 2,000 vertical feet to Fall River Reservoir.

View west toward Parry Peak from Fall River Reservoir

View north toward Parry Peak from Mount Eva

(13,130')

Mount Eva

Difficulty/Quality .... Intermediate or Advanced / ☺☺☺
Season .... May, June
Distance .... 4.5 miles or more
Starting Elevation ...... 10,700' or lower
Elevation Gain .... 2,400' or more
Access .... Fall River Reservoir Road, Page 128
Maps
U.S.G.S. .... *Empire*
Trails Illustrated .... #103, *Winter Park, Central City, Rollins Pass*
Guidebook .... Page 199

Mount Eva is the snowy temptress that comes in and out of view as one heads up the Fall River Road from I-70. Actually it is Eva's jutting east ridge that is erroneously identified as Eva, for Eva's true summit is hidden further west. Early in the season with her flanks streaked by steep strips of snow (go ahead — say it fast), we have pondered the potential for sensational ski and snowboard descents. But with time these apparent descents proved ephemeral as these lines melted quickly and were prone to slide on their slabby rock beds. So how does one climb and ski Eva? There are two ways. On the south face below and slightly east of the summit there are 1,200 vertical feet of advanced skiing. One can also climb Eva and ski down the intermediate bowl ("Eva Bowl") that faces east between Eva and Witter Peak, the mountain directly south of Eva.

Follow the directions to Fall River Reservoir dam as described for Parry Peak (Route 39). From the dam, turn left (south) up the steep wooded slope for 200 vertical feet to Chinns Lake. Continue west along the north shores of both Chinns and Sherwin Lakes. From the west end of Sherwin Lake climb steeply west up the open drainage to where it flattens (11,400'); then turn northwest and climb another 400 vertical feet into the Eva-Witter Bowl.

From the flat bottom of the bowl, there are two routes to the summit of Eva. You can head west up Eva Bowl to the Continental Divide and then follow the southwest ridge to the summit. Or climb north-northwest up the snow slopes that lead to the 12,800' saddle slightly east of the summit. From here the summit is less than 200 yards away. The summit has excellent close-up views of Parry Peak to the north. The top of Berthoud Pass is also visible as are the Winter Park Ski area and the entire Fraser Valley.

The southeast face route (advanced) descends 1,200 vertical feet. Another way to descend from the summit begins at the U-notch in front of the steel tower along the southwest ridge. The U-notch provides a break in the cornice that rims the summit ridge and clearly is safer than wrestling with the cornice. The easiest way down is via Eva Bowl (Intermediate), which retraces the first ascent route described above.

Because the approach for Eva is relatively short, you might consider following a descent of Eva with an ascent and descent of Witter Peak. There is a pleasant snow slope on the north flank of Witter Peak (12,884'). This obvious slope is directly opposite Eva's summit and provides a convenient route to Witter's west ridge. From the top of the west ridge, the summit is only a quarter mile stroll to the east.

Mount Eva from the east

(12,400')

Stanley Slide Path

Difficulty/Quality	Expert (at top) / Advanced ☺☺☺
Season	May
Distance	1.6 miles
Starting Elevation	10,946'
Elevation Gain	1,560'
Access	Stanley Slide Path Parking, Page 128
Maps	
U.S.G.S.	*Berthoud Pass*
Trails Illustrated	#103, *Winter Park, Central City, Rollins Pass*
Guidebook	Page 200

The Stanley slide is a classic avalanche path that receives a lot of attention from the highway department's winter avalanche crew. This is because the runout zone of the path crosses U.S. 40 and occasionally blocks traffic in the winter. The wide starting zone of the path is located high on a ridge top that lies east of Stanley Mountain (12,521'). During May when the snow in the slide path has consolidated, one can ski the path safely. This is an excellent descent that offers easy access and a ski descent of more than 2,000 feet back to the highway. A quick car shuttle or hitchhike brings you back to the start of the tour.

From the parking area cross the highway and hike or ski uphill through the trees heading generally west toward timberline. At timberline continue toward the southeast ridge of Point 12,507'. Follow this ridge in a northwest direction to its top at 12,400'. The slope (Advanced) that lies directly to the east makes a fine warm-up run of about 500 vertical feet.

The top of the slide path is quite steep but has a safe runout. It is easy to enter the path at a lower point and avoid the steep upper headwall. Ski as far as the highway. The snow often deteriorates within fifty yards of the road. Drive or hitchhike back to the upper parking area. Because of the south-facing exposure, an early start is recommended.

Peter Bridge

Hanging on for dear life at the top of the Stanley Slide

Cruising the mid-section of the Stanely Slide

(13,641')

Bard Peak

Difficulty/Quality .... Advanced / ☺☺
Season .... Late May, early June
Distance .... 9 miles
Starting Elevation ...... 10,200'
Elevation Gain .... 3,400'
Access .... Bard Creek Trailhead, Page 129
Maps
U.S.G.S. .... *Grays Peak, Georgetown*
Trails Illustrated .... #104, *Idaho Spgs, Georgetown, Loveland Pass*
Guidebook .... Page 201

A tour to the summit of Bard Peak offers skiers and snowboarders the opportunity to log 1,800 vertical feet of excellent skiing in a remote and scenic setting. Since most of the trail lies on the sunny north side of Bard Creek, it is usually possible to hike the first two or three miles on a dry trail. The final half-mile along the southeast ridge to the summit is exceptionally beautiful.

From the Bard Creek Trailhead, hike west along a rocky trail that gradually meets and follows along the north bank of Bard Creek. At 10,800' the trail switchbacks up and west along an open hillside interspersed with aspen groves. The trail traverses high above the valley, crosses two major drainages from the north, and reaches flatter terrain around 12,000'. There is usually snow at this point, and except for an occasional cairn, it is difficult to follow the trail. This isn't a problem since the peak is in full view and it is easy to dead reckon. Take note of the left side of the long southeast ridge and head for it by the easiest way possible. With careful route selection it is possible to encounter a minimum of snow and to reach the summit ridge via grassy slopes intermixed with talus. Once on top of the southeast ridge, hike to the summit. There are excellent views of Grays Peak, Torreys Peak, and Kelso Mountain to the south.

Ski directly down the northeast slope of the peak. Where the slope flattens significantly, traverse directly north for several hundred yards to reach another excellent steeper slope. To avoid a wide patch of brush, ski north again and enter the snow-filled creek bed that flows from the saddle between Robeson and Engelmann Peaks. Ski down the creek bed to where the Bard Creek Trail crosses the creek. Remove skis here and hike out on the trail.

Three skiers approach the east slope of Bard Peak.

South Ridge of Bard Peak
To the left of the hiker is Kelso Mountain, on the right are Grays Peak and Torreys Peak.

(13,794')

Square Top Mountain

Difficulty/Quality .... Advanced or Expert / ☺☺☺
Season .... May, early June
Distance .... 6 miles
Starting Elevation ...... 11,669'
Elevation Gain .... 2,100'
Access........................... Guanella Pass Parking, Page 129
Maps
U.S.G.S. .... *Mount Evans, Montezuma*
Trails Illustrated .... #104, *Idaho Spgs, Georgetown, Loveland Pass*
Guidebook .... Page 202

From Guanella Pass the imposing mass of Mount Bierstadt (14,050') and the neighboring Sawtooth dominate the landscape on the east side of the road. On the west side of the highway and only 250 feet lower is Square Top Mountain. So, why should you head for Square Top when an opportunity to bag a fourteener is almost as close? Because Square Top has an excellent ski descent, and Bierstadt doesn't. From the Guanella Pass parking area a snow slope with a vertical drop of 1,600' is clearly visible on Square Top's east side.

East Slope — Advanced

From the Guanella Pass parking area, cross the road and locate the South Park Trail, an old double track road. The trail heads west and crosses a shallow, willow-infested, drainage. The trail then heads south and traverses higher ground eventually reaching the lower of the two Square Top Lakes after 1.8 miles. Cross the outlet of the lake and head uphill toward the east ridge of Square Top (no trail). Once on the ridge follow it toward the summit. On the way to the summit, watch for the east slope ski run which begins at around 13,500'. Below 13,500' you will pass steeper ski slopes that drop directly downward into upper Square Top Lake. Avoid these. Also, above 13,500' you will pass very steep slopes and gullies that drop down the north face into Silver Dollar Lake. Avoid these as well. Leave your skis at the top of the east slope ski run, which can be recognized by the fact that it is fairly wide and not very steep, and continue to the summit, if you wish.

Return to your skis and enjoy 1,400 vertical feet to upper Square Top Lake. Skirt the south edge of the lake and ski 150 more feet to lower Square Top

Lake. Skirt the north edge of this lake and continue skiing (or hiking, if necessary) to the outlet of the lake and the South Park Trail. Return to your car via the South Park Trail.

Squaretop Mountain from the east. The descent route is clearly visible below the summit ridge.

North Couloir — Expert

This is a steeper alternative to the east slope. It also involves a lengthy but enjoyable tour down a different valley to the highway further north from where you parked. From the summit of Square Top, hike west to where the northwest ridge drops downhill. The north couloir is located at this point. The top is the widest part of the route and the rest of the couloir is wide enough for comfortable turning. From the bottom of the couloir, turn right (east) and head for Silver Dollar Lake. Pass this lake on the north and continue skiing to Naylor Lake. Ski or hike along the south bank of Naylor Lake to a cluster of summer cabins. There is a trail (buried in snow) uphill and 300 yards south of the lake's outlet. The trail will be hard to locate at first. Look around for old snowshoe and ski tracks. Using the map on page 202 and good route-finding, it should be possible to locate the trail and eventually the 4WD road (probably snowcovered) that brings you to the Guanella Pass Road. You may want to park a car at the end of this route to use as a shuttle. Hitchhiking back to the Pass is feasible on weekends when there is more traffic.

North face of Square Top Mountain viewed from Mount Wilcox. The North Couloir begins at the right (west) end of the summit plateau. Silver Dollar Lake is on the left side of the photo.

Skiing Square Top's east slope

(13,164')

Kelso Mountain

Difficulty/Quality .... Expert (at top), Advanced / ☺☺☺
Season .... May
Distance .... 2.5 miles
Starting Elevation ...... 10,800'
Elevation Gain .... 2,360'
Access .... Kelso Mountain Parking, Page 129
Maps
U.S.G.S. .... *Grays Peak*
Trails Illustrated .... #104, *Idaho Spgs, Georgetown, Loveland Pass*
Guidebook .... Page 203

The couloir that splits Kelso's north face is plainly visible from Exit #221 on Interstate 70. Incidentally there is also an excellent view of the northwest couloir on Torreys Peak from this exit. Kelso is the perfect mountain for skiers who prefer to hike less and ski more. The approach to the base of the couloir is minimal, and there are 2,200 vertical feet of skiing and snowboarding. As a bonus Kelso's summit has jaw-dropping views of Grays and Torreys Peaks as well as upper Stevens Gulch and upper Grizzly Gulch. On weekends you can expect company on the summit.

From your roadside parking spot, hike up the road and locate an abandoned, rust-colored, two-story building on the right. Immediately after this building, turn onto a closed road that peels off to the right and drops downhill to the main creek. Rock hop across the shallow creek. On the other side of the creek, the road turns west and uphill, eventually crossing the Kelso couloir at 10,800'. You have two options at this point. You can ski or hike directly up the snow in the gully. Or you can hunt for a herd path on the left (east) side of the gully. Your goal, eventually, is to attain the ridge that flanks the east side of the couloir. Regardless of which option you choose, be prepared for a long and tedious ascent.

From the summit, ski the couloir, tending at first toward skier's left for the best snow. The return to the Steven's Gulch road is quick, short, and obvious.

View looking south toward Kelso Mountain from Exit #221 (Bakerville) along Interstate 70. The brightly sunlit North Couloir is plainly visible.

Nothing deters the true ski or snowboard mountaineer from making a descent.

(14,270')

Grays Peak

Difficulty/Quality	Expert or Advanced / ☺☺
Season	June
Distance	6.5 miles
Starting Elevation	11,300'
Elevation Gain	3,000'
Access	Stevens Gulch Parking, Page 130
Maps	
U.S.G.S.	*Grays Peak*
Trails Illustrated	#104, *Idaho Spgs, Georgetown, Loveland Pass*
Guidebook	Page 203

If you are determined to ski one of Colorado's "Fourteeners," either Grays Peak or Quandary Peak (Route 54) is a sensible first choice. A high elevation trailhead, moderate to steep terrain with a safe runout, and lots of spectators to marvel at your skiing prowess are just a few of the features of a ski descent on Grays' northeast slope. If you're lucky, a band of photogenic mountain goats may greet you at the summit.

From the parking area cross the road to the Grays Peak trailhead. The wide, well-maintained trail ascends gradually to the southwest and leads into the basin between Grays and Torreys. After two miles the trail, marked with large cairns, steepens and switchbacks its way to the summit. When dry trail gives way to snow, hike up the snowfield following one of several previous boot tracks. The snowfield will probably not reach the summit, so drop your skis at the height of the snow and hike the rest of the way to the summit. First timers to the area often descend to the Grays-Torreys saddle and make an easy ascent of Torreys, thereby bagging two Fourteeners in a single day.

The descent requires no explanation. You should be able to log at least 1,600 vertical feet of skiing. The bowl is usually streaked with runnels where climbers have glissaded. The skier's left (west) side of the bowl is steeper than the right side, so you can choose a level of difficulty that suits you.

Photo next page

Bowl between Grays Peak (out of the photo on the left) and Torreys Peak (partially visible on the right).

(14,267')

Torreys Peak

Difficulty/Quality	Expert / ☺☺☺
Season	Late May, June
Distance	6 miles via Grizzly Gulch 7 miles via Stevens Gulch
Starting Elevation	10,340' at Grizzly Gulch 11,300' at Stevens Gulch
Elevation Gain	4,000' via Grizzly Gulch 3,000' via Stevens Gulch
Access	Grizzly Gulch Parking, Page 129 Stevens Gulch Parking, Page 130
Maps	
U.S.G.S.	*Grays Peak*
Trails Illustrated	#104, *Idaho Spgs, Georgetown, Loveland Pass*
Guidebook	Page 203

A spring ski descent of Torreys is understandably among the most popular and coveted tours in the state. In prime conditions the reward is 1,700 or 2,800 vertical feet of lung-busting skiing, more vertical, by far, than any other descent in this guide. On the summit during weekends, there is usually a throng of expectant skiers, snowboarders and just-plain-folks hanging out and telling tall tales of derring-do. The gnarliest of the bunch may be planning to ski the "Dead Dog Couloir," a steep, narrow, and more technical (and shorter) descent down the east face into Stevens Gulch.

From the Bakerville exit overpass, most of the northwest couloir is plainly visible along the right (northwest) edge of the peak. This is a stunning view of Torreys. Another view of the long northwest couloir appears at the point where the Grizzly Gulch Road turns right from the Stevens Gulch Road. The Dead Dog Couloir, which is inset into the east face, is not completely visible unless you are standing in the bowl between Grays and Torreys.

Northwest Couloir — Expert

The hike to the bottom of the northwest couloir is relatively short but the mile-long ascent of the couloir can seem interminable. From the Grizzly Gulch Parking, hike for two miles along the bottom of Grizzly Gulch to the base of the northwest couloir at 11,200'. Ascend the couloir. Many climbers use crampons, but if the snow is soft enough you can kick steps. Some climbers ascend the stable talus slope to the right (west) of the couloir to avoid kicking steps. From the top of the couloir, which peters out without any cornice, continue up to the southwest ridge and eventually to the summit.

The return to the couloir, the descent, and hike out simply follow the approach. Because of the large vertical change along the couloir, it is not unusual to find three types of snow in this couloir: Hard snow is the norm in the top section. Excellent corn comprises most of the midsection. Bottomless slush is almost inevitable on the lower, flatter section that extends to the creek.

Alternative approach: It is easier to park in the Stevens Gulch parking area, hike the Grays Peak Trail to 13,800' and then traverse to the Grays-Torreys saddle and up to the summit. This involves hiking out Grizzly Gulch 2.3 miles to the intersection with the Stevens Gulch road where a second car can be placed at the outset of the trip. Even without a second car, there is enough weekend traffic that it should be possible to hitch a ride back to the Stevens Gulch parking area.

View to the southwest toward Torreys Peak from Kelso Mountain. Dead Dog Couloir drops down and to the left from the summit. The northwest couloir runs along the right-hand skyline.

Dead Dog Couloir — Expert +

This descent is a more serious undertaking than the northwest couloir. The maximum angle is 45 degrees. From a vantage point directly below Torreys east face, three couloirs are visible. The D.D. Couloir is the one on the right dropping from a point slightly right of the summit. Ascend Torreys via the "alternative approach" in the previous paragraph. More detailed information about the Grays Peak Trail can be found under "Grays Peak" (Route 45). From the summit carry your skis down the northeast ("Kelso") ridge for about 100 feet. The couloir is on the right (south) side of the ridge. The inset portion of the couloir is relatively short (600 vertical feet) before spilling out onto the wide, open slope of the bowl between Grays and Torreys. If you are confused about where to ski, ask for directions and definitely ski with a partner.

Riding the upper section of Torrey's northwest couloir and…

…only 2,000 vertical feet to go.

(13,553')

Pettingell Peak

Difficulty/Quality .... Advanced or Expert / ☺☺☺
Season .... May, early June
Distance .... 8.5 miles
Starting Elevation ...... 10,300'
Elevation Gain .... 3,300'
Access .... Herman Gulch Trailhead, Page 130
Maps
U.S.G.S. .... *Loveland Pass*
Trails Illustrated .... #104, *Idaho Spgs, Georgetown, Loveland Pass*
Guidebook .... Page 204

Front Range hikers and winter ski tourers are familiar with Herman Gulch as a pristine valley that culminates at Herman Lake (12,000') and two thirteeners (Pettingell and Citadel). Along the Herman Gulch Trail, views of the upper valley are plentiful and make it possible to plan your choice of descent from the summit of Pettingell. (Note that the Herman Gulch Trail is only partially shown on the U.S.G.S. map but is shown completely on the Trails Illustrated map.)

From the Herman Gulch Parking, hike up the trail, and after a quarter mile switchback left (west) at an intersection with the trail to Watrous Gulch. After another half mile the trail levels off and finally you are free from the noise of traffic on the interstate. The trail ascends gradually through trees and meadows. Intermittent snow begins at about 11,000 feet. Use your map and altimeter to maintain your course toward Herman Lake, which is located in a steep-walled depression below Pettingell.

From the east side of Herman Lake, cross to the west side on the ice/snow. Hike or ski up a short, steep draw west of the lake and reach flatter terrain at around 12,300'. Continue west toward a steep, fairly wide couloir slightly south of Point 13,418' and climb this relatively short couloir to the ridgeline. The top of the couloir is quite steep. From the ridge at the top of the couloir, there are three options for ski descents.

The first option is to ski east down the couloir and then turn southeast and ski to the creek that runs along Herman Gulch. Ski along the creek until the snow runs out. Then hike northeast to catch the main trail back to the parking area.

The second option is to hike north along the ridge about 200 yards to a snow bowl between the summit of Pettingell and Point 13,418'. Then ski the bowl east and southeast to join the ascent track, then continue as in option one.

The third option is to hike north to the summit and ski the large snowfield on the southeast face and drop down to the north end of Herman Lake. This snowfield melts out earlier than the other two options. Only the descent down the couloir is rated Expert. The other two options are Advanced. Keep in mind that it is possible to ascend to the summit by reversing any of the three descent options. We prefer the couloir as an ascent route because it is the most esthetic. (See photo below.)

Above — Pettingell from Herman Gulch. The summit is on the right. Point 13,418' is left of center. The ascent couloir is visible slightly left of Point 13,418'.

Left — Topping out on the ascent couloir.

(13,294')

"Citadel"

Difficulty/Quality .... Advanced / ☺☺☺
Season .... May, early June
Distance .... 7 miles
Starting Elevation ...... 10,600'
Elevation Gain .... 2,700'
Access .... Dry Gulch Parking, Page 130
Maps
U.S.G.S. .... *Loveland Pass*
Trails Illustrated .... #104, *Idaho Spgs, Georgetown, Loveland Pass*
Guidebook .... Page 204

The peak referred to as "Citadel" is Point 13,294' and lies between Hagar Mountain and Pettingell Peak at the west end of the long ridge that separates Herman Gulch to the north from Dry Gulch to the south. Because of its position on this ridge, it makes a natural destination for a tour from Dry Gulch, over the ridge into Herman Gulch. The unique craggy summit towers set Citadel apart from its more-rounded neighbors, which were covered over and smoothed by Pleistocene glaciers. Citadel's summit remained a tiny island above the ice and escaped this grinding fate.

The previous description of the route to Pettingell Peak can be used, in part, to access the excellent ski slope on the northeast face of Citadel. However, we prefer to access Citadel from Dry Gulch because of the higher starting point, the shorter approach, and the chance to visit two beautiful valleys, not just one. The approach from Dry Gulch requires that a second car be parked at the Herman Gulch Trailhead to use as a shuttle. It is also possible to hitchhike or to walk along the interstate for 1.3 miles back to the Dry Gulch parking.

From the Dry Gulch parking area walk past the gate and up the road into Dry Gulch. After a half mile the road peters out and turns into a faint double-track through a meadow on the north side of the creek. This path soon changes to a foot trail. Early in the spring the trail will be snow-covered and difficult to follow. To avoid becoming entangled in willows and marshy ground, make a gradually-ascending traverse westward to drier ground. Your goal is to reach the bottom of a wide, open slope at 11,000'. Since the snow on this slope melts early, it makes an ideal ascent route. Hike up this slope tending a bit to the west to reach a snow-covered bench (11,900') below Point 12,671'. Hike northwest along this bench until you are below the saddle (clearly visible) that lies west of Point 12,671'. Hike up to the saddle where there is a view of upper Herman Gulch, Herman Lake, and Pettingell Peak.

From the saddle hike steeply uphill along Citadel's east ridge, passing any rocky obstacles on their left (south) sides. The top of the ski descent route is at 13,000' and is bounded on the west by cliffs. There is a blunted cornice that can be passed on skier's right. The top of the slope is not as steep as it appears from the drop in. From the bottom of the slope continue skiing east along the south side of the creek at the bottom of Herman Gulch until the snow runs out. Plan ahead where you will cross to the north side of the creek. Obviously it is easier to cross on a snow bridge than to rock-hop or wade across. Once on the north side of the creek, traverse uphill to the east to locate the Herman Gulch Trail. (Note that the Herman Gulch Trail is only partially shown on the U.S.G.S. map but is shown completely on the Trails Illustrated map.) Follow the Herman Gulch Trail to the trailhead parking area along I-70.

Northeast face of Citadel from Herman Gulch

The beautiful, and surprisingly moderate, descent route on Citadel's northeast face

(13,195')

Hagar Mountain

Difficulty/Quality .... Advanced / ☺☺☺
Season .... May, early June
Distance .... 7 miles
Starting Elevation ...... 10,600'
Elevation Gain .... 2,600'
Access .... Dry Gulch Parking, Page 130
Maps
U.S.G.S. .... *Loveland Pass*
Trails Illustrated .... #104, *Idaho Spgs, Georgetown, Loveland Pass*
Guidebook .... Page 204

If you are looking for an excellent ski descent with a relatively short and straightforward approach, head for Hagar. Hagar is the broad-shouldered mountain at the head of Dry Gulch. A significant amount of snow accumulates in this mile-wide cirque and many ski slopes will be evident when you reach the base of Hagar. This tour can be completed in a half day, unless you choose to hang around in the upper bowl enjoying additional lines.

From the Dry Gulch parking, follow the route description for "Citadel" (Route 48). However, instead of turning uphill at 11,000', cross over to the south side of the creek wherever there is a break in the vegetation, and continue on snow to timberline at 11,600'. Continue hiking or skiing west up the drainage to about 12,100', turn north, and gain a wide bench at 12,400'. Climb west up to the saddle (12,730') just south of the summit ridge, then up a steep snow slope to the summit.

To locate the top of the descent route continue north past the summit for one hundred feet or so to a notch and the top of the descent route. As usual the top is fairly steep, but the angle lessens quickly. Ski to a flat bench, turn south and retrace the ascent route. Usually good skiing can be enjoyed down to 11,400' for a total vertical descent of 1,800 feet. Continue skiing along the south bank of the creek, eventually retracing the approach route to the parking spot.

Approaching Hagar Mountain from the head of Dry Gulch. The summit is the hump on the left. The route to the summit ridge ascends the triangular snow slope on the left. The descent starts in the notch to the right of the summit.

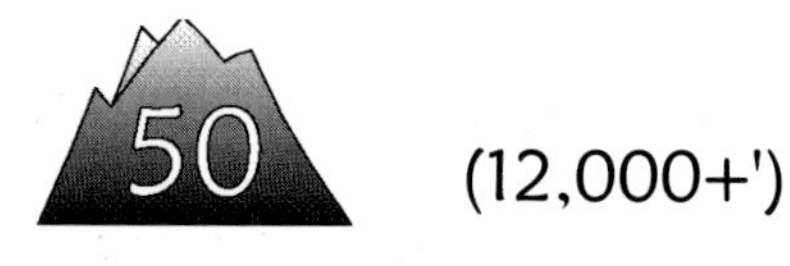

(12,000+')

Loveland Pass

Difficulty/Quality .... Intermediate, Advanced, or Expert / ☺☺☺
Season .... May, most of June
Distance .... 50 feet up to 2 miles
Starting Elevation ...... 11,990'
Elevation Gain .... 3 feet up to 1,100'
Access .... Loveland Pass Parking, Page 130
Maps
U.S.G.S. .... *Loveland Pass*
Trails Illustrated .... #104, *Idaho Spgs, Georgetown, Loveland Pass*
Guidebook .... Page 205

Panoramic view of West Bowl from the north while driving along U.S. 6. Loveland Pass is at the left edge of the photo.

Mention spring skiing to a skier or snowboarder and "Loveland Pass" is sure to be mentioned. The pass offers the highest and quickest access to spring and summer skiing of any area in this book. An abundance of skiing is apparent to anyone driving toward the pass from the north or the south. By arranging car shuttles or by hitchhiking back to the pass, it is possible to make multiple runs in a day. From the pass it also possible to scope out snow conditions on three mountains to the north (Hagar, Citadel, and Pettingell), so bring your binoculars if you are interested in skiing these peaks. There are only descriptions below for routes that tend to hold snow for most of the spring corn season.

West Bowl — Intermediate and Advanced

The easiest way into West Bowl is to cross the highway, put on your skis, and ski the fall line into the drainage that leads north back to the highway at 11,260'. This is called the "cabin run" and is extremely popular. For more skiing in West Bowl, cross to the west side of the road and hike along the west side of the ridge that extends north from Point 12,585'. Continue in a slightly ascending traverse until you reach the saddle between Point 12,585' and Point 12,414'. You can ski downhill from here or you can continue hiking along the Continental Divide to Point 12,479' and the point to the north. Good drops are abundant from many places along the ridge crest.

There is terrain for every level of ability in this one mile wide bowl. All runs lead to the hairpin turn at the bottom of this photo.

Kearney Bowl — Expert and Advanced

If you are looking for a bit of privacy away from the highway, hike over to Kearney Bowl. A day or two after a late spring storm, you may be lucky and find powder snow (and avalanche hazard) in the bowl. From the sign that reads "Loveland Pass," hike northeast uphill along an unmarked trail. At 12,400', break away from the ridge and traverse right (southeast) toward the saddle marked "12,714." It's a mile from the Pass to this saddle. This saddle overlooks Kearney Bowl to the east. The best snow is accessible from the south rim of the bowl about 200 yards south from the saddle. The only way out of the bottom of the bowl is to hike back up. A couple of grassy and rocky ribs between snow slopes should make the hike easier.

Dave's Wave — Advanced and Intermediate

Very popular, very long, but never very steep. Its only drawback is that the ski and/or hike from the bottom of the run through the forest to the highway can be tedious. You will end up at the highway slightly north of the Arapahoe Basin ski area where hitchhiking back to the pass is necessary, unless you've parked a second vehicle. From the saddle marked "12,714" (see previous paragraph), continue south and ascend Point 13,117'. Just before you reach the summit of this point, turn right (west) and descend 100 feet or more to the top of the ski slope. Be careful not to get out of control and ski off the left (south) edge of the route into a ravine that parallels the slope. Later in the season the ski slope narrows. Ski until the slope drops off steeply. Turn left (south) and traverse for a couple of hundred yards across a drainage. Turn downhill into the forest where the skiing will be difficult, at best. Watch for landmarks and you should have no trouble hitting the highway.

Life is full of difficult choices.

Region 6

Stripping skins — summit of Bald Mountain

Summit County

Summit County is world famous for its downhill ski areas. So it's no wonder that on Saturday mornings in the winter half the population of Denver roars up I-70, squeezes into the Eisenhower Tunnel, and oozes out the other end into Summit County on the west slope of the Continental Divide. On Sunday evening the traffic pattern reverses. However, in late April, May, and early June ("mud season" to the locals) the skier frenzy dies down. This is the best time to head for Summit County, to enjoy the sun, the warmth, and some fine peak descents. Buffalo Mountain, Mount Guyot, Bald Mountain, and Quandary Peak are all within close range of Lake Dillon, Silverthorne, and Breckenridge.

To get to Summit County from the Fort Collins, Denver metro area, drive west on Interstate-70 through the Eisenhower Tunnel. It's about 70 miles from Denver to Lake Dillon. From Colorado Springs and points south, use U.S. 24 West to U.S. 9 North over Hoosier Pass. From Colorado Springs it's about 110 miles to Lake Dillon. The descriptions to the various access points assume one is driving to Summit County on I-70 west.

Approaching Mount Guyot

Parking and Trailheads

Buffalo Cabin Trailhead (9,780')

Use this trailhead to climb Buffalo Mountain. Get off at I-70 Exit #205, "Silverthorne, Dillon." At the end of the exit ramp, turn right and drive 150 yards, then take the first left onto Wildernest Road. Wildernest Road soon changes its name to Ryan Gulch Road. Drive 3.3 miles past densely-packed condos to an unsigned parking area on the left. The signed trailhead is on the opposite side of the road.

French Creek Parking (10,400')

Get off at I-70 Exit #203, "9 S. Frisco, Breckenridge." At the end of the exit ramp, turn left and drive south on U.S. 9. At 9.4 miles turn left onto C.R. 450, slightly north of Breckenridge. Drive 1.1 miles to a "T" intersection and turn left onto French Creek Road. At 4.1 miles along French Creek Road there is an excellent view of Guyot. At 4.6 miles a steel gate blocks the road. There is a parking area on the right side of the road. The road beyond the steel gate accesses Mount Guyot and Bald Mountain. If you encounter snow before reaching the steel gate, pull over, park, and walk the rest of the way

The Tenmile Range from the west. Summit County is home to over a dozen high thirteeners.

Quandary Peak Trailhead (11,100')

From Breckenridge drive south on U.S. 9. At 6 miles there is a good view on the right of Quandary. At 8 miles turn right onto Blue Lakes Road (2WD dirt). Drive 0.1 mile and turn right onto McCullough Gulch Road. Drive 1 mile to a small, unsigned parking spot on the right shoulder. A small sign indicating the trailhead is on the opposite side of the road. The trail starts out as a steep 4WD road.

(12,777')

Buffalo Mountain

Difficulty/Quality .... Expert / ☺☺☺
Season .... Late May, early June
Distance .... 4.5 miles
Starting Elevation ...... 9,780'
Elevation Gain .... 3,000'
Access .... Buffalo Cabin Trailhead, Page 168
Maps
U.S.G.S. .... *Willow Lakes, Vail Pass,* (opt. *Dillon, Frisco*)
Trails Illustrated .... #108, *Vail, Frisco, Dillon*
Guidebook .... Page 206

As you emerge from the Eisenhower Tunnel on I-70 the massive hump of a mountain that is directly in front of you to the west is Buffalo Mountain. It is part of the Gore Range, one of Colorado's less traveled mountain ranges. Embedded into its north flank is a 2,000 vertical foot, mile-long ski descent that has long been popular with local downhill skiers. The best place to view this impressive line is from U.S. 9 two miles north of I-70. If you prefer a spring ski descent with a short, but steep, approach, then you should add Buffalo Mountain to your tick list.

From the trailhead, hike northwest along the Buffalo Cabin Trail about a half mile to a signed junction. Turn left onto the continuation of the Buffalo Cabin Trail and hike another half mile to the end of the trail at the ruins of a tiny log cabin. Notice that an unmaintained trail turns left (west) and uphill directly from the cabin ruins. (Fifty feet before the cabin a second trail also heads in the same general direction. This trail is severely eroded higher up and is not recommended. The eroded trail joins the preferred trail at timberline.) From the cabin turn left onto the unmaintained trail, which ascends steeply and efficiently to timberline. Near timberline there is usually snow and you will lose the trail. Just continue to battle your way to timberline. None of the aforementioned trails is indicated on the U.S.G.S. Frisco map, but they are shown on the T.I. map, although here the S. Willow Creek Trail is erroneously labeled as the Buffalo Cabin Trail. You should also note that improvements are planned for the steep trail to the summit, so added signage and more switchbacks may be added in the future.

Above timberline walkable boulders are interspersed with snowfields. Continue west toward the obvious north ridge. The top of the descent couloir will become visible on your right (north) as a football field-sized snow field that funnels into the main couloir. There is no cornice. About 100 yards before reaching the descent couloir, there is a smaller, steeper couloir that can be mistaken for the descent couloir. When you find the descent couloir, you can drop your gear and hike south along the north ridge to the summit. If you are not content with the easterly view of the mini-metropolis of Silverthornedillonfriscokeystone, then turn your gaze west and north onto the beautiful Eagles Nest Wilderness.

The broad slope at the top of the ski descent funnels into a rock walled couloir that turns out not to be as steep as it appears from the highway. In early June the snow typically melts out at about 10,000'.

For the return, bushwhack east and slightly downhill across deadfall and willows for a few hundred yards to 9,600' where you can pick up the South Willow Creek Trail. Hike south on this trail for about two miles to the parking area.

Buffalo Mountain viewed from U.S. 9 north of Dillon and Silverthorne.
The north couloir is the longer of the two couloirs that split the north flank of the mountain.

(13,370')

Mount Guyot

Difficulty/Quality .... Advanced / ☺☺
Season .... May, early June
Distance .... 5 miles
Starting Elevation ...... 10,400'
Elevation Gain .... 3,000'
Access .... French Gulch Parking, Page 168
Maps
U.S.G.S. .... *Boreas Pass*
Trails Illustrated .... #109, *Breckenridge, Tennessee Pass*
Guidebook .... Page 207

A "guyot" (pronounced GEE-oh) is an underwater sea mount with a truncated summit. Minus the ocean, Mount Guyot is aptly named. Mount Guyot lies east of the town of Breckenridge and is one valley east of its partner, Bald Mountain. The north side of Mount Guyot has a fine ski descent that is visible, along with Bald Mountain, from the Scenic Area pullout on I-70 between Exits 205 and 203. The pair of mountains stands out clearly across Lake Dillon, so you can check out the snow conditions from the interstate.

From the parking area, pass the steel gate and walk southeast up French Creek. After about half a mile an old road leading into Little French Gulch bears left away from the main trail. The turnoff is in a clearing. This turnoff is often snowcovered, so keep your map handy. Hike or ski into Little French Gulch for almost a mile until the small valley bottom opens up. Guyot's north ski slope is directly in front of you. Ascend directly up this slope to its top, which is slightly west of the summit. Drop your gear and boulder hop about 75 yards to the summit. The summit affords an outstanding view of the couloirs on the east face of Bald Mountain to the west.

The descent and return trip to the parking area follow the ascent route. You can ski 1,600 vertical feet to the base of the slope. Often it is possible to keep skiing as far as the junction with the French Gulch Road.

Mount Guyot from the north. The lower third of the descent route is hidden behind the ridge in the foreground.

Going for the Gold on Guyot

(13,684')

Bald Mountain

Difficulty/Quality .... Expert / ☺☺☺
Season .... May, mid June
Distance .... 7.6 miles
Starting Elevation ...... 10,400'
Elevation Gain .... 3,300'
Access .... French Gulch Parking, Page 168
Maps
U.S.G.S. .... *Boreas Pass*
Trails Illustrated .... #109, *Breckenridge, Tennessee Pass*
Guidebook .... Page 207

As mentioned under Mount Guyot (Route 52) section, Bald Mountain, which is east of the town of Breckenridge, can be seen from the Scenic Area pullout on I-70 between Exits 205 and 203 where Guyot and Bald Mountain stand out clearly across Lake Dillon. The steep east face of Bald Mountain contains an excellent couloir with a vertical drop of 1,800 feet that holds snow into June. Unlike its partner on Guyot, this ski descent requires more effort to access.

From the parking area, pass the steel gate and walk or ski southeast up the continuation of the French Creek Road. At 2.5 miles you can see the east face couloir across the wide valley bottom. One option is to cross the valley and ascend the couloir. Another more interesting option that will turn the trip into a complete tour of the mountain is to continue up the valley for another half mile then turn right (west) and gain the ridge that leads to Point 13,634'. Hike up this ridge to its top then head north a short distance to the actual summit.

To access the couloir from the summit, head north along the ridge for a few yards. The couloir drops off to the right, is a consistent grade, and has a gentle runout. Beyond the runout there is a stretch of forest leading to the valley bottom. This forest may be unpleasant to travel through due to soft snow. In addition you may have to battle through soft snow and willows across the valley bottom to reach the snow-covered road that you used for the approach. When you finally reach this road turn left and retrace your steps back to the parking area. This descent faces east, so an early start is essential.

View west toward Bald Mountain from Mount Guyot. More than one descent route is visible near the summit.

(14,265')

Quandary Peak

Difficulty/Quality	East Ridge - Int./Adv. at the top / ☺☺☺
	Cristo Couloir - Expert / ☺
Season	May, early June
Distance	5 miles
Starting Elevation	11,100'
Elevation Gain	3,200'
Access	Quandary Peak Trailhead, Page 169
Maps	
U.S.G.S.	*Breckenridge*
Trails Illustrated	#109, *Breckenridge, Tennessee Pass*
Guidebook	Page 208

Quandary is one of the most accessible Fourteeners to climb and ski. It is a great choice for a first Fourteener ski descent. Along with a cluster of other high peaks, it forms the southern terminus of the Tenmile Range. It lies a few miles south of the Breckenridge ski resort and town. It has the advantage of an easy drive to a high elevation trailhead plus a relatively gentle hike to the summit.

East Ridge — Intermediate/Advanced at the top

The upper east face has a superb slope that is understandably popular on spring weekends. Early in the season it is usually possible to ski the entire face and east ridge to timberline, a vertical drop of over 2,000 feet covering a mile and a half. For a preview of Quandary, drive six miles south of Breckenridge on U.S. 9 to a road sign that points out the peak.

The trail to Quandary starts out as a double track that ascends up through the forest and soon reaches timberline. At timberline the trail gains the east ridge, which is followed, with intermittent snow, to the elongated summit. The entire line of descent can be previewed during the hike to the summit. The descent back to the parking retraces the ascent.

Cristo Couloir — Expert

If you are looking for a more challenging (Expert) alternative to the East Ridge, you can check out the wide gully that drops down the south face from the summit. To access this descent route you have two options. You can drive two miles on Blue Lakes Road (rough 2WD) until you reach a dam and park here. The second option is to park at the Quandary Peak Trailhead, hike the east ridge, and drop down the couloir. If you choose to park at the dam, you can check out the descent route by walking to the south end of the dam along the road that runs below the dam. If you are satisfied with the condition of the snow, hike up and onto the north end of the dam, then up and west into the gully, which can be climbed to the summit. If you choose the east ridge option, pick a weekend since then there will be enough cars by the dam to give you a lift back to your car. Another option is to stash a bike at the dam and ride back. The drawbacks of the Cristo Couloir are that it is south-facing, so the snow softens quickly, and that it is a popular route among glissaders and deep runnels can exist. Also since it is a popular snow climb, you run the risk of "taking out" a climber or two.

Quandary Peak from the northeast. The snowcovered, sprawling east ridge is one of the finest advanced and intermediate descents on a fourteener.

Remember ... It's not all hard work!

Some Guy Who Offered To Take Our Picture

TOPOGRAPHIC MAPS

Credit ... The color maps on the following pages were printed from National Geographic TOPO! ® software. A complete set of seamless U.S.G.S. 1:24,000 scale topographic maps covering the entire state of Colorado is available on CD-ROM.

Visit *www.nationalgeographic.com/topo* for more information.

The contour interval for all maps is 40 feet.

Map...180

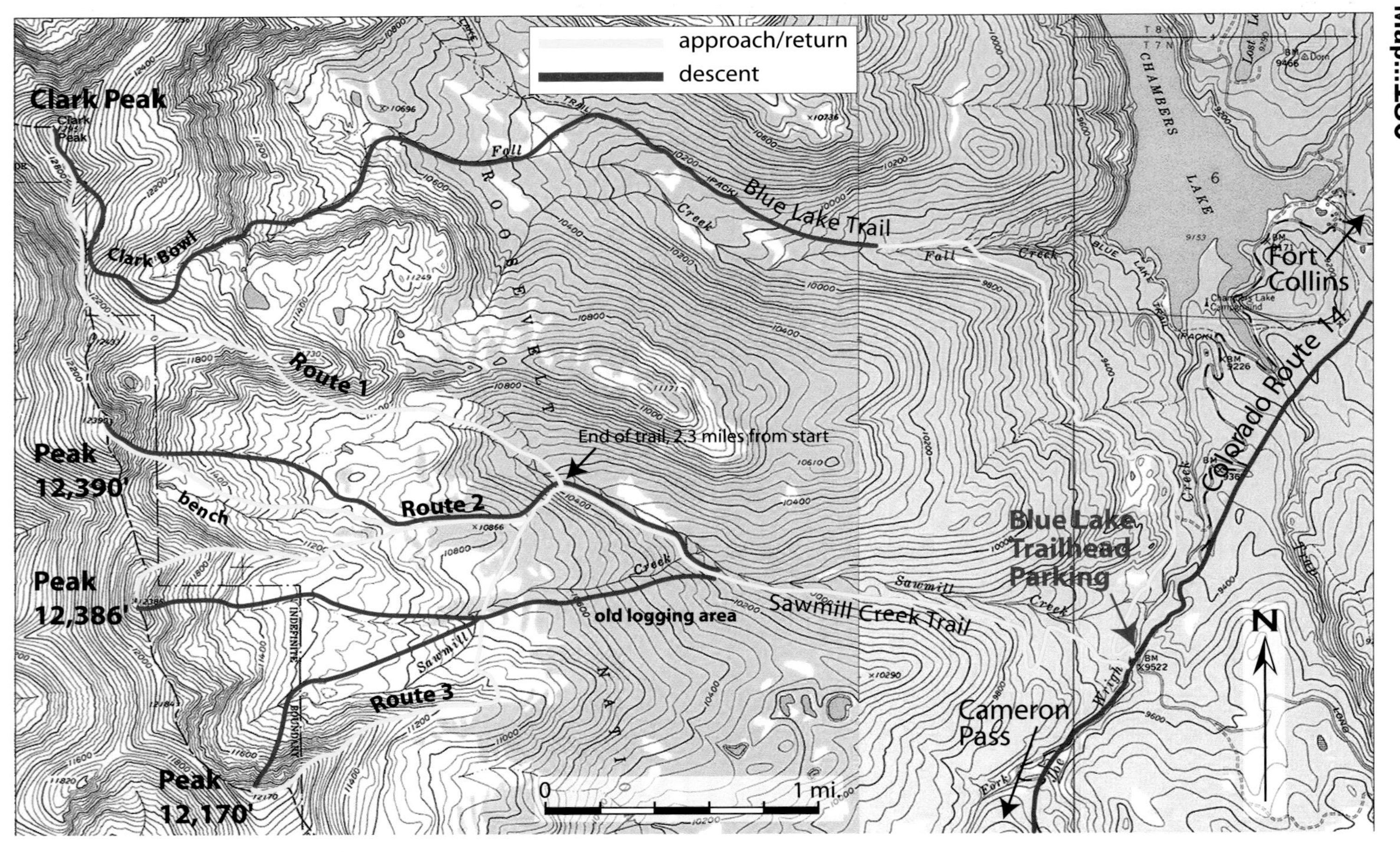

approach/return
descent
Clark Peak
Clark Bowl
Blue Lake Trail
CHAMBERS LAKE
Fort Collins
Colorado Route 14
Route 1
End of trail, 2.3 miles from start
Peak 12,390'
bench
Route 2
Blue Lake Trailhead Parking
Peak 12,386'
old logging area
Sawmill Creek Trail
INDEFINITE BOUNDARY
Route 3
N
Cameron Pass
Peak 12,170'
0
1 mi.

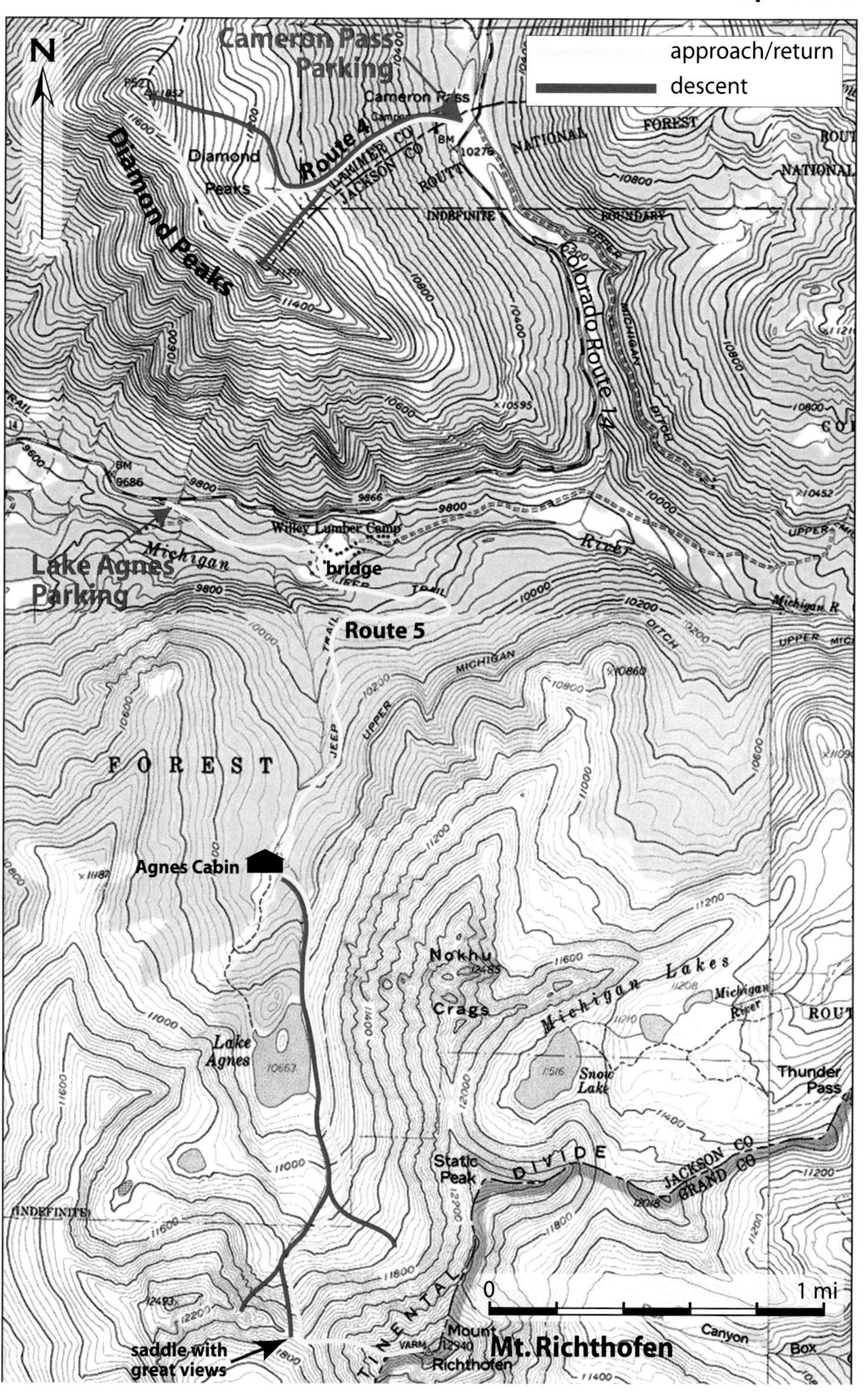

N
Cameron Pass Parking
approach/return
descent
Cameron Pass
Route 4
Diamond Peaks
Diamond Peaks
LARIMER CO
JACKSON CO
ROUTT
NATIONAL
FOREST
INDEFINITE
BOUNDARY
Colorado Route 14
UPPER
MICHIGAN
DITCH
Willey Lumber Camp
Michigan
River
Lake Agnes Parking
bridge
JEEP
TRAIL
Route 5
FOREST
Agnes Cabin
Nokhu
Crags
Michigan Lakes
Michigan River
Lake Agnes
Snow Lake
Thunder Pass
Static Peak
DIVIDE
JACKSON CO
GRAND CO
INDEFINITE
0
1 mi
Mount Richthofen
Mt. Richthofen
Canyon
Box
saddle with great views

Map...182

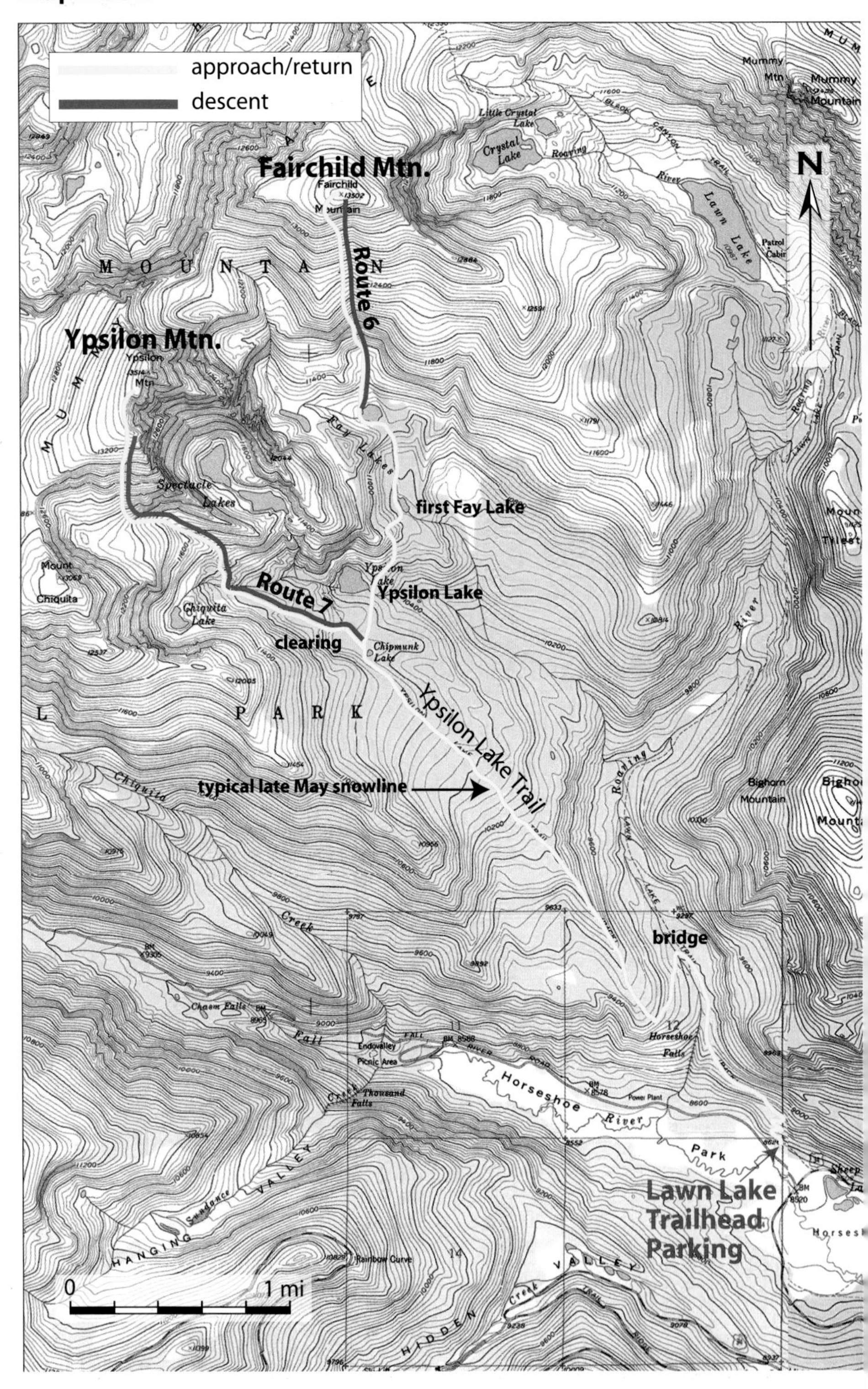

approach/return
descent
Fairchild Mtn.
Route 6
Ypsilon Mtn.
Route 7
first Fay Lake
Ypsilon Lake
clearing
Ypsilon Lake Trail
typical late May snowline
bridge
Lawn Lake Trailhead Parking
N
0
1 mi

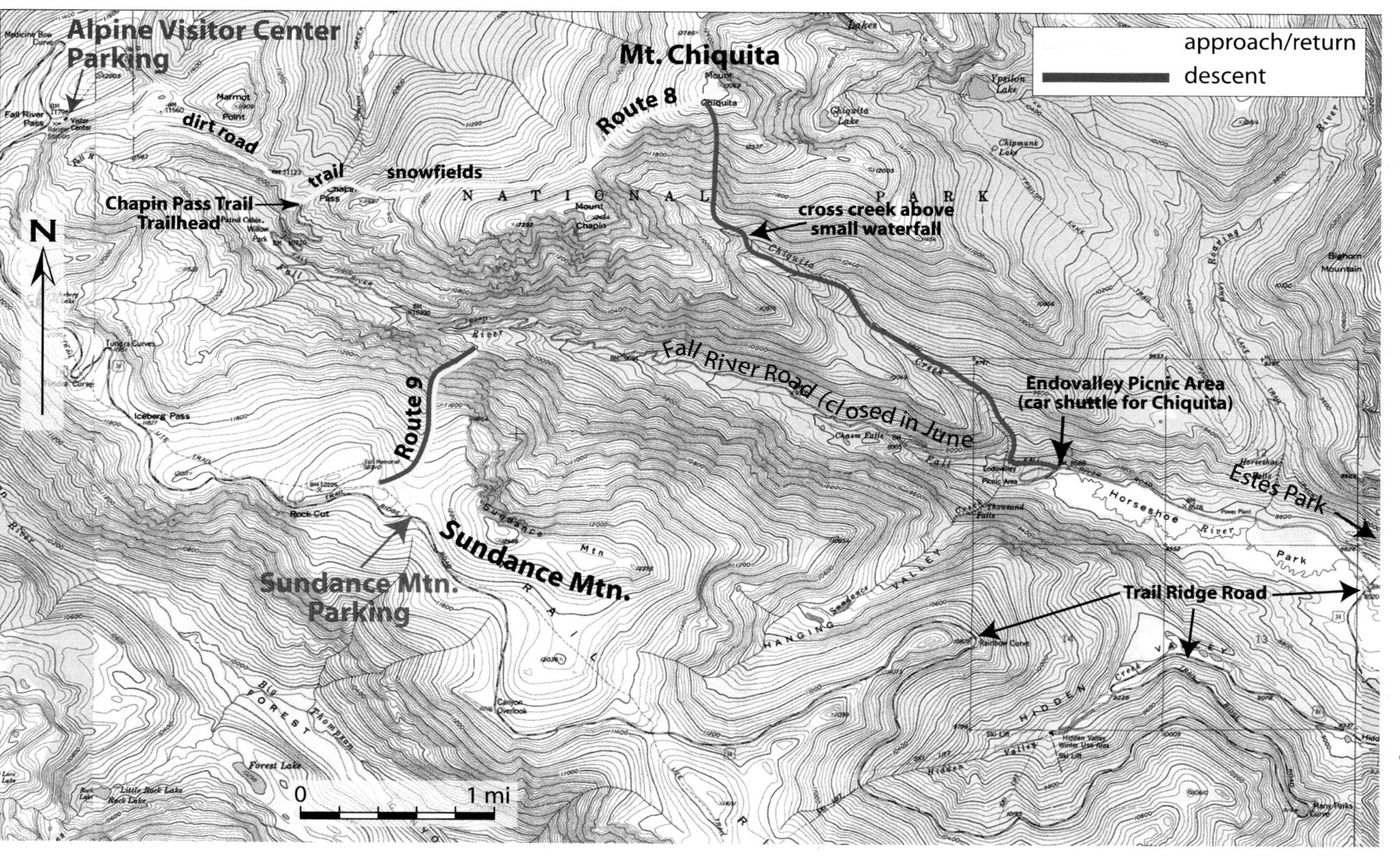
approach/return
descent
Alpine Visitor Center Parking
dirt road
trail
snowfields
Chapin Pass Trail Trailhead
N
Mt. Chiquita
Route 8
cross creek above small waterfall
Fall River Road (closed in June
Endovalley Picnic Area (car shuttle for Chiquita)
Estes Park
Route 9
Sundance Mtn.
Sundance Mtn. Parking
Trail Ridge Road
0
1 mi

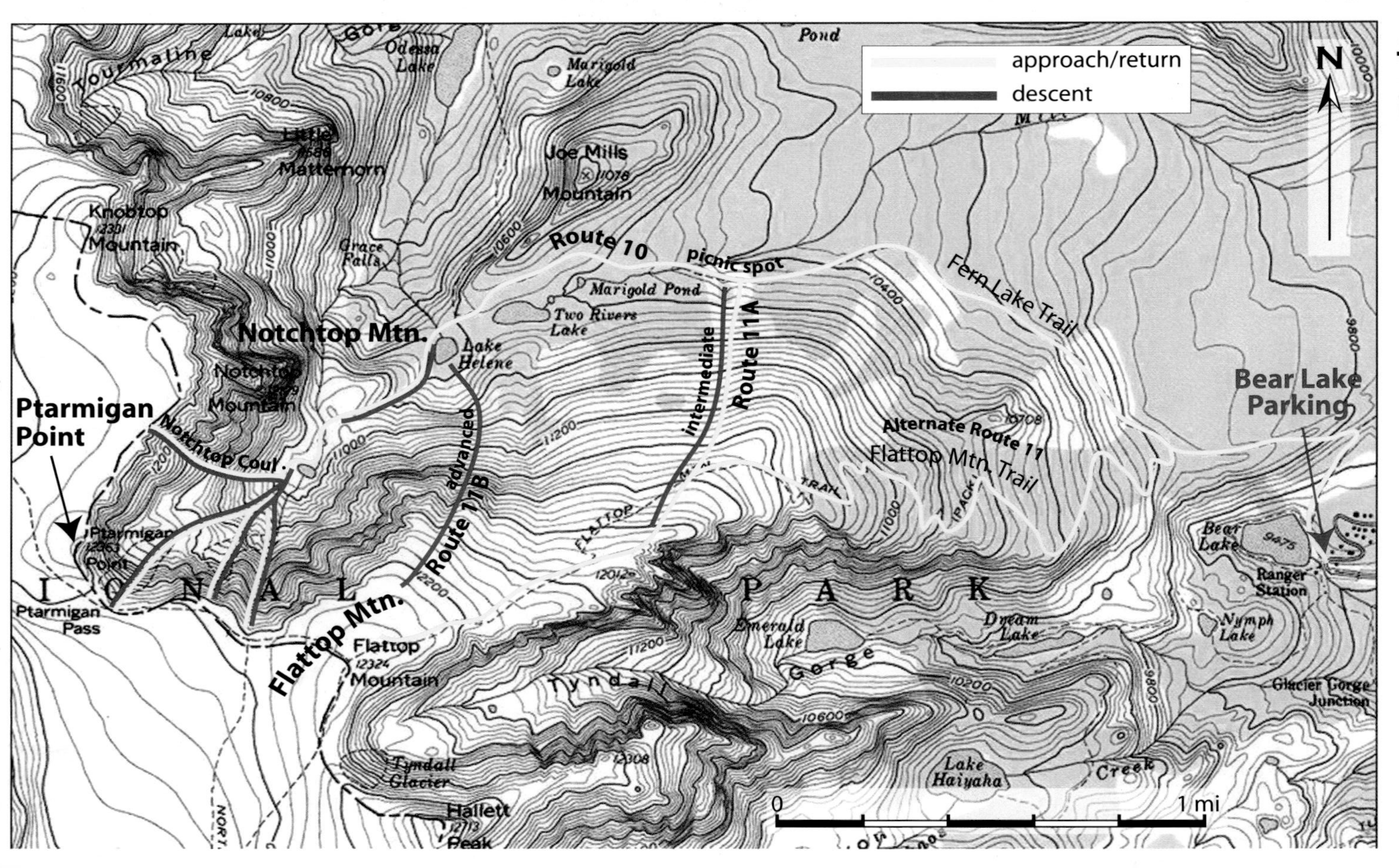
approach/return
descent
N
Tourmaline
Odessa Lake
Pond
Marigold Lake
Little Matterhorn
Joe Mills Mountain
Knobtop Mountain
Grace Falls
Route 10
picnic spot
Fern Lake Trail
Marigold Pond
Two Rivers Lake
Notchtop Mtn.
Lake Helene
Notchtop Mountain
Ptarmigan Point
Notchtop Coul.
advanced
Route 11B
intermediate
Route 11A
Alternate Route 11
Flattop Mtn. Trail
Bear Lake Parking
Bear Lake
Ranger Station
Ptarmigan Point
Ptarmigan Pass
Flattop Mtn.
Flattop Mountain
P A R K
Emerald Lake
Dream Lake
Nymph Lake
Tyndall Gorge
Glacier Gorge Junction
Tyndall Glacier
Hallett Peak
Lake Haiyaha
Creek
0
1 mi

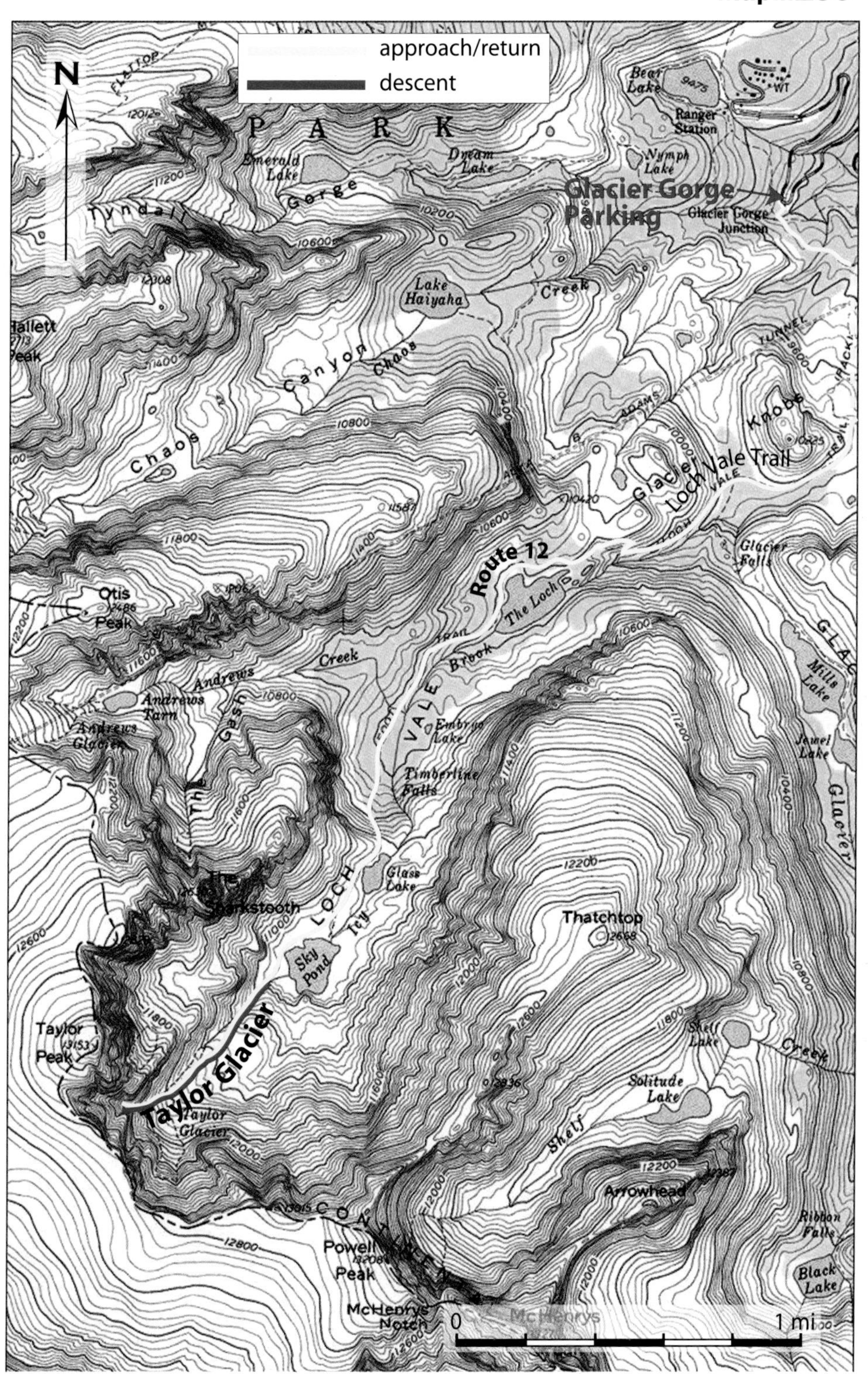
approach/return
descent
N
Glacier Gorge Parking
Loch Vale Trail
Route 12
Taylor Glacier
Thatchtop
Arrowhead
Powell Peak
McHenrys Notch
Taylor Peak
Otis Peak
Hallett Peak
The Sharkstooth
0
1 mi

Map...186

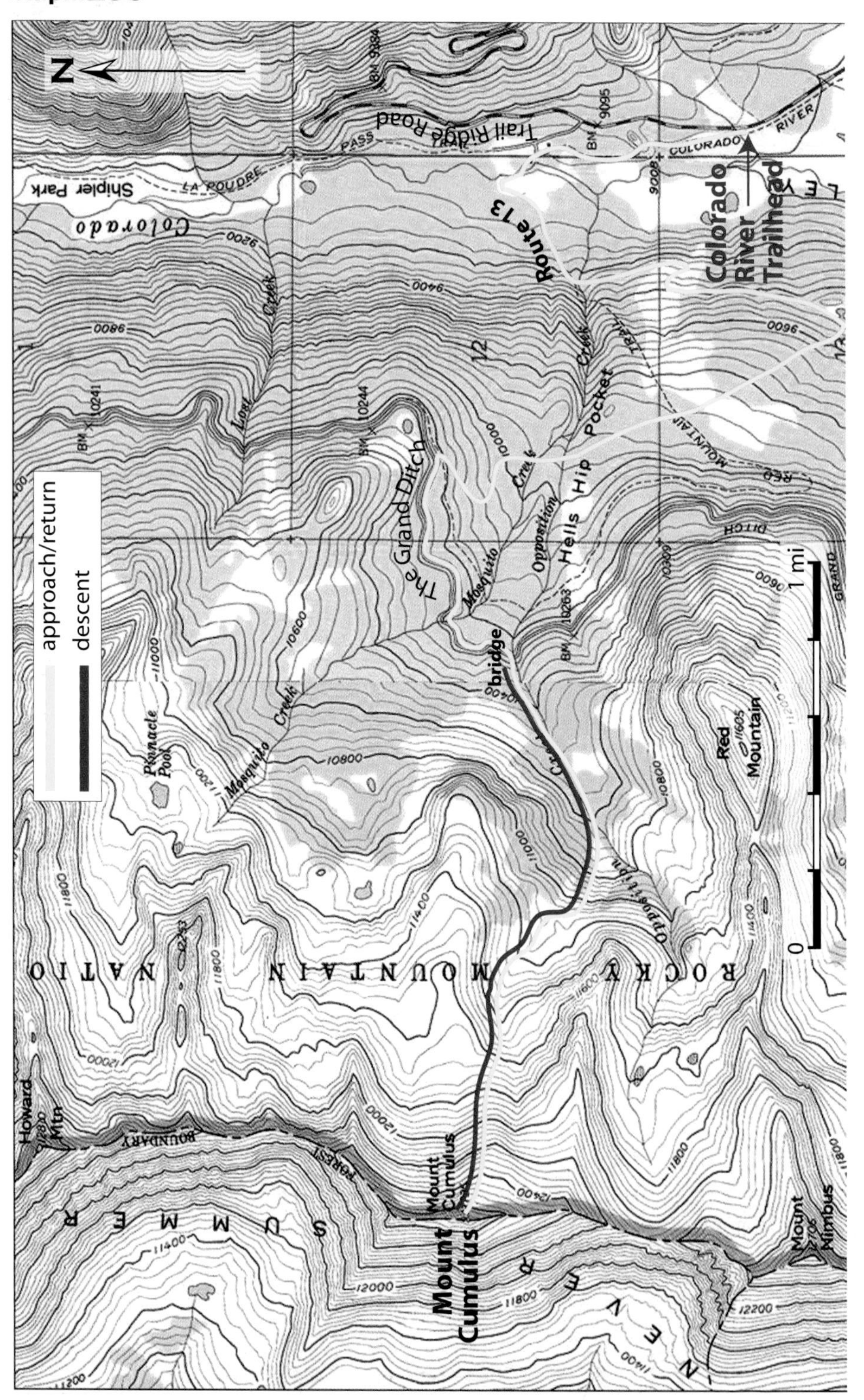
N
approach/return
descent
Route 13
Colorado River Trailhead
Trail Ridge Road
Shipler Park
The Grand Ditch
Hells Hip Pocket
bridge
Mount Cumulus
Red Mountain
Pinnacle Pool
Howard Mtn
Mount Nimbus
0
1 mi

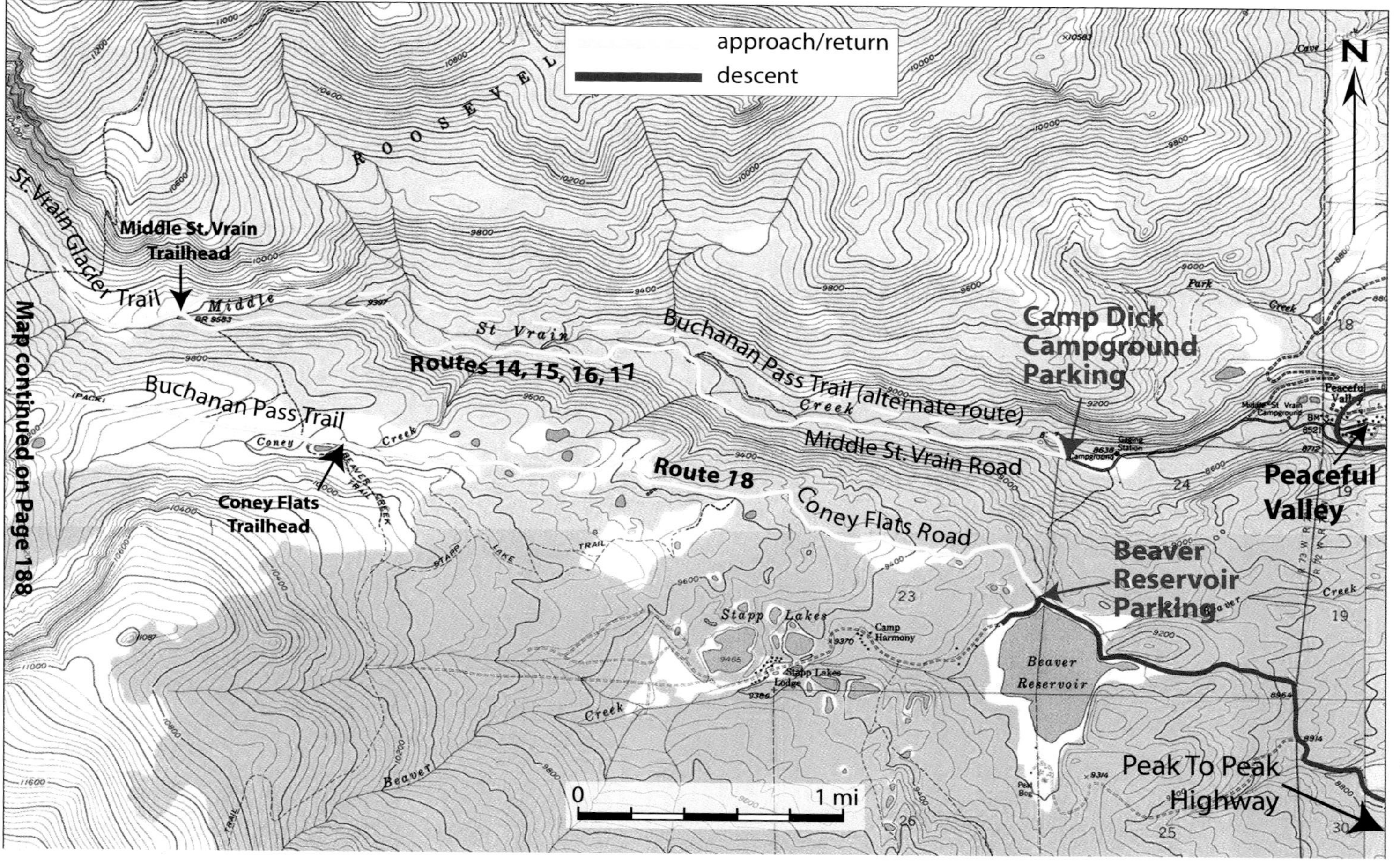
approach/return
descent
N
Middle St. Vrain Trailhead
St. Vrain Glacier Trail
Buchanan Pass Trail
Routes 14, 15, 16, 17
Buchanan Pass Trail (alternate route)
Camp Dick Campground Parking
Middle St. Vrain Road
Route 18
Coney Flats Road
Coney Flats Trailhead
Peaceful Valley
Beaver Reservoir Parking
Beaver Reservoir
Stapp Lakes
Camp Harmony
Stapp Lakes Lodge
Peak To Peak Highway
0
1 mi
Map continued on Page 188

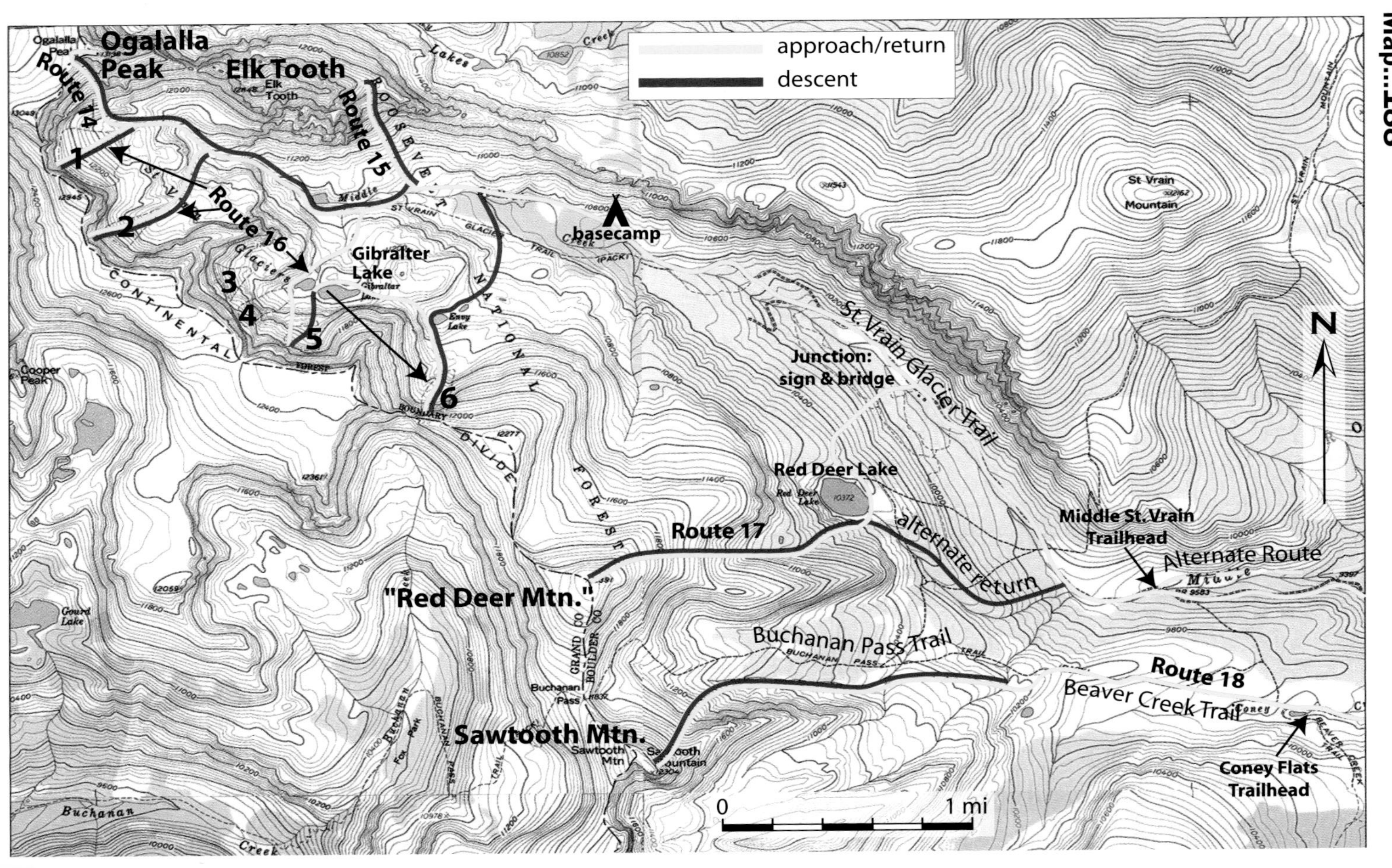
Ogalalla Peak
Elk Tooth
Route 14
Route 15
Route 16
1
2
3
4
5
6
Gibralter Lake
basecamp
approach/return
descent
St. Vrain Mountain
Junction: sign & bridge
St. Vrain Glacier Trail
N
Red Deer Lake
Route 17
alternate return
Middle St. Vrain Trailhead
Alternate Route
"Red Deer Mtn."
Buchanan Pass Trail
Route 18
Beaver Creek Trail
Sawtooth Mtn.
Coney Flats Trailhead
0
1 mi

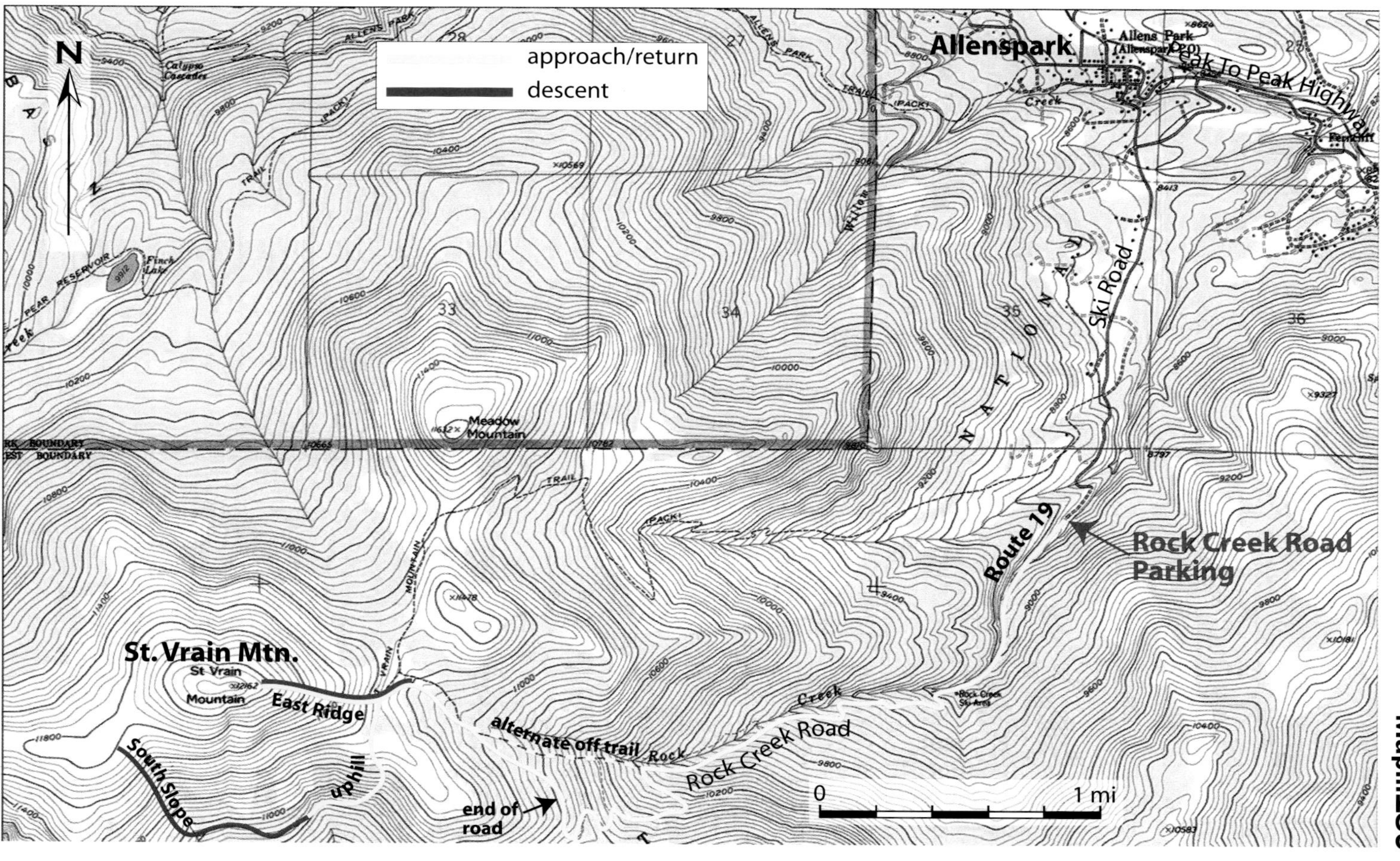

N
approach/return
descent
Allenspark
Peak To Peak Highway
Ski Road
Meadow Mountain
Route 19
Rock Creek Road Parking
St. Vrain Mtn.
East Ridge
South Slope
uphill
alternate off trail
Rock Creek Road
end of road
0
1 mi

Map...190

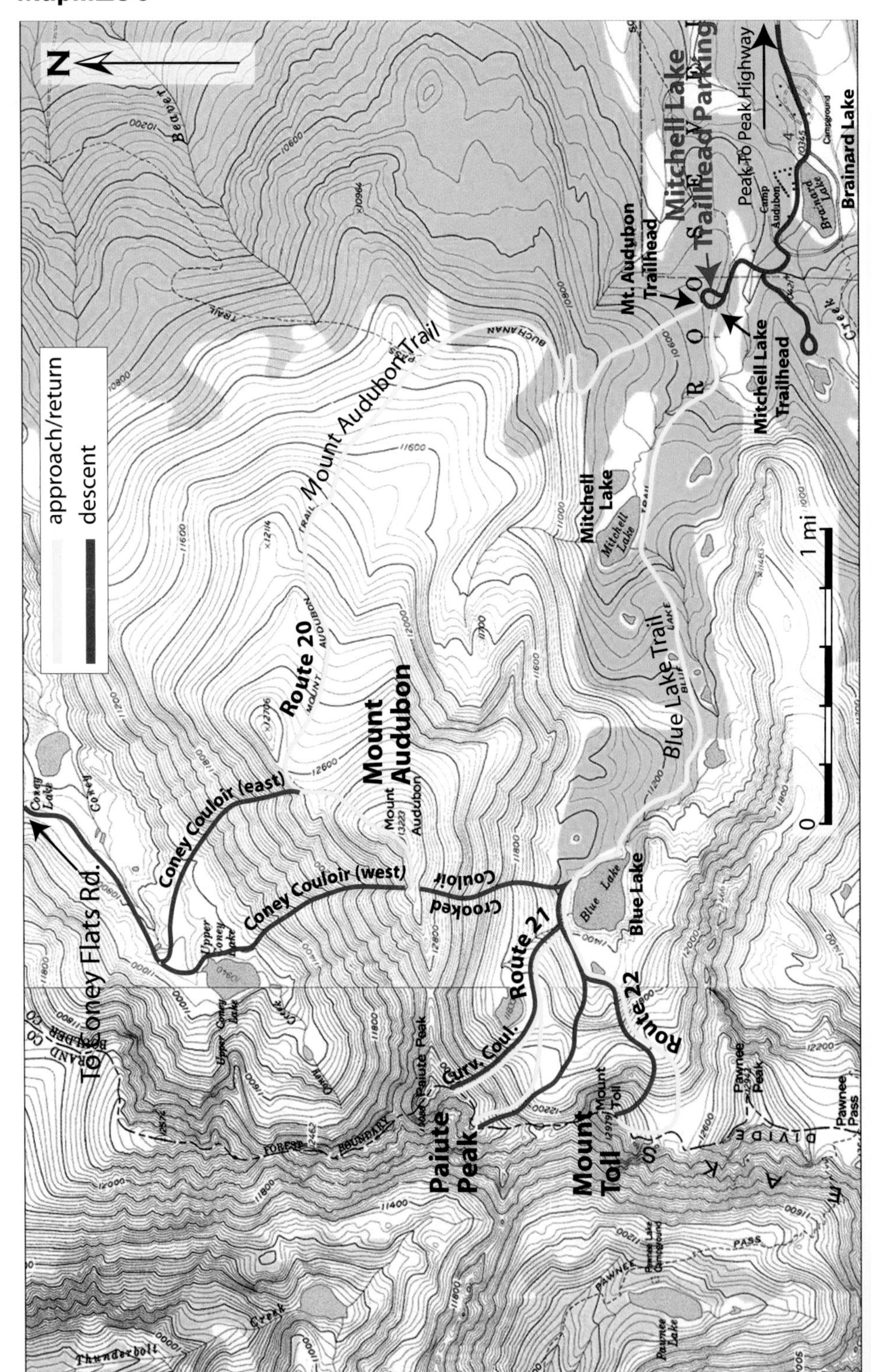
N
approach/return
descent
Route 20
Mount Audubon
Mount Audubon Trail
Coney Couloir (east)
Coney Couloir (west)
Crooked Couloir
To Coney Flats Rd.
Route 21
Route 22
Curv. Coul.
Paiute Peak
Mount Toll
Blue Lake
Blue Lake Trail
Mitchell Lake
Mt. Audubon Trailhead
Mitchell Lake Trailhead
Mitchell Lake Trailhead Parking
Peak to Peak Highway
Brainard Lake
0
1 mi

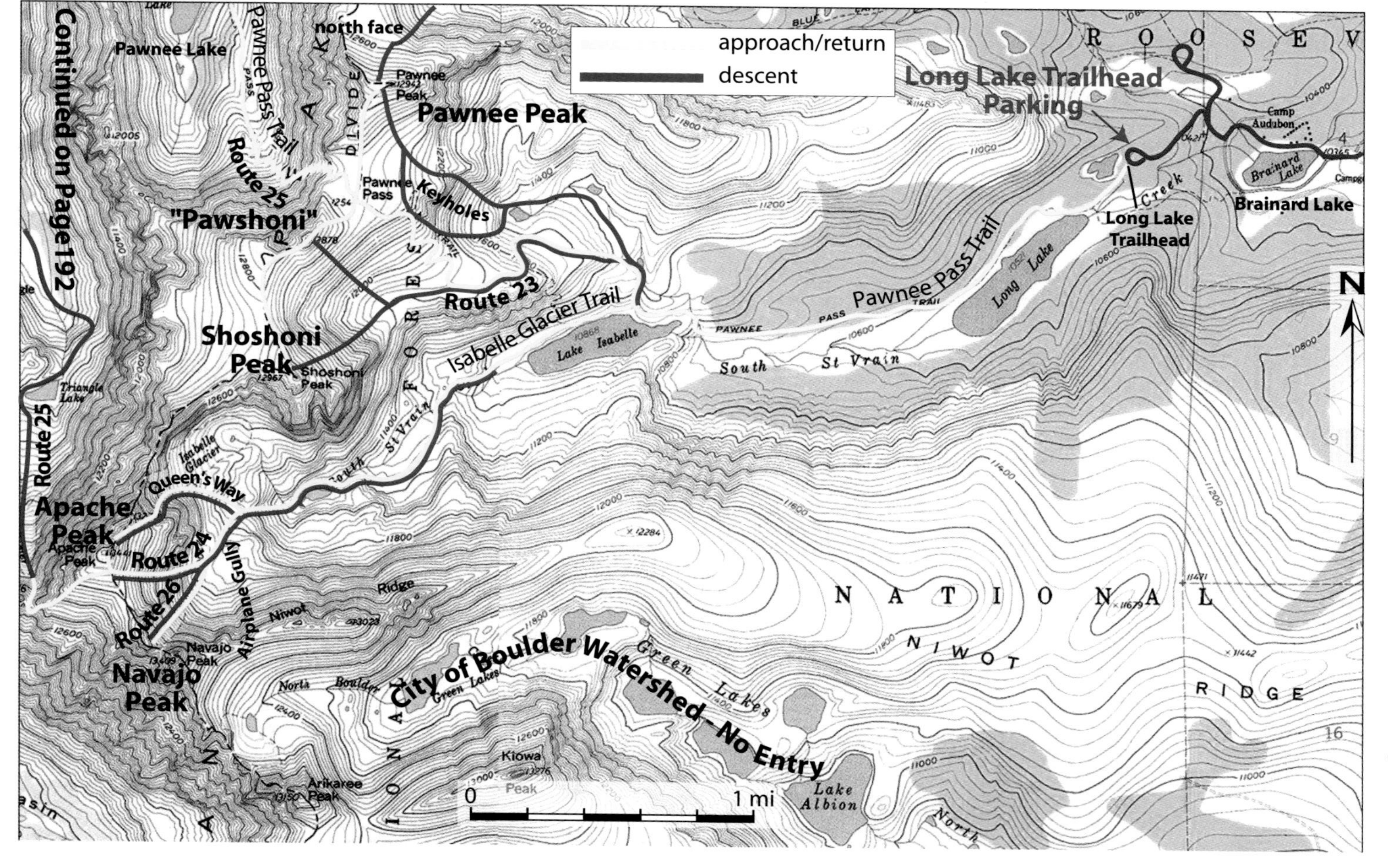

approach/return
descent
Long Lake Trailhead Parking
Long Lake Trailhead
Brainard Lake
Camp Audubon
Creek
Pawnee Pass Trail
Long Lake
N
Isabelle Glacier Trail
Lake Isabelle
South St Vrain
Route 23
Pawnee Peak
Keyholes
north face
Pawnee Pass
Pawnee Pass Trail
Route 25
"Pawshoni"
Shoshoni Peak
Queen's Way
Airplane Gully
Route 24
Route 26
Apache Peak
Navajo Peak
Pawnee Lake
Triangle Lake
Route 25
Continued on Page192
City of Boulder Watershed - No Entry
Green Lakes
Lake Albion
Kiowa Peak
Arikaree Peak
Niwot Ridge
NATIONAL
NIWOT RIDGE
0
1 mi

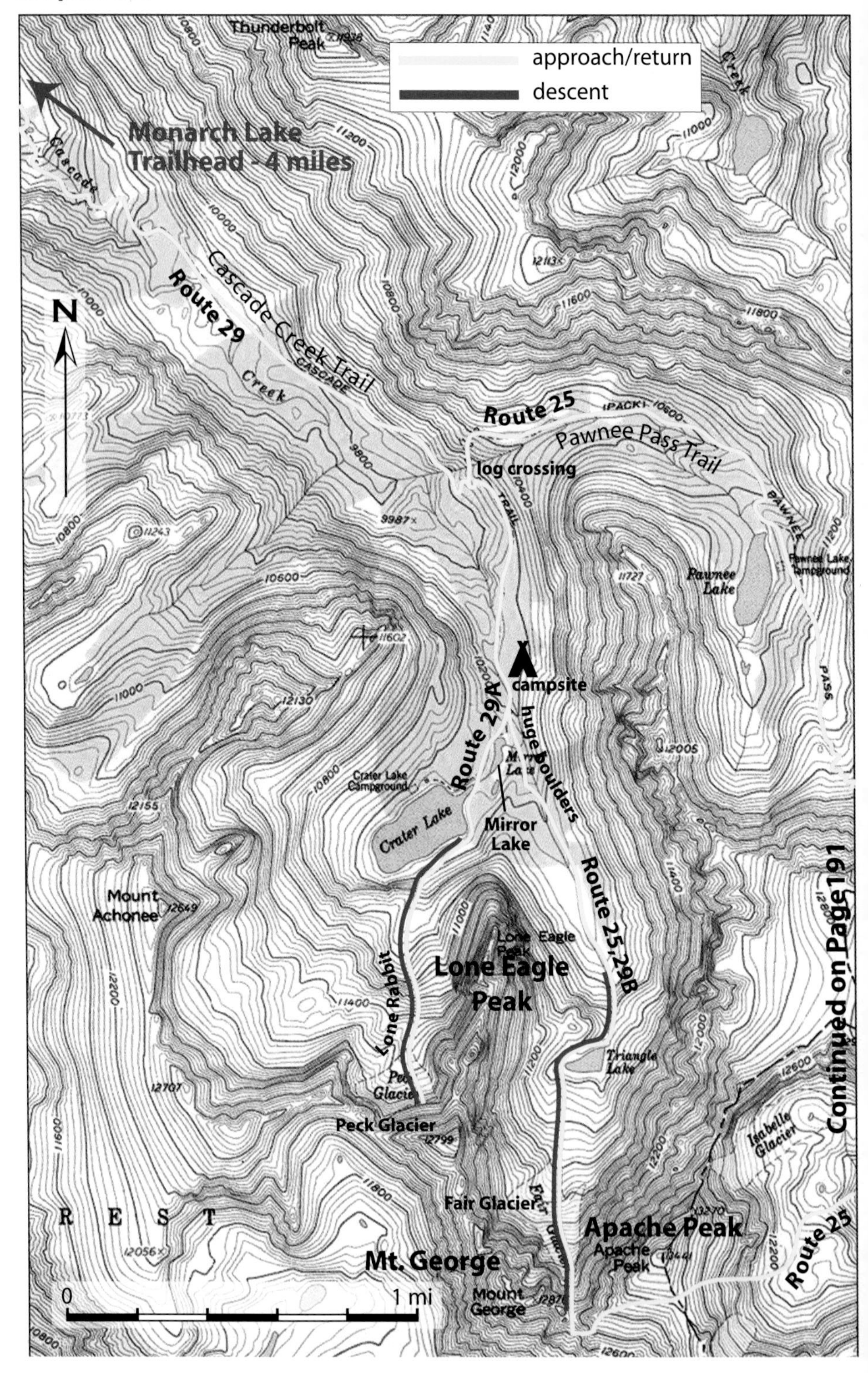

Continued on Page 191

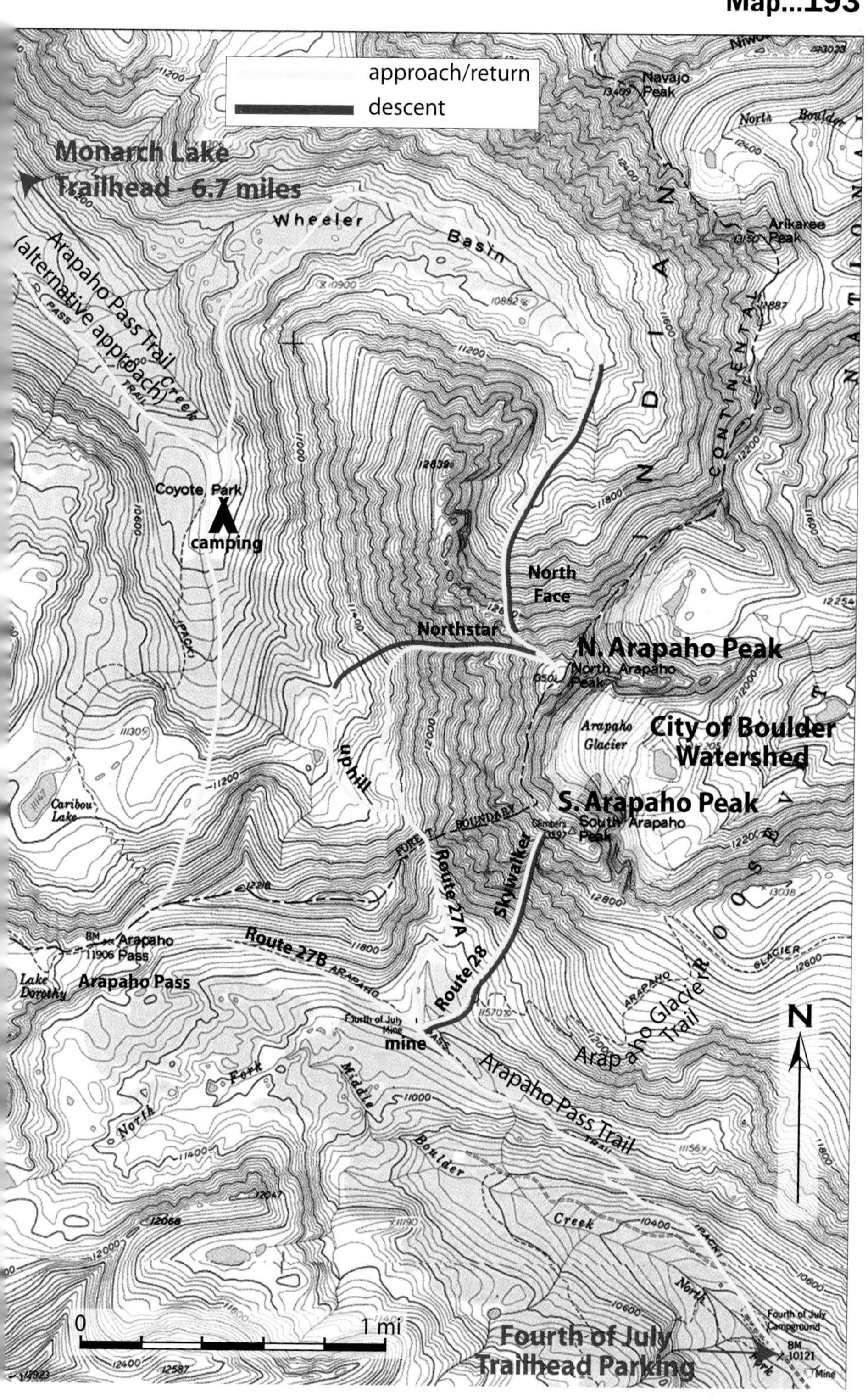
approach/return
descent
Monarch Lake Trailhead - 6.7 miles
Arapaho Pass Trail (alternative approach)
Wheeler Basin
Coyote Park
camping
Northstar
North Face
N. Arapaho Peak
City of Boulder Watershed
uphill
S. Arapaho Peak
Route 27A
Skywalker
Route 27B
Route 28
Arapaho Pass
mine
Arapaho Pass Trail
Arapaho Glacier Trail
N
0
1 mi
Fourth of July Trailhead Parking
Navajo Peak
Arikaree Peak
North Arapaho Peak
South Arapaho Peak
Arapaho Glacier
Caribou Lake
Lake Dorothy
Fourth of July Mine
Fourth of July Campground

Map...194

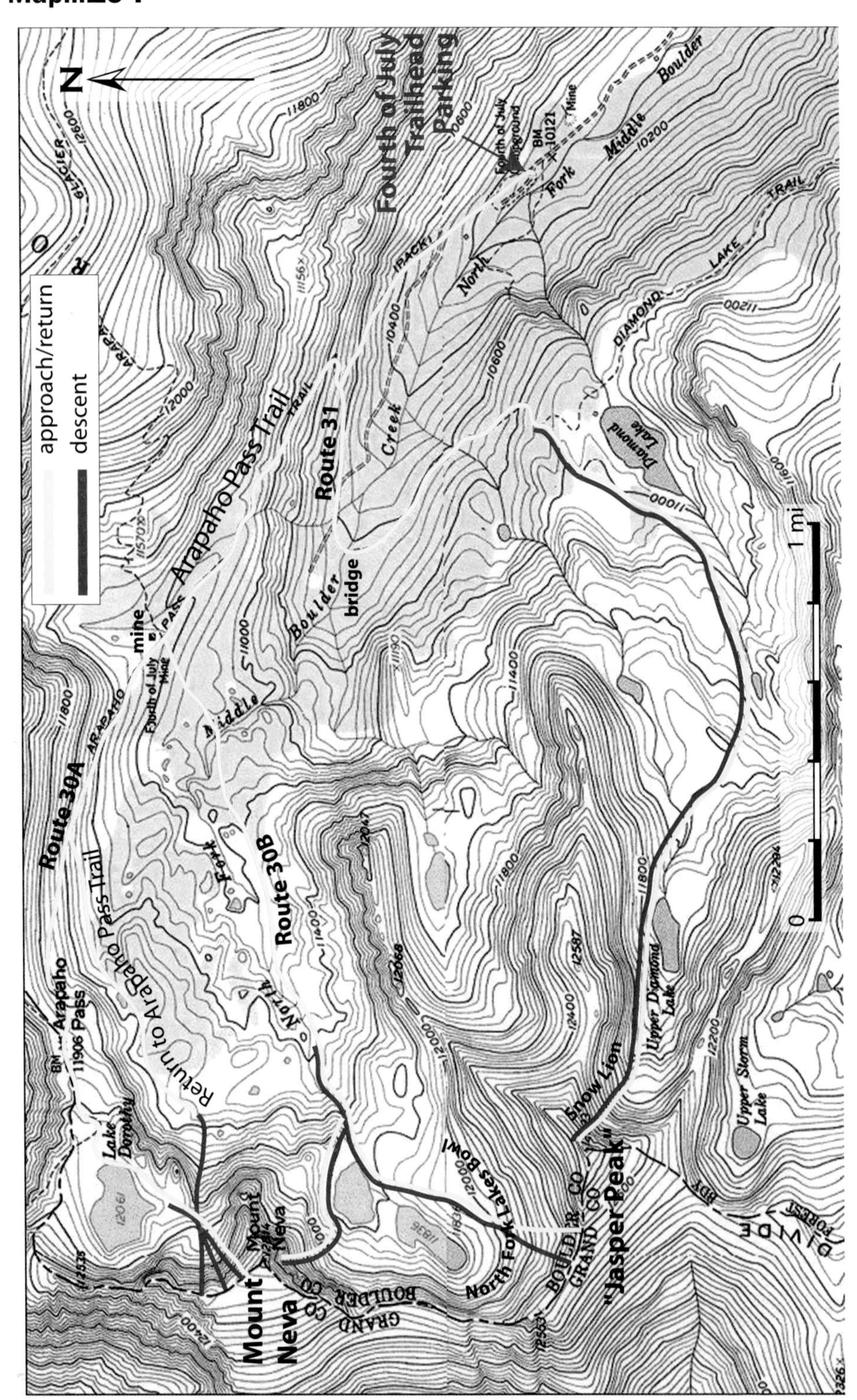

N
approach/return
descent
Fourth of July Trailhead Parking
Arapaho Pass Trail
Route 31
bridge
mine
Route 30A
Route 30B
Arapaho Pass Trail
Return to Arapaho Pass Trail
Arapaho 11906 Pass
Lake Dorothy
Mount Neva
North Fork Lakes Bowl
Snow Lion
"Jasper Peak"
Diamond Lake
Upper Diamond Lake
Upper Storm Lake
0
1 mi

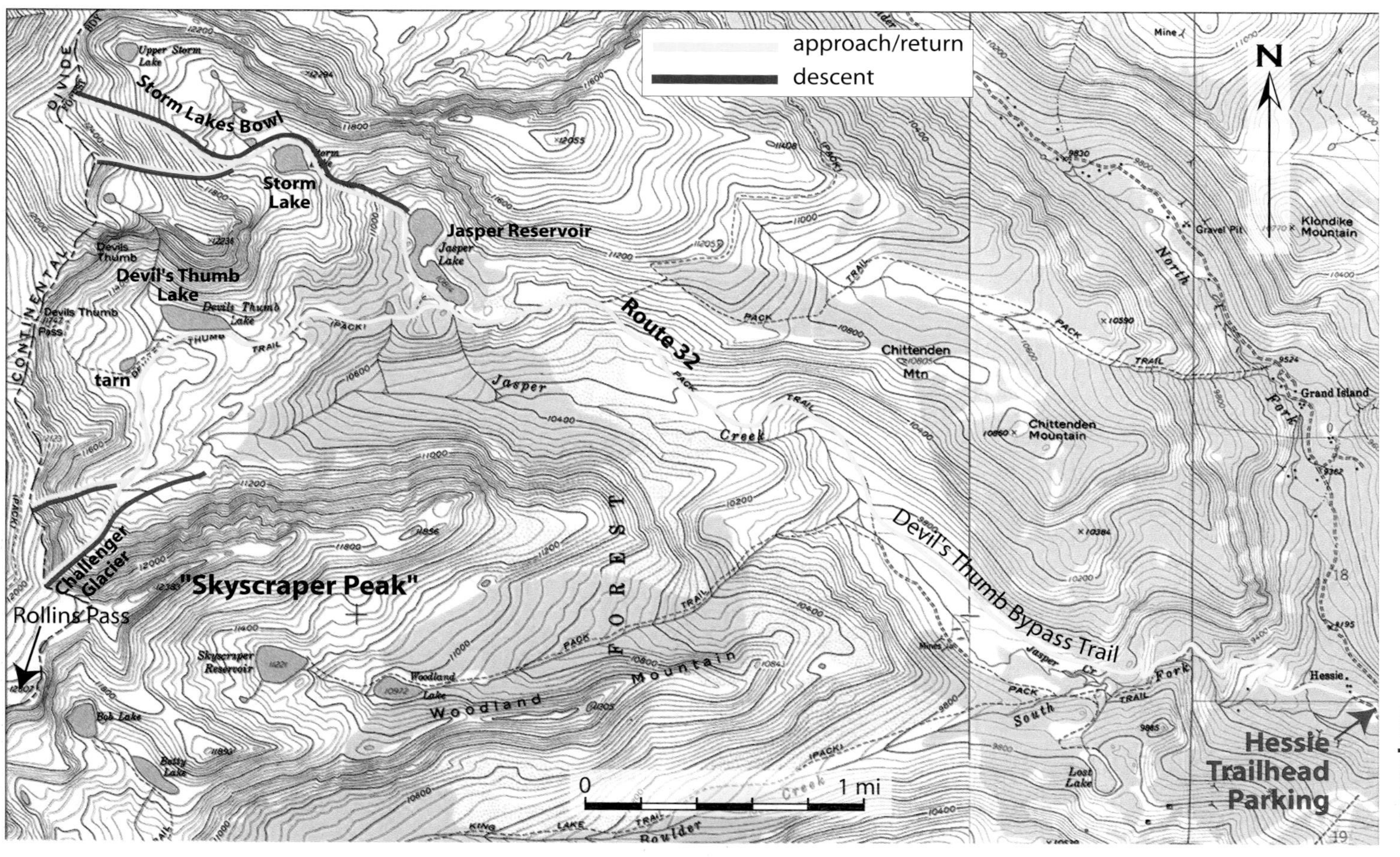
approach/return
descent
N
Storm Lakes Bowl
Storm Lake
Upper Storm Lake
Jasper Reservoir
Jasper Lake
Devil's Thumb Lake
Devils Thumb Lake
Devils Thumb
Devils Thumb Pass
tarn
Route 32
Jasper
Creek
Chittenden Mtn
Chittenden Mountain
Klondike Mountain
Gravel Pit
Mine
Grand Island
North
Fork
Devil's Thumb Bypass Trail
Challenger Glacier
"Skyscraper Peak"
Rolling Pass
Skyscraper Reservoir
Woodland Lake
Woodland
Mountain
FOREST
Bob Lake
Betty Lake
South
Lost Lake
Hessie
Hessie Trailhead Parking
PACK
TRAIL
KING
LAKE
Boulder
CONTINENTAL
DIVIDE
0
1 mi

Map...196

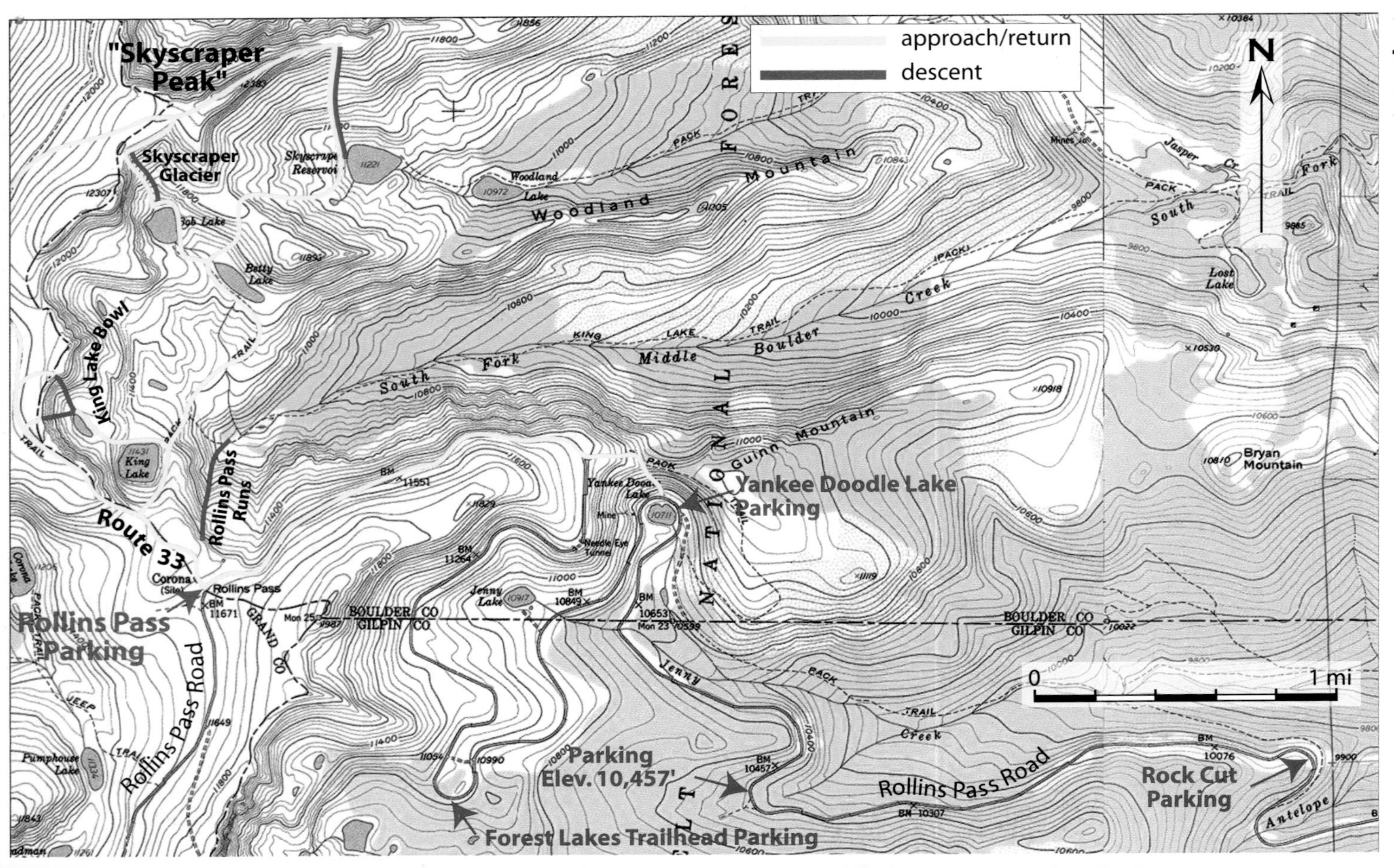
"Skyscraper Peak"
approach/return
descent
N
Skyscraper Glacier
Skyscraper Reservoir
Woodland Lake
Woodland Mountain
Bob Lake
Betty Lake
King Lake Bowl
King Lake
Rollins Pass Runs
Route 33
Corona (Site)
Rollins Pass
Rollins Pass Parking
Rollins Pass Road
South Fork Middle Boulder Creek
King Lake Trail
Guinn Mountain
Yankee Doodle Lake
Yankee Doodle Lake Parking
Needle Eye Tunnel
Jenny Lake
BOULDER CO
GILPIN CO
GRAND CO
Lost Lake
Bryan Mountain
Jasper Cr
Pumphouse Lake
Parking
Elev. 10,457'
Forest Lakes Trailhead Parking
Rock Cut Parking
0
1 mi
Antelope

Map...197

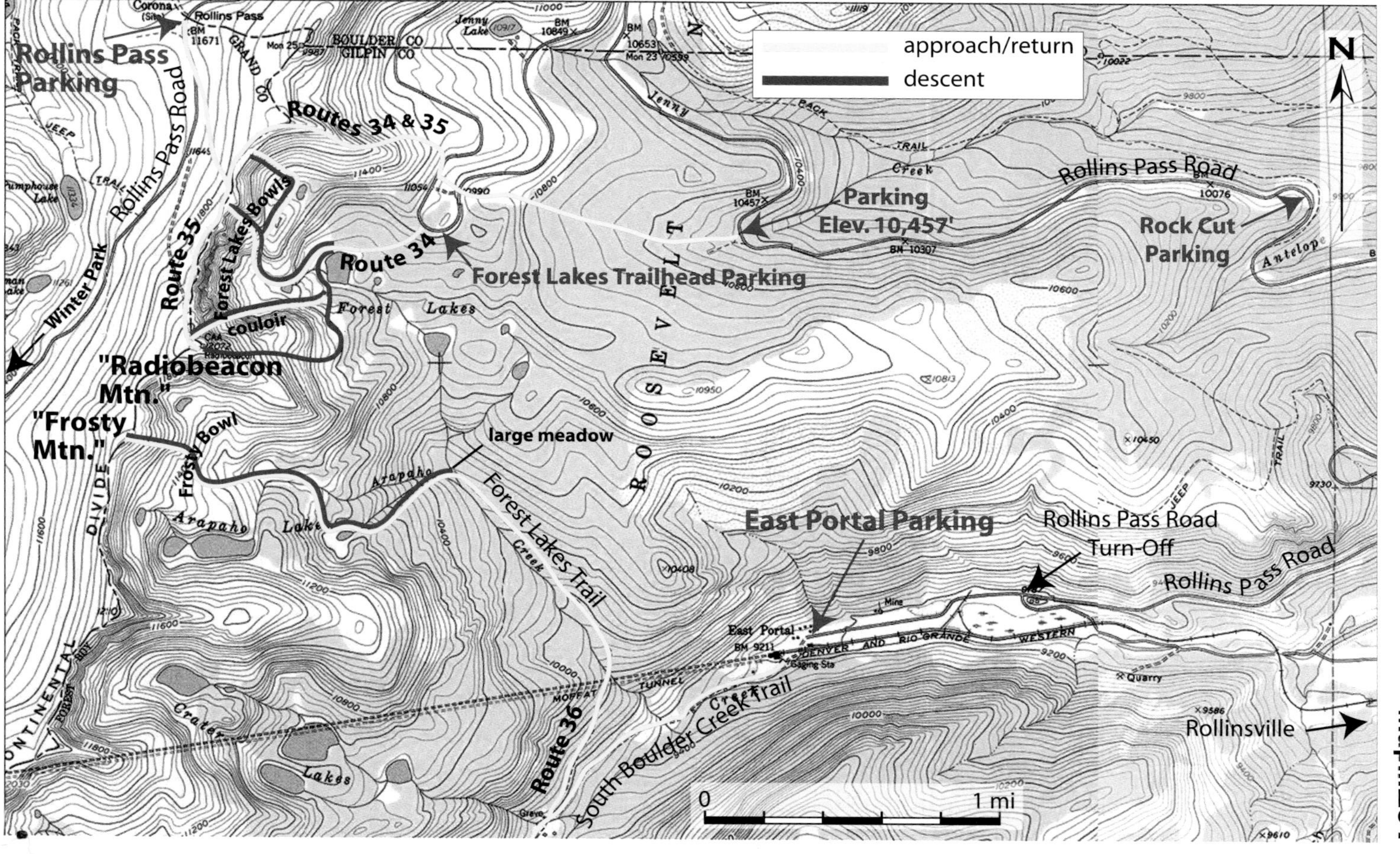

approach/return
descent
N
Rollins Pass Parking
Rollins Pass Road
Routes 34 & 35
Route 35
Forest Lakes Bowls
couloir
Route 34
Forest Lakes Trailhead Parking
Parking
Elev. 10,457'
Rollins Pass Road
Rock Cut Parking
"Radiobeacon Mtn."
"Frosty Mtn."
Frosty Bowl
Winter Park
large meadow
Forest Lakes Trail
East Portal Parking
Rollins Pass Road Turn-Off
Rollins Pass Road
Route 36
South Boulder Creek Trail
Rollinsville
0
1 mi

Map...198

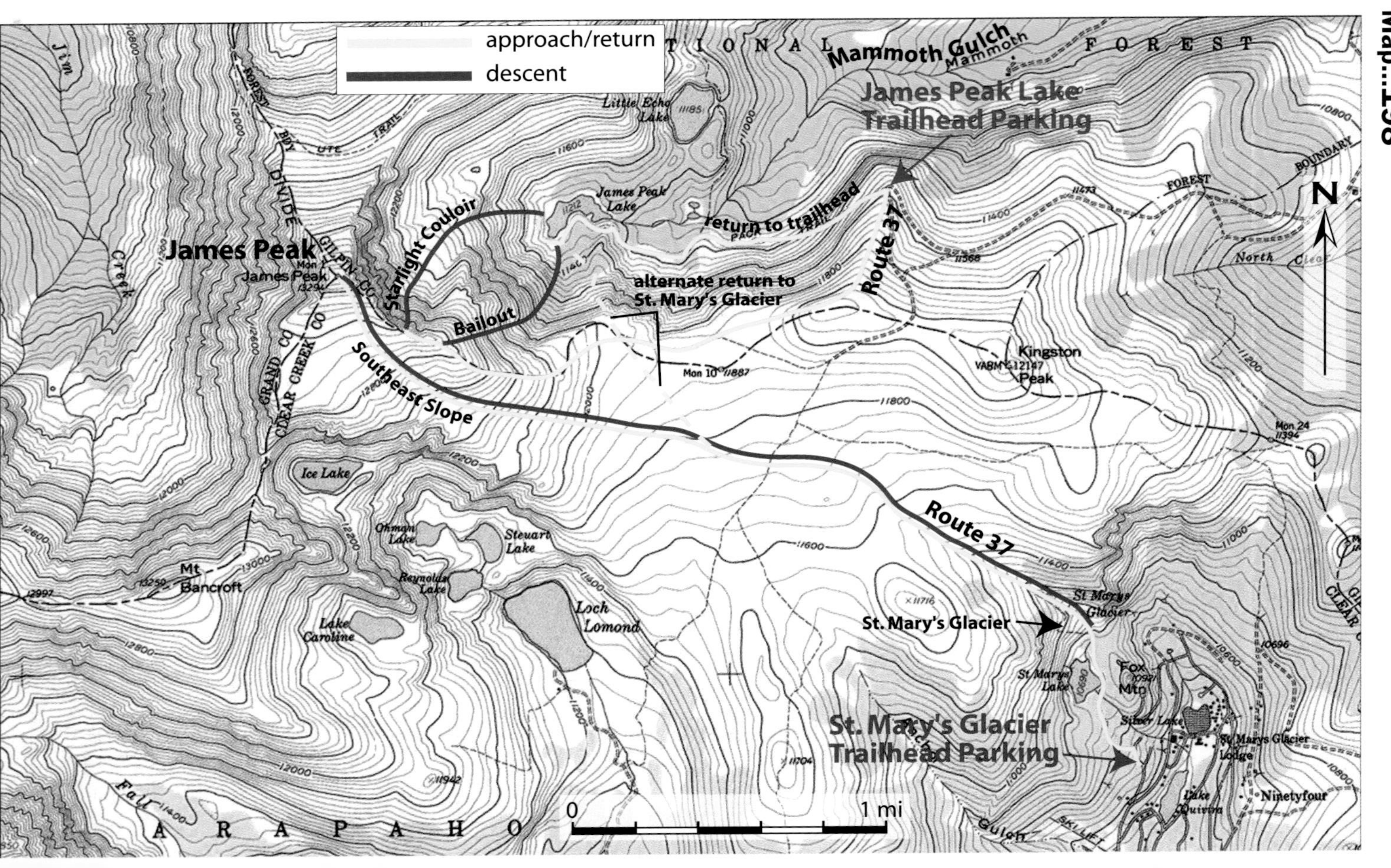

approach/return
descent
N
James Peak
Starlight Couloir
Bailout
Southeast Slope
Route 37
return to trailhead
alternate return to St. Mary's Glacier
James Peak Lake Trailhead Parking
Mammoth Gulch
St. Mary's Glacier
St. Mary's Glacier Trailhead Parking
Kingston Peak
James Peak Lake
Little Echo Lake
Loch Lomond
Steuart Lake
Reynolds Lake
Ohman Lake
Lake Caroline
Ice Lake
Mt Bancroft
Fox Mtn
St Marys Lake
Silver Lake
St Marys Glacier Lodge
Lake Quivira
Ninetyfour
Jim Creek
0
1 mi

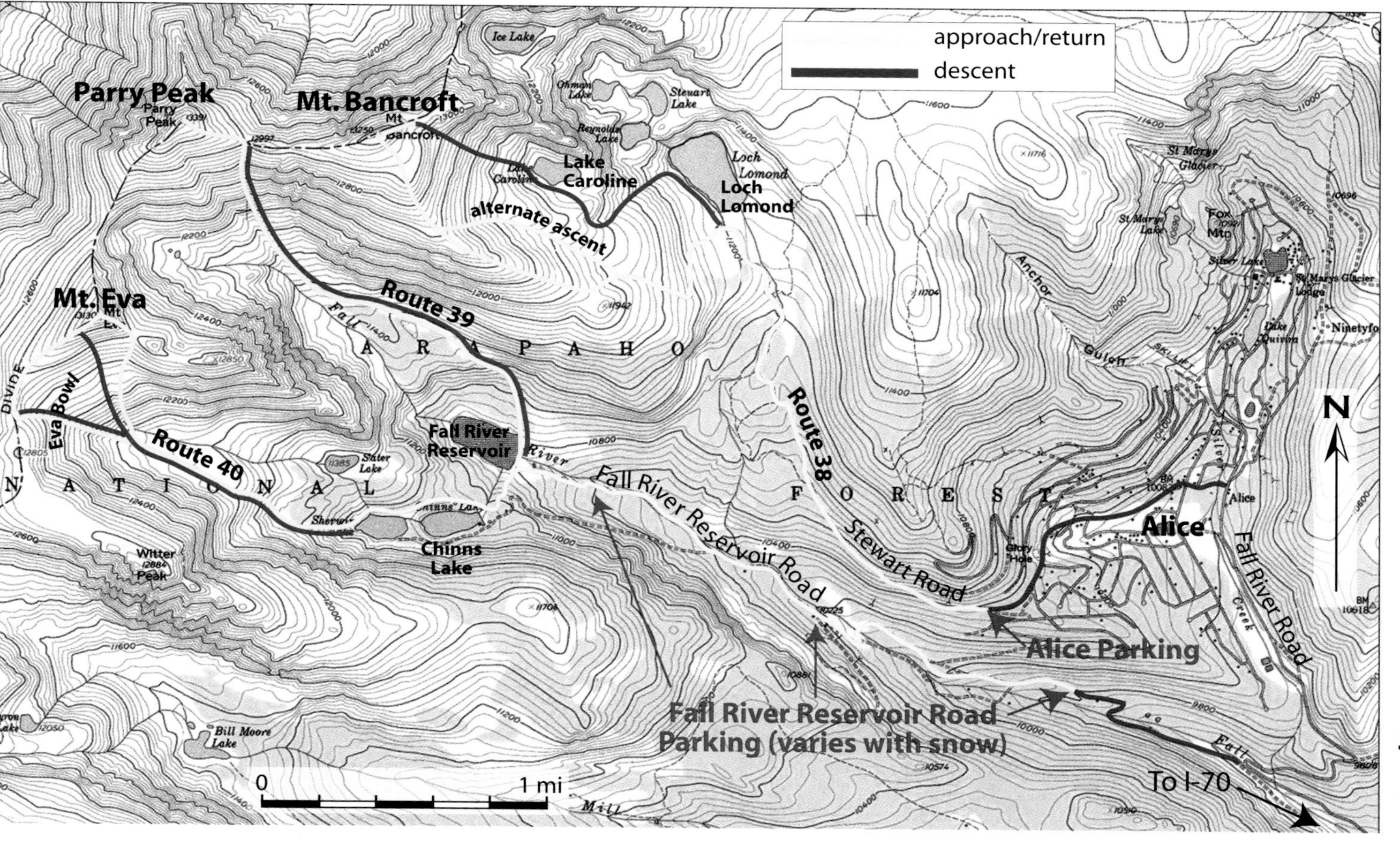
approach/return
descent
Parry Peak
Mt. Bancroft
Lake Caroline
Loch Lomond
alternate ascent
Mt. Eva
Route 39
Eva Bowl
Route 40
Fall River Reservoir
Route 38
Chinns Lake
Fall River Reservoir Road
Stewart Road
Alice
Fall River Road
N
Alice Parking
Fall River Reservoir Road Parking (varies with snow)
0
1 mi
To I-70

Map...200

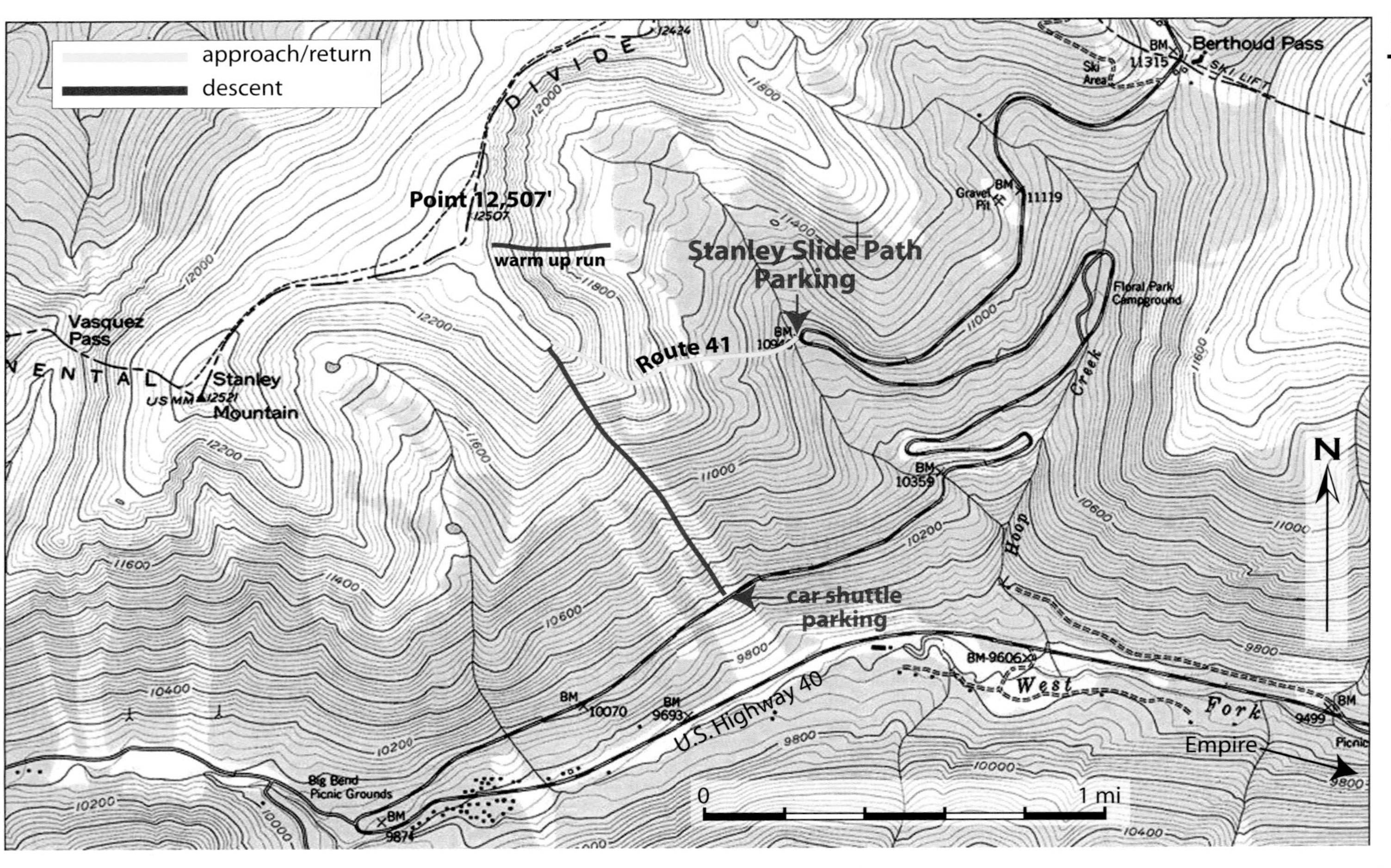

approach/return
descent
DIVIDE
Point 12,507'
warm up run
Vasquez Pass
Stanley Mountain
Route 41
Stanley Slide Path Parking
Berthoud Pass
Ski Area
SKI LIFT
Gravel Pit
Floral Park Campground
Creek
Hoop
N
car shuttle parking
West
Fork
Empire
Picnic
U.S. Highway 40
Big Bend Picnic Grounds
0
1 mi

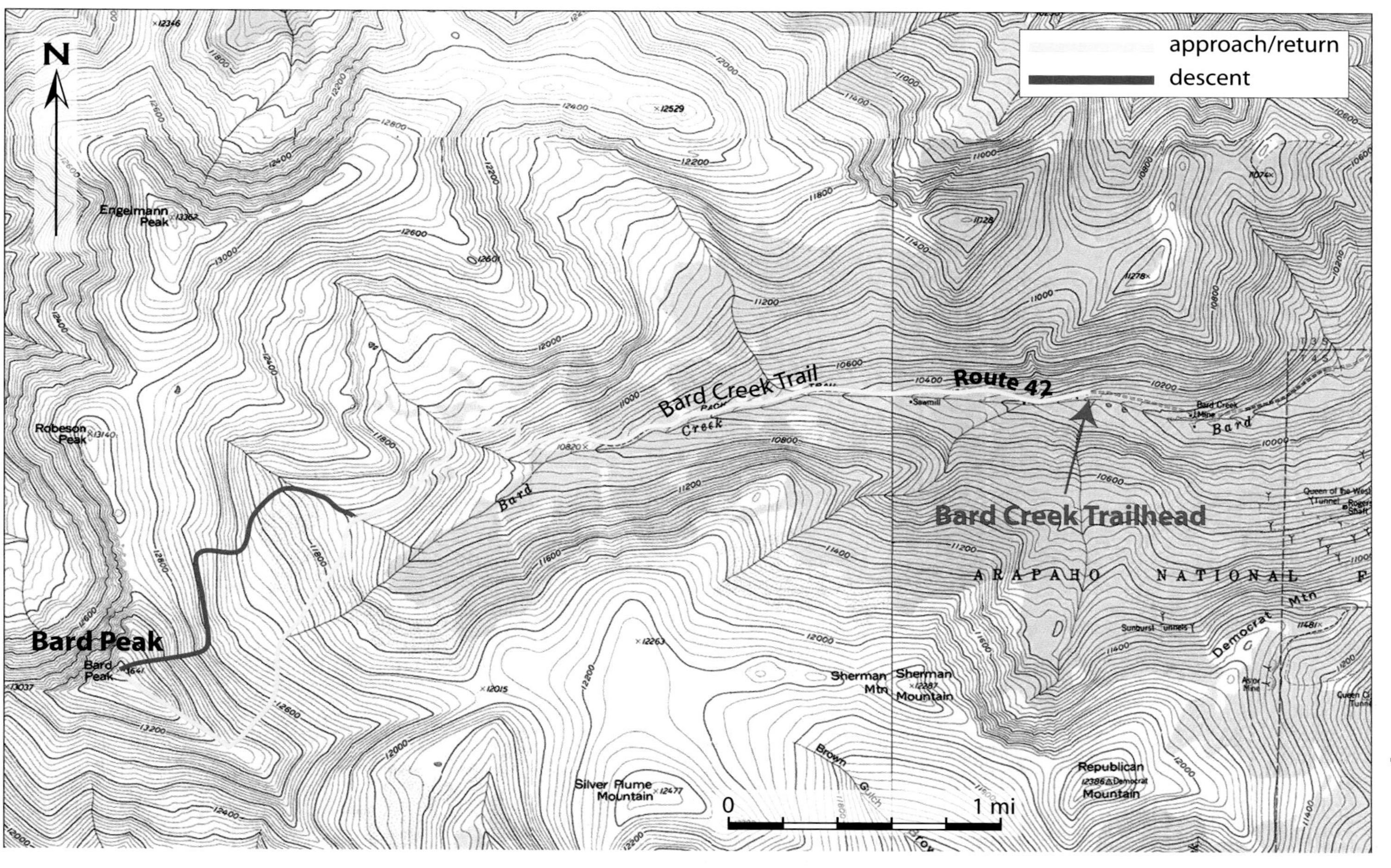
approach/return
descent
N
Engelmann Peak
Robeson Peak
Bard Peak
Bard Creek Trail
Route 42
Bard Creek Trailhead
ARAPAHO NATIONAL F
Sherman Mtn
Sherman Mountain
Silver Plume Mountain
Republican Mountain
Democrat Mtn
Brown Gulch
0
1 mi

Map...202

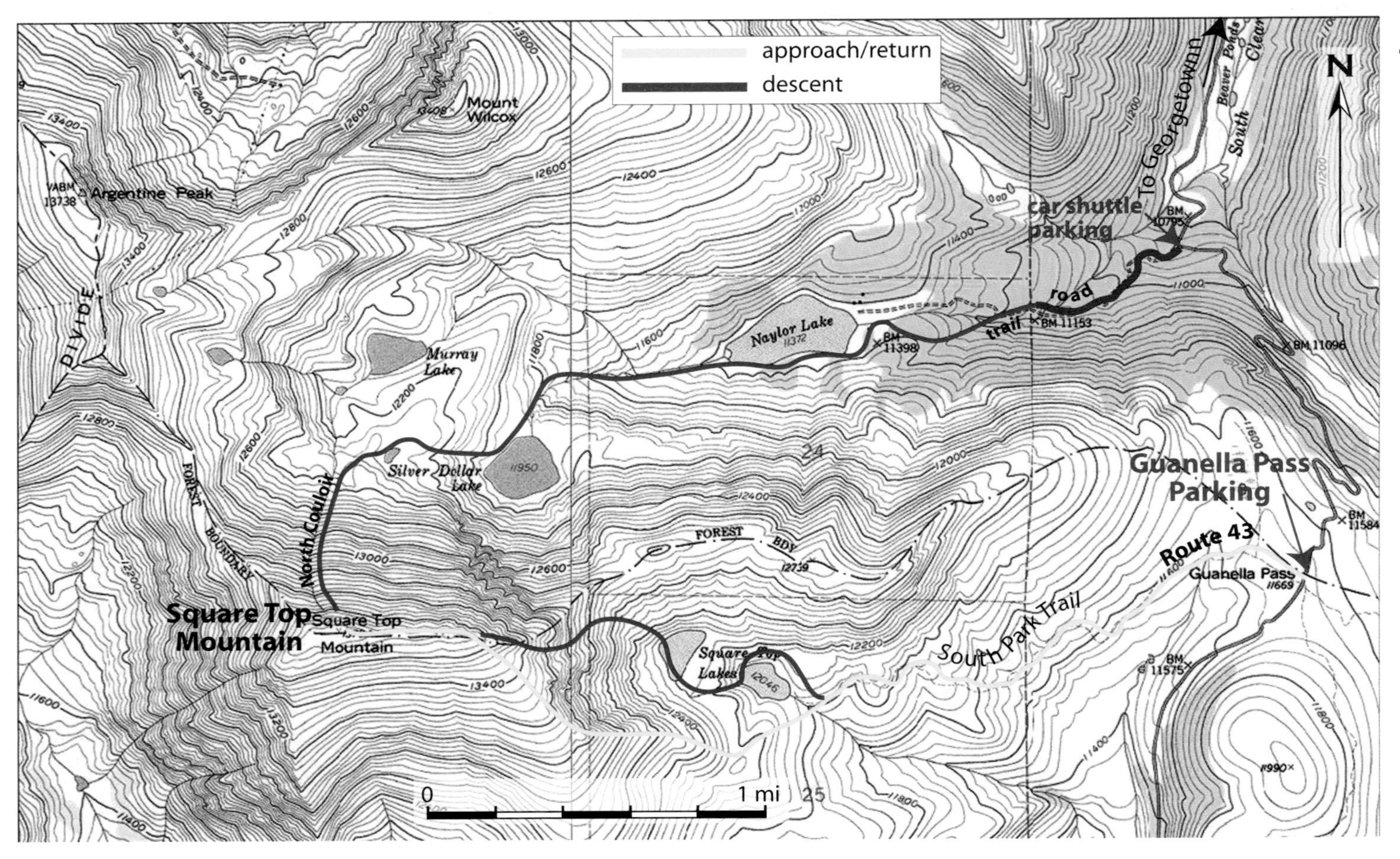

N
approach/return
descent
To Georgetown
car shuttle parking
road
trail
Naylor Lake
Murray Lake
Mount Wilcox
Argentine Peak
DIVIDE
Silver Dollar Lake
North Couloir
Square Top Mountain
FOREST BOUNDARY
Square Top Lakes
South Park Trail
Guanella Pass Parking
Route 43
Guanella Pass
0
1 mi

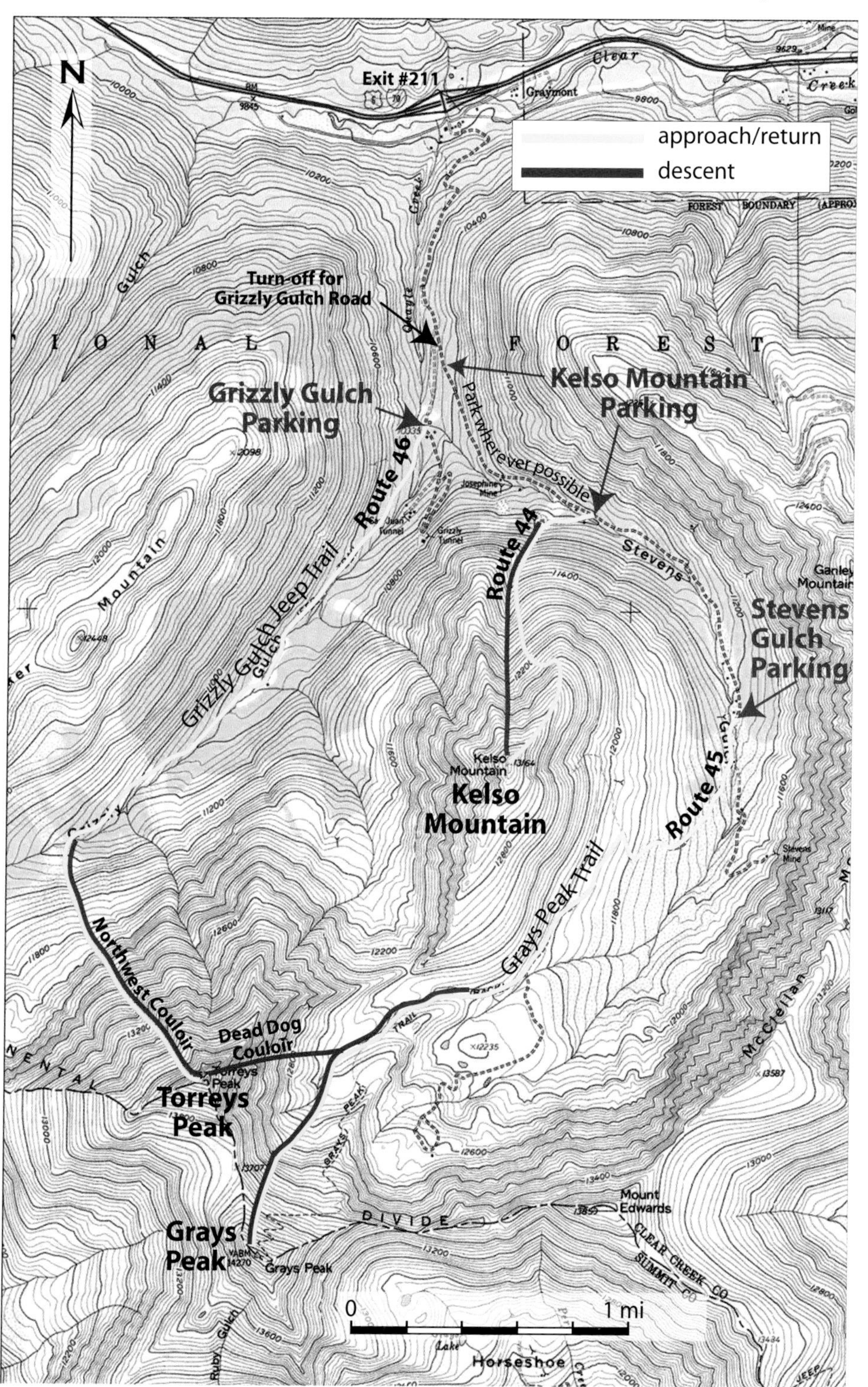
N
Exit #211
approach/return
descent
Turn-off for
Grizzly Gulch Road
Grizzly Gulch
Parking
Kelso Mountain
Parking
Park wherever possible
Route 46
Route 44
Grizzly Gulch Jeep Trail
Stevens
Gulch
Parking
Route 45
Kelso
Mountain
Grays Peak Trail
Northwest Couloir
Dead Dog
Couloir
Torreys
Peak
Grays
Peak
Mount
Edwards
DIVIDE
CLEAR CREEK CO
SUMMIT CO
0
1 mi
Horseshoe
Graymont
FOREST BOUNDARY (APPROX)
Ganley
Mountain
Stevens
Mine
Josephine
Mine
Grizzly
Tunnel
McClellan
Mountain

Map...204

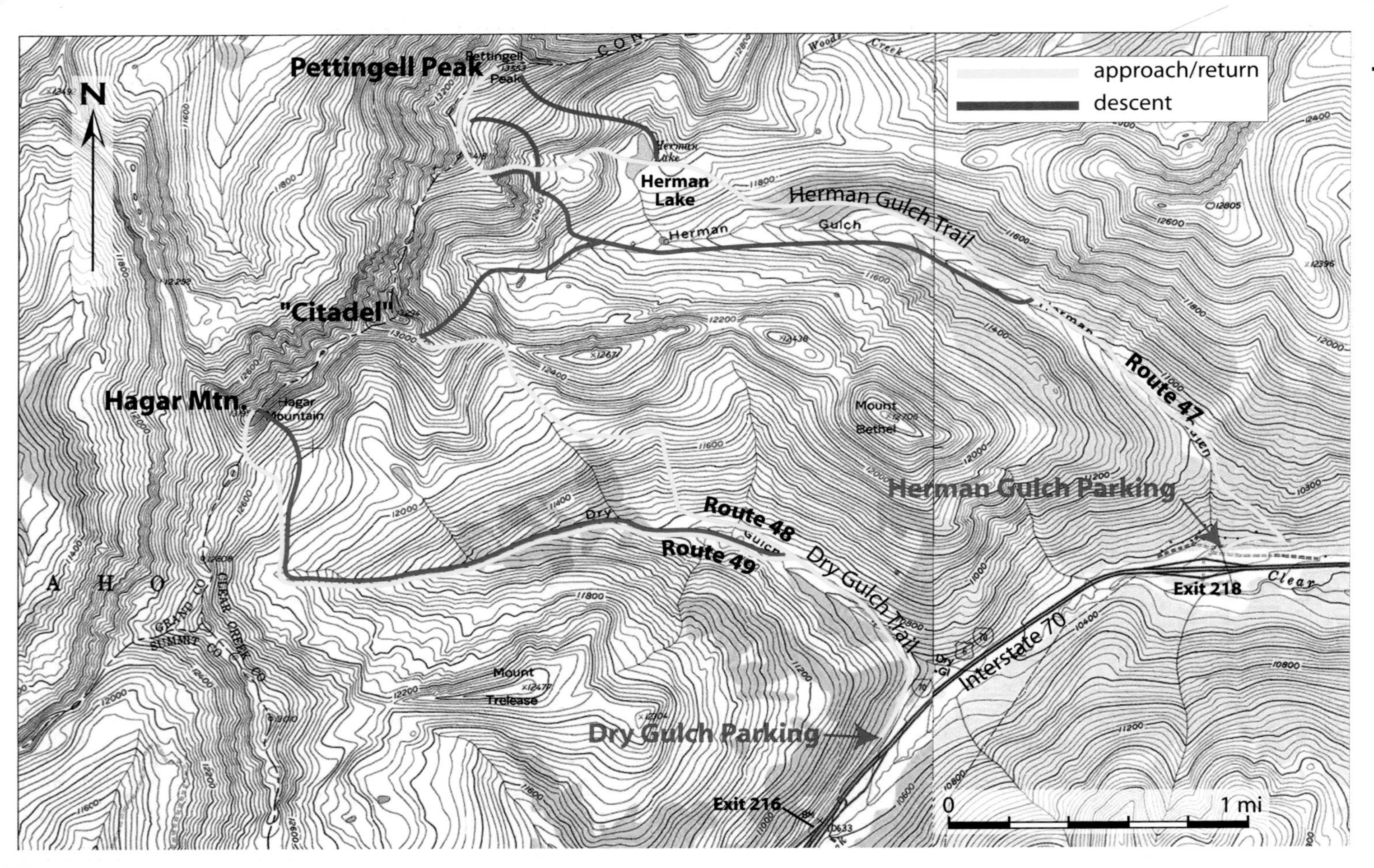

approach/return
descent
N
Pettingell Peak
Herman Lake
Herman Gulch Trail
"Citadel"
Hagar Mtn.
Mount Bethel
Route 47
Herman Gulch Parking
Route 48
Route 49
Dry Gulch Trail
Exit 218
Interstate 70
Mount Trelease
Dry Gulch Parking
Exit 216
CLEAR CREEK CO
GRAND CO
SUMMIT CO
0
1 mi

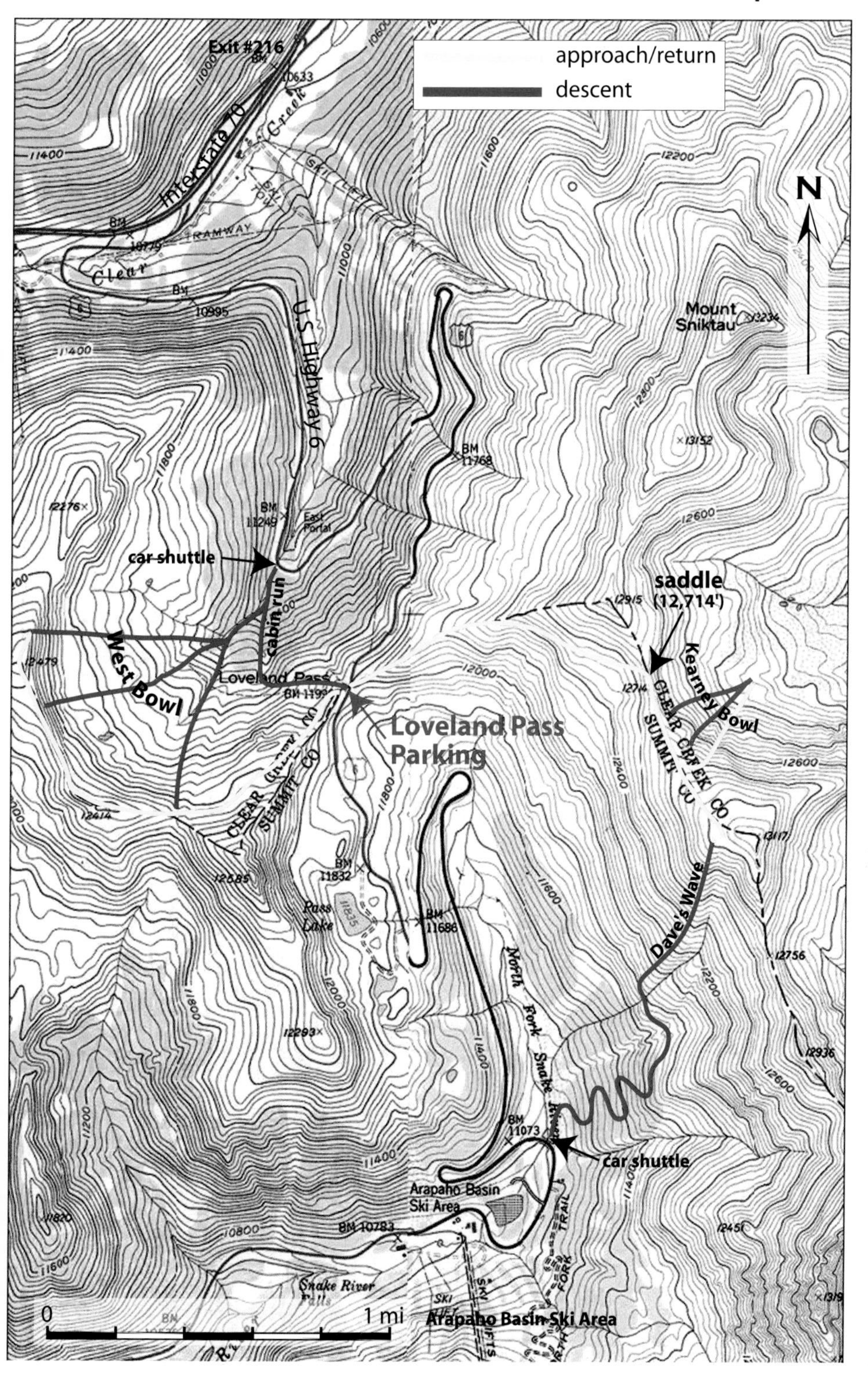

approach/return
descent
Exit #216
Interstate 70
U.S. Highway 6
N
Mount Sniktau
car shuttle
cabin run
West Bowl
Loveland Pass
Loveland Pass Parking
saddle
(12,714')
Kearney Bowl
Dave's Wave
car shuttle
Arapaho Basin Ski Area
Pass Lake
North Fork Snake River
0
1 mi
Arapaho Basin Ski Area

Map...206

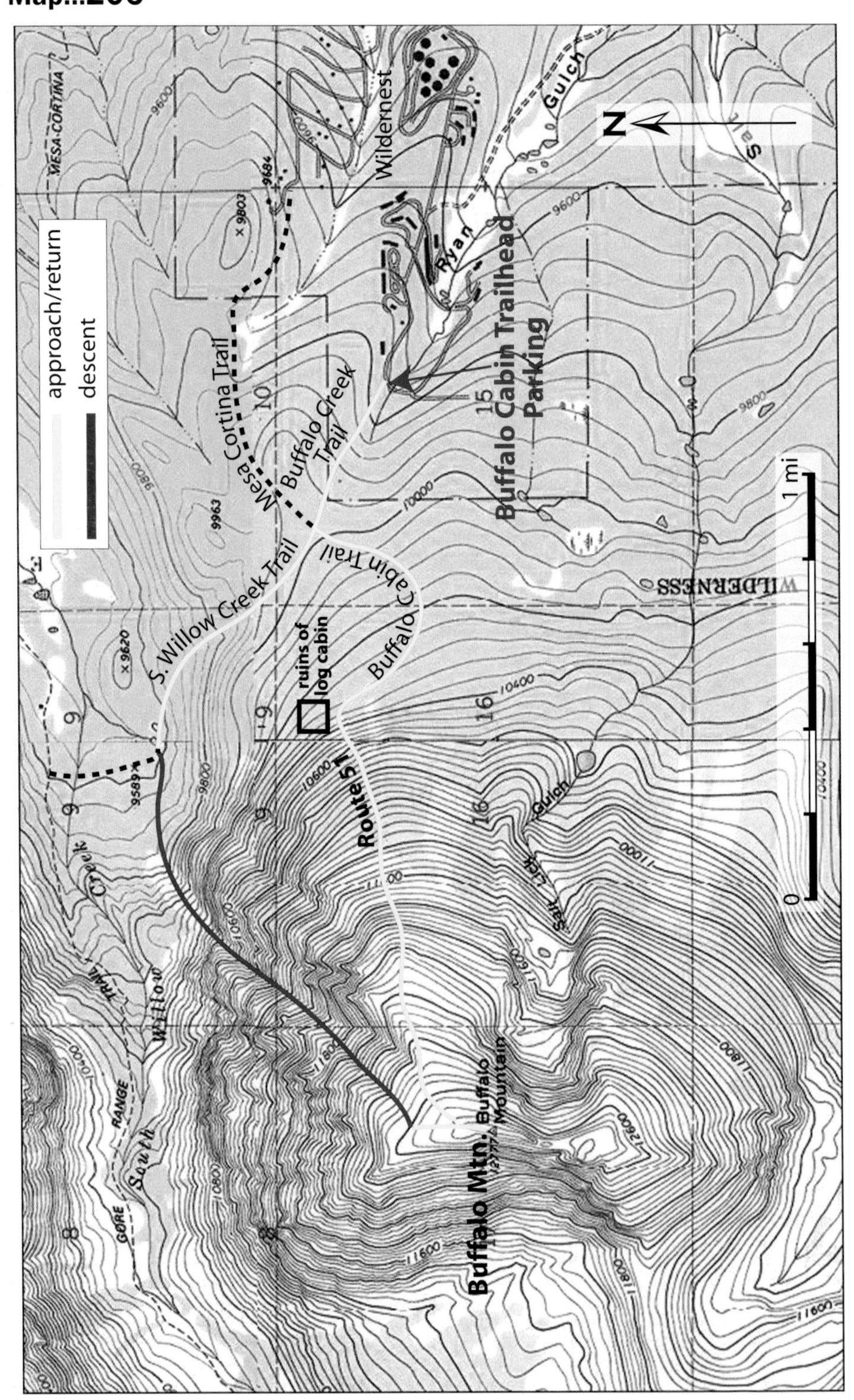
approach/return
descent
Mesa Cortina Trail
Buffalo Creek Trail
S. Willow Creek Trail
Buffalo Cabin Trail
ruins of log cabin
Route 51
Buffalo Mtn.
Buffalo Cabin Trailhead Parking
Wildernest
N
0
1 mi

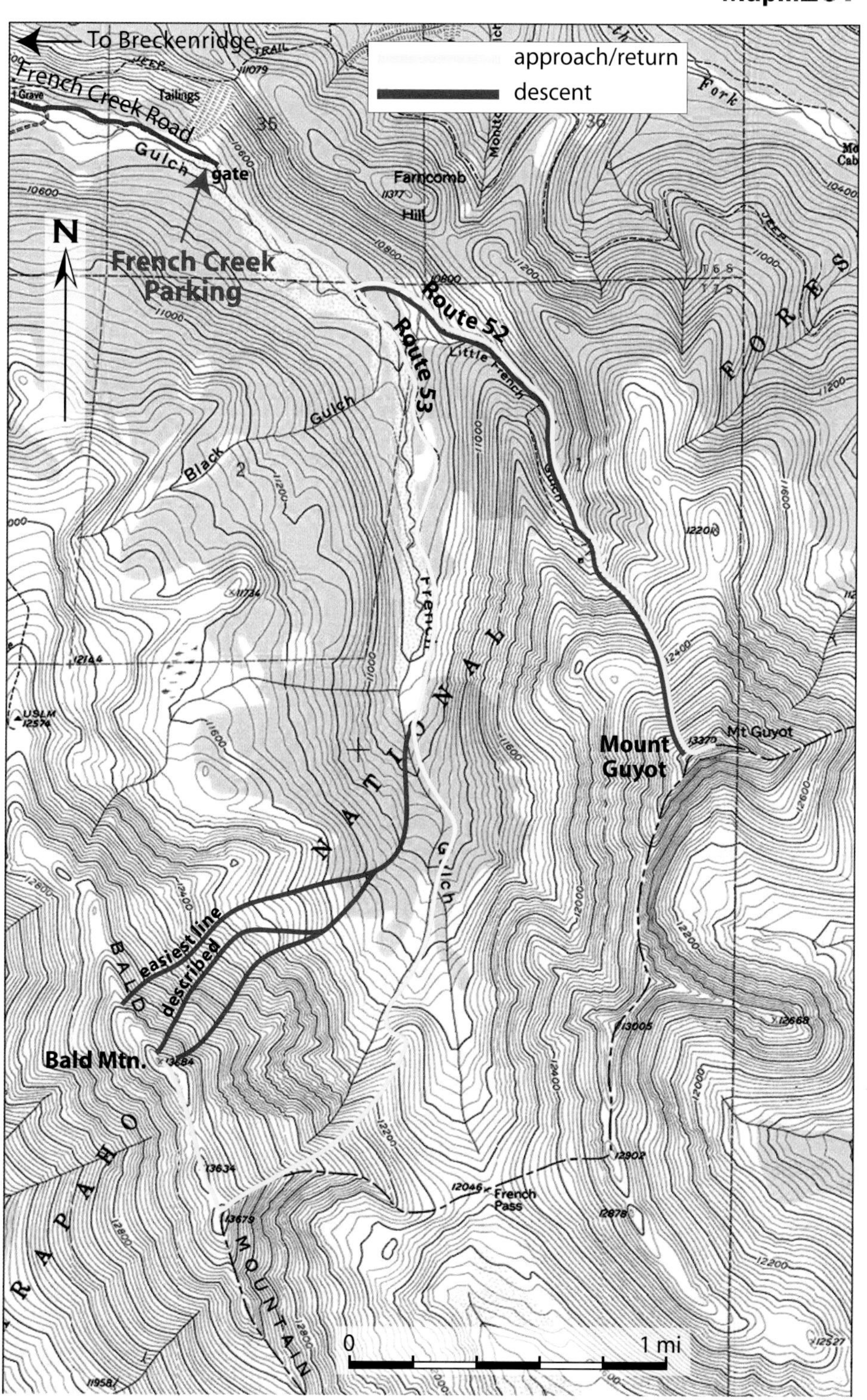
To Breckenridge
approach/return
descent
French Creek Road
Gulch
gate
French Creek Parking
Farncomb Hill
Route 52
Route 53
Little French
Gulch
Black
French
Mount Guyot
Mt Guyot
easiest line described
Bald Mtn.
Bald
French Pass
Mountain
0
1 mi

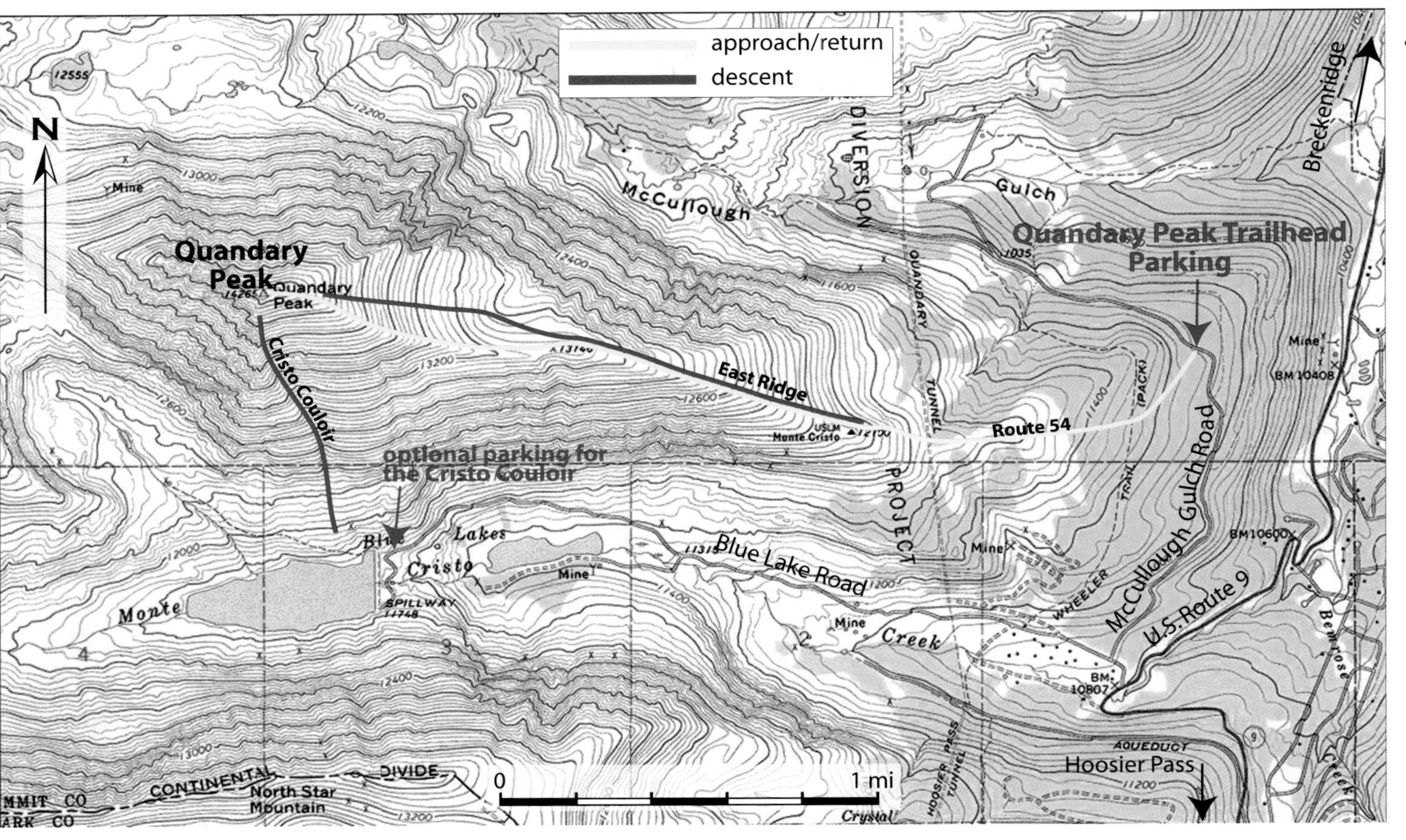

approach/return
descent
N
Quandary Peak
Quandary Peak
14265
Cristo Couloir
East Ridge
Route 54
Monte Cristo
Quandary Peak Trailhead Parking
McCullough Gulch Road
U.S. Route 9
Breckenridge
Hoosier Pass
optional parking for the Cristo Couloir
Blue Lake Road
Blue Lakes
Monte Cristo Creek
SPILLWAY
McCullough
Gulch
DIVERSION
QUANDARY TUNNEL
PROJECT
WHEELER TRAIL (PACK)
HOOSIER PASS TUNNEL
AQUEDUCT
Bemrose Creek
CONTINENTAL DIVIDE
North Star Mountain
0
1 mi

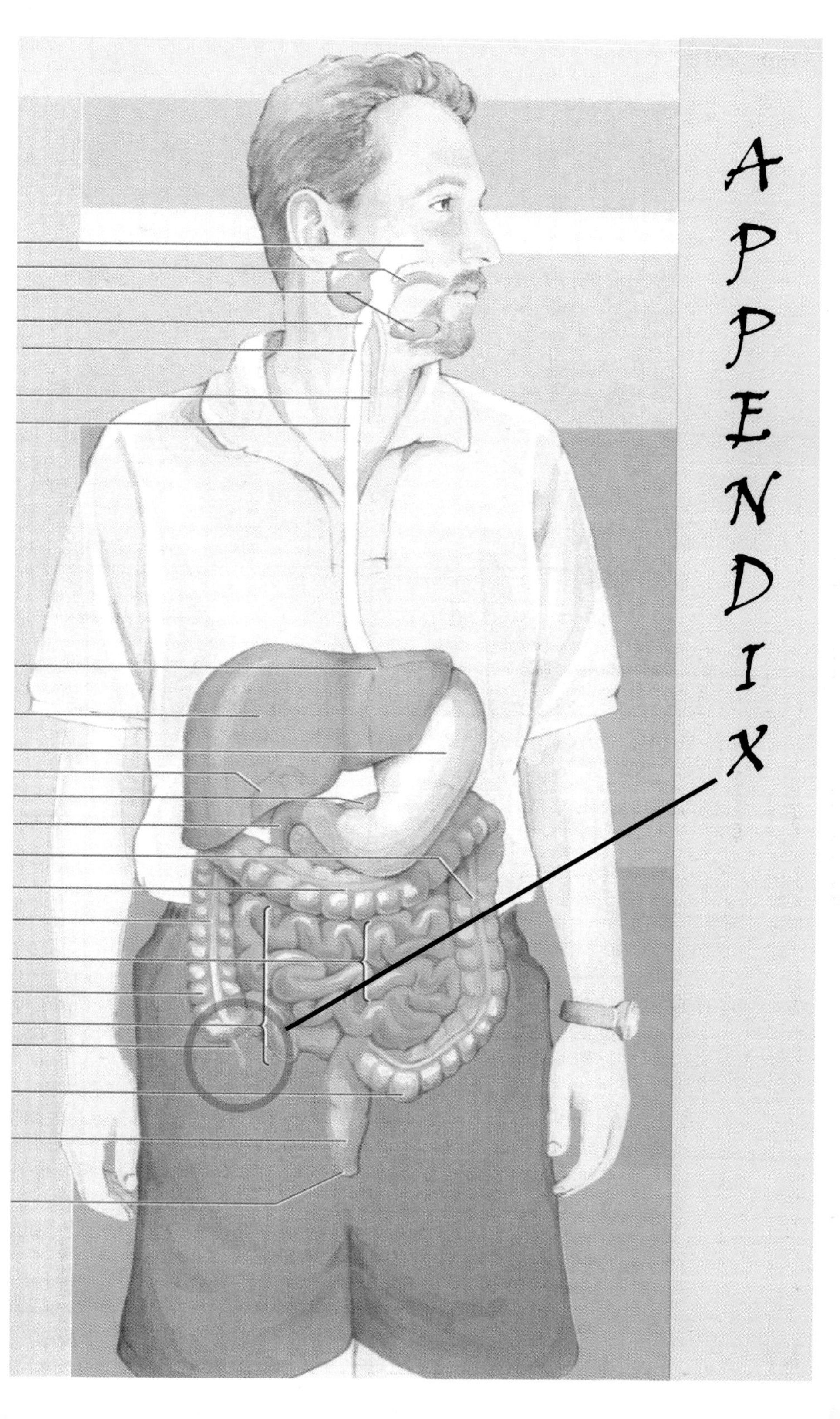
APPENDIX

Ski Descents In Order of Quality

Route	Location	Quality
3	Upper Sawmill Creek: Peak 12,170'	☺☺☺
4	Diamond Peaks	☺☺☺
5	Lake Agnes Bowl & Mt. Richthofen	☺☺☺
8	Mount Chiquita	☺☺☺
9	Sundance Mountain Bowl	☺☺☺
10	Ptarmigan Point Cirque	☺☺☺
11	Flattop Mountain	☺☺☺
16	Saint Vrain Glaciers Tour	☺☺☺
20	Mount Audubon	☺☺☺
21	Paiute Peak	☺☺☺
22	Mount Toll	☺☺☺
23	Pawnee Peak	☺☺☺
24	Apache Peak	☺☺☺
25	Indian Peaks Super Tour	☺☺☺
29	Crater Lake & Lone Eagle Cirques	☺☺☺
35	"Radiobeacon Mountain"	☺☺☺
38	Mount Bancroft	☺☺☺
39	Parry Peak	☺☺☺
40	Mount Eva	☺☺☺
41	Stanley Slide Path	☺☺☺
43	Square Top Mountain	☺☺☺
44	Kelso Mountain	☺☺☺
46	Torreys Peak	☺☺☺
47	Pettingell Peak	☺☺☺
48	"Citadel"	☺☺☺
49	Hagar Mountain	☺☺☺
50	Loveland Pass	☺☺☺
51	Buffalo Mountain	☺☺☺
53	Bald Mountain	☺☺☺
54	Quandary-East Face	☺☺☺

Ski Descents In Order of Quality

Route	Location	Quality
1	Clark Peak	☺☺
2	Upper Sawmill Crk: Pks 12,390' & 12,386'	☺☺
12	Taylor Glacier	☺☺
15	Elk Tooth	☺☺
17	Red Deer Mountain	☺☺
18	Sawtooth Mountain	☺☺
19	St. Vrain Mountain	☺☺
26	Navajo Peak	☺☺
27	North Arapaho Peak-Northstar	☺☺
28	South Arapaho Peak	☺☺
30	North Fork Lakes Bowl	☺☺
32	Upper Jasper Creek	☺☺
34	Forest Lakes Bowls and Couloir	☺☺
36	Arapaho Lakes & "Frosty Mountain"	☺☺
37	James Peak	☺☺
42	Bard Peak	☺☺
45	Grays Peak	☺☺
52	Mount Guyot	☺☺
6	Fairchild Mountain	☺
7	Ypsilon Mountain	☺
13	Mount Cumulus	☺
14	Ogalalla Peak	☺
27	North Arapaho Peak-North Face	☺
30	Mount Neva	☺
31	"Jasper Peak"	☺
33	"Skyscraper Peak" etc.	☺
54	Quandary-Cristo Couloir	☺

Ski Descents In Order of Difficulty

Route	Location	Difficulty *
17	Red Deer Mountain	Int.
11	Flattop Mountain	Int. or Adv.
19	Saint Vrain Mountain	Int. or Adv.
36	Arapaho Lakes & "Frosty Mtn."	Int. or Adv.
40	Mount Eva	Int. or Adv.
9	Sundance Mountain Bowl	Int. & Adv. & Exp.
23	Pawnee Peak	Int. or Adv. or Exp.
32	Upper Jasper Creek	Int. or Adv. or Exp.
33	"Skyscraper Peak" etc.	Int. or Adv. or Exp.
37	James Peak	Int. or Adv. or Exp.
50	Loveland Pass	Int. or Adv. or Exp.
1	Clark Peak	Adv.
5	Lk Agnes Bowl & Mt. Richthofen	Adv.
6	Fairchild Mountain	Adv.
7	Ypsilon Mountain	Adv.
13	Mount Cumulus	Adv.
21	Paiute Peak	Adv.
30	North Fork Lakes Bowl	Adv.
35	"Radiobeacon Mountain"	Adv.
38	Mount Bancroft	Adv.
39	Parry Peak	Adv.
42	Bard Peak	Adv.
48	"Citadel"	Adv.
49	Hagar Mountain	Adv.
52	Mount Guyot	Adv.
2	Up. Sawmill Crk: Pks 12,390' & 12,386'	Adv. or Exp.
4	Diamond Peaks	Adv. or Exp.
10	Ptarmigan Point Cirque	Adv. or Exp.
16	Saint Vrain Glaciers Tour	Adv. or Exp.
34	Forest Lakes Bowls & Couloir	Adv. or Exp.

Ski Descents In Order of Difficulty

Route	Location	Difficulty *
43	Squaretop Mountain	Adv. or Exp.
47	Pettingell Peak	Adv. or Exp.
54	Quandary	Adv. or Exp.
3	Upper Sawmill Creek: Peak 12,170′	Exp.
12	Taylor Glacier	Exp.
14	Ogalalla Peak	Exp.
15	Elk Tooth	Exp.
18	Sawtooth Mountain	Exp.
20	Mount Audubon	Exp.
22	Mount Toll	Exp.
24	Apache Peak	Exp.
25	Indian Peaks Super Tour	Exp.
26	Navajo Peak	Exp.
27	North Arapaho Peak	Exp.
28	South Arapaho Peak	Exp.
29	Crater Lake & Lone Eagle Cirques	Exp.
30	Mount Neva	Exp.
31	"Jasper Peak"	Exp.
46	Torreys Peak	Exp.
51	Buffalo Mountain	Exp.
53	Bald Mountain	Exp.
8	Mount Chiquita	Exp. & Adv.
41	Stanley Slide Path	Exp. & Adv.
44	Kelso Mountain	Exp. & Adv.
45	Grays Peak	Exp. & Adv.

* When **"or"** separates difficulty ratings, there are separate descents within the route number that are rated separately.

When **"&"** separates difficulty ratings, there is a single descent that has two or three sections of varying difficulty, with the most difficulty usually occurring at the top of the descent.

Books

Geology, Natural History, and Human History

Arps, Louisa W., and Elinor Kingery. *High Country Names.* Johnson Books, 1994...For trivia lovers and local history buffs. [Out of print, but used copies available from Amazon.com.]

Benedict, Audrey D. *A Sierra Club Naturalist's Guide: The Southern Rockies.* Sierra Club Books, 1991...Beautifully written, comprehensive guide to geology, meteorology, and natural history. [Out of print, but used copies available from Amazon.com.]

Chronic, Halka. *Roadside Geology of Colorado.* Mountain Press, 1980...A great way to get the "big picture." Keep it in your car.

Craighead, John J., Frank C. Craighead, Jr., and Ray Davis. *A Field Guide To Rocky Mountain Wildflowers.* (Peterson Field Guide Series) Houghton Mifflin Co. 1998...Color photographs along with written descriptions and line drawings. Ninety percent of the flowers that you'll see can be quickly identified.

Mutel, Cornelia and John C. Emerick. *From Grassland To Glacier: The Natural History of Colorado.* Johnson Books, 1992...A classic that focuses on the diversity of Colorado's major ecosystem units.

Skiing, Climbing, and Hiking in the Front Range

Dawson, Louis W. *Dawson's Guide To Colorado Backcountry Skiing,* Vol 1. Blue Clover Press, 2000...Tours for skiers of every persuasion in central Colorado's Elk and West Elk Mountains.

Dawson, Louis W. *Guide To Colorado's Fourteeners*: Vols. 1 & 2. Blue Clover Press, 1994/6...Meticulously documented and extremely well researched. Contains information on technical routes, snow climbs and ski descents. Lou has climbed and skied every Fourteener.

D'Antonio, Bob. *Hiking Colorado's Indian Peaks Wilderness.* Falcon, 2002...Comprehensive, up-to-date guide to all of the trails between Rocky Mountain National Park and Rollins Pass.

Roach, Gerry. *Colorado's Indian Peaks: Classic Hikes and Climbs.* Fulcrum, 1998...Although not a guide to skiing, still a terrific resource to every nook and cranny of the Indian Peaks. Perfect for peak-baggers.

Barton, Harlan. *Peak to Peak: Colorado's Front Range Ski Trails,* Guidebook and Map. Quality Press, 1995...Use this guide in the winter to scope out your spring ski descents. Includes a meticulously annotated topo map.

Ski Mountaineering Outside Colorado

Moynier, John. *Backcountry Skiing California's High Sierra*. Falcon, 1999...Contains a section on mouth-watering spring ski descents.

Burgdorfer, Rainer. *100 Classic Backcountry Ski and Snowboard Routes In Washington*. The Mountaineers. 1999...Challenging routes for intermediate and advanced backcountry skiers and snowboarders.

Richins, Paul. *50 Classic Backcountry Ski and Snowboard Summits In California*, Mount Shasta to Mount Whitney. The Mountaineers...Covers the Cascade Range to the Sierra Nevada.

Waag, David. *Oregon Descents: Backcountry Skiing Southern Cascades*. Free Heel Skiing: 1997...Covers the southern Cascades.

Dawson, Louis W. *Wild Snow*. The Mountaineers. 1998...A history as well as a guide to 54 North American ski mountaineering classics. Inspirational.

Skiing Techniques and General Mountaineering

Van Tilburg, Christopher. *Backcountry Snowboarding*. The Mountaineers. 1998...The first book to introduce snowboarders to the techniques and concerns of backcountry snowboarding.

Vives, Jean. *Backcountry Skier: The Complete Guide To Ski Training*. Human Kinetics. 1998...More than just a technique book, this thorough, accurate guide to the sport also focuses on nutrition and conditioning for the backcountry.

Graydon, Don (Editor), et al. *Mountaineering: The Freedom of the Hills*. The Mountaineers. 1997...The best single source for information and techniques related to mountain travel. A well respected classic with the editions to prove it.

Parker, Paul. *Free-Heel Skiing: Telemark and Parallel Techniques for All Conditions*. The Mountaineers. 2001...The next best thing to a private lesson with Paul.

O'Bannon, Allen and Mike Clelland. *Allen & Mike's Really Cool Telemark Tips*. Chockstone. 1998. This book's outrageous caricatures and memorable mnemonics have something to offer free-heelers of all ability levels. This is the best ski technique book we've seen.

Periodicals

BackCountry Magazine, Four issues per year. Subscribe to Backcountry Publishing, Inc. P.O. Box 190, 168 Main Street, Jeffersonville, VT 05464.

www.backcountrymagazine.com

Couloir, Five issues per year. Subscribe to Couloir Publications, P.O. Box 2349, Truckee, CA 96161.

www.earnyourturns.com

Alpine Guiding Services

Alpine World Ascents, Professional Mountain Guides

- Instruction and guiding (locally and internationally)
- Ski and snowboard mountaineering
- Rock, ice, and alpine climbing
- Avalanche courses

www.alpineworldascents.com

National Forest, Wilderness, and Backcountry Information

The Arapaho National Forest and the Roosevelt National Forest maintain a joint website (*www.fs.fed.us/r2/arnf/*) that contains excellent information about road access, hiking trails, camping and campgrounds, and issuance of permits for camping in the Indian Peaks Wilderness. You can also get information by telephone: 303.541.2500.

Similarly the Medicine Bow and Routt National Forests also maintain a joint website *(www.fs.fed.us/r2/mbr/)* with the same sorts of information. Or telephone: 307.745.2300.

The Backcountry Skiers Alliance

The B.S.A. is a Colorado not-for-profit organization that "represents winter backcountry recreationists by advocating the creation, preservation, and management of non-motorized areas on public lands." According to their mission statement: "The Backcountry Skiers Alliance is committed to preserving and protecting, a quiet, non-motorized winter recreational experience for backcountry skiers, snowboarders and snowshoers, and finding lasting solutions to user conflicts." Readers who are interested in learning more about this valuable organization and who may be interested in joining can visit the B.S.A. website. *www.backcountryalliance.org.*

Skiers, Riders & Climbers Pictured In This Book

Peter Bridge, Bob Cauthen, Tom Conway, Al Desetta, Henry Gibb, Al Huck, Terry Huck, Dave Farrell, Eileen Faughey, Ron Haddad, Greg Hood, Stan Ladd, Owen Lunz, Mystery Man, Todd Mead, Ace Reid, Wolfgang Schnitzhofer, Abdominal Snowman, Carl Zimmer, Robert Zink.

The Authors

Ron Haddad and Eileen Faughey live in Boulder, Colorado. Ron is a high school science teacher and Eileen is a nutrition consultant. During the past twenty-five years, they have enjoyed outdoor adventures together in eighteen states and seven countries. They have twenty years of backcountry skiing experience in the northeast, the west, and in western Canada. Ron has skied almost every route described in this book and is always on the prowl for new routes wherever his ski adventures take him.

David Schwartz

"A huge mountain cannot be denied —
it speaks in silence to the very core of your being."
Ansel Adams